THE
GREAT DEBATE

THE
GREAT DEBATE

Edmund Burke, Thomas Paine,
and the
Birth of Right and Left

YUVAL LEVIN

BASIC BOOKS
A Member of the Perseus Books Group
New York

Books published by Basic Books are available at special discounts
for bulk purchases in the United States by corporations, institutions,
and other organizations. For more information, please contact the Special
Markets Department at the Perseus Books Group, 2300 Chestnut
Street, Suite 200, Philadelphia, PA 19103, or call (800) 810-4145,
ext. 5000, or e-mail special.markets@perseusbooks.com.

Designed by Linda Mark

The Library of Congress has catalogued the hardcover as follows:
Levin, Yuval.
    The great debate : Edmund Burke, Thomas Paine, and the
birth of right and left / Yuval Levin.
       pages cm
    Includes bibliographical references and index.
    ISBN 978-0-465-05097-0 (hardcover)
    ISBN 978-0-465-04094-0 (e-book)
1. United States--Politics and government. 2. Right and left
(Political science) 3. Political science—Philosophy. 4. Burke,
Edmund, 1729–1797—Political and social views. 5. Paine, Thomas,
1737–1809—Political and social views. I. Title.
    JK275.L5 2013
    320.50973—dc23

10 9 8 7 6 5 4 3

For Cecelia, with love

CONTENTS

PREFACE

O N ITS SURFACE, AMERICAN POLITICS THESE DAYS CAN seem impossibly complicated. We confront a bewildering array of public policy problems, each impenetrably convoluted in itself and largely disconnected from the others. Who could simultaneously understand the intricacies of our tax code, the inefficiencies of our entitlement system, the inadequacies of our transportation infrastructure, the moral challenges presented by the abortion debate, and the ins and outs of the dozens of other prominent public questions demanding our attention?

I make my living as a combatant in these policy debates. I am the editor of a quarterly journal about domestic policy and a think-tank scholar who studies health care, entitlement reform, the federal budget, and similarly wonkish fare. I have worked on these issues as a policy staffer at the White House (under George W. Bush) and as a member of the staffs of several Republican members of Congress. And in doing so, I have found that making sense of these debates requires more than an immersion in the technical details. It requires a sense of how the different policy dilemmas that confront our society relate to one another and why they so frequently divide us as they do.

The way they divide us, after all, is hardly arbitrary. It is not by coincidence that people who tend to agree with one another on one set of issues (say, how to deal with the deficit) often also agree on others (like how to reform American education) that do not seem obviously connected. There are exceptions, to be sure, but conservatives and liberals—and therefore often Republicans and Democrats—fairly consistently find themselves on opposite sides of contentious debates on a very broad range of subjects, from economic policy to social policy to the environment, the culture, and countless other public questions. The political right and left often seem to represent genuinely distinct points of view, and our national life seems almost by design to bring to the surface questions that divide them.

I have long been intrigued by the sources and nature of those distinct points of view. And since the thick of the fight is not always the best vantage point for understanding what moves our politics, the search for some answers at one point took me away from Washington for a time, to pursue a Ph.D. in political philosophy at the University of Chicago. In studying the work of the West's great political thinkers, I became persuaded that the complicated policy debates that take place on the surface of our politics are moved not just by partisan passions or economic interests but by deeper questions that, perhaps ironically, can be much more accessible to average citizens. These debates pose moral and philosophical questions regarding what each of us takes to be true and important about human life and how this influences our expectations of politics. We may not think about these deeper questions explicitly every time we approach a contemporary political issue, but how we answer such questions shapes the great political debates of our day.

That such questions should underlie our political life, however, does not itself explain why the citizens of our republic should coalesce around two clearly discernible and fairly coherent sets of answers. Why, then, is there a left and a right in our politics? This book hopes to offer the beginning of an answer to that question. That beginning is both historical and philosophical, and so this book is, too.

It is historical in that it seeks to understand where we are by considering where we came from. And in our particular political tradition, seeking out where we came from often means beginning our search in the late eighteenth century—that extraordinary era of the American Revolution and the French Revolution that together helped to shape the modern world.

It is philosophical because it contends that what we can learn from that era is above all a way of thinking about the most basic and timeless dilemmas of society and politics. This book therefore looks at Anglo-American politics during the age of America's founding—a subject of justifiably unending fascination—from an unusual angle and tries to expose some unfamiliar features of it.

The historical and the philosophical in this case intersect not in the abstract but in the real lives of two people whose thoughts and actions helped define the right and the left at their origins. This book tells the stories of their lives and times and carefully considers their ideas and arguments. Edmund Burke and Thomas Paine lived in an era defined by a seemingly interminable succession of intense political crises, and both men were deeply involved in a great many of them both as thinkers and as actors. In the process, each laid out a vision of the world and especially a way of thinking about political change. In some important ways, Burke and Paine laid out the beginnings of the right and the left, respectively. The implicit and often explicit debate between them therefore offers us a glimpse into the origins of our political divisions. This book is thus a case study in how ideas move history and in where some of the key ideas that have moved, and still move, our history came from.

To point to the historical and philosophical roots of our political debates is not to stand apart from or above those debates. On the contrary, I have been drawn to the questions that animate this book precisely because I have played a modest part in some political debates myself. I'm a conservative, and I would not pretend to leave my worldview at the door while I explore the foundations of our political order. But a conservative must take an interest in his own society's traditions, and our political tradition has always contained both the left and the right—each passionately advancing its understanding of the common good. I am therefore a conservative who is deeply interested in understanding both the left and the right as they truly are, and I strive here to tell their stories in a way that both liberals and conservatives today might recognize as meaningful and true, and from which both might learn something about themselves and their political adversaries.

The origins of the left-right divide, of course, are not the same as its current incarnation. The differences between today's political divisions and those of Burke and Paine's era are at least as fascinating and numerous as their similarities. I hope to encourage both sides of our political divide to reflect on the path we have traveled. What might we each learn from our (and our opponents') intellectual progenitors, and what crucial insights might we have forgotten with time but would do well to recall? Above all, though, I hope this story might help fellow citizens of any political persuasion approach American politics with greater understanding and confidence. I hope to help the reader see that although many arguments that boil at the surface are technical and complicated, they are moved by deep permanent questions that are not only important but also awfully interesting.

INTRODUCTION

NYONE TRACING THE PEDIGREE OF OUR POLITICAL ideas must be struck by the importance, and by the sheer eventfulness, of the late eighteenth century. Between about 1770 and 1800, many of the crucial concepts, terms, divisions, and arguments that still define our political life seemed to burst into the world in fierce and fiery succession.

This was the era of the American Revolution and the French Revolution, and we have long since fallen into the comfortable habit of attributing the explosion of political philosophy and drama of that time to those monumental upheavals. The American Revolution—the first successful colonial revolt in history—gave birth to a creedal nation embodying the idealism of the Enlightenment, whereas the French Revolution launched in earnest the modern quest for social progress through unyielding political action guided by uncompromising philosophical principle. In these great crucibles of revolution was forged the frame of modern politics, or so the argument goes.

There is of course much truth to this cliché, but it is a partial, or perhaps a secondhand, truth. In fact, the late eighteenth century was the scene of a great Anglo-American debate about the meaning of modern liberalism—a debate that has since shaped the political life of Britain and America, and by now that of a great and growing portion of humanity beyond them. The American Revolution embodied that debate, and the French Revolution intensified it, but the debate preceded them both and has long outlasted them.

The ideals of the American founding were championed by statesmen-revolutionaries who disagreed among themselves about the practical significance of those ideals. The disagreements did not take long to surface and to break the politics of the new republic into distinct camps that in many ways have endured. The actual parties to the struggle in France, meanwhile, the Jacobins and Girondists, monarchists and aristocrats, have no real parallels in contemporary politics. But the parties to the intense Anglo-American debate *about* the French Revolution—a party of justice and a party of order, or a party of progress and a party of conservation—bear a plain paternal resemblance to the parties that now compose the politics of many liberal democracies, including our own. In both cases, the parties to the great debate of the late eighteenth century clearly prefigured key elements of the left-right divide of our time. The arguments between them had to do with much more than the particular promise and peril of the American or French revolutions, and they have lasted because they brought to the surface a disagreement within liberalism that has never lost its salience.

There are no perfect representatives of the two major parties to the great debate of that age, but there may well be no better representatives than Edmund Burke and Thomas Paine. Burke was an Irish-born English politician and writer, a man of intense opinions with an unrivaled gift for expressing them in political rhetoric. He was his era's most devoted and able defender of the inherited traditions of the English constitution. A patient, gradual reformer of his country's institutions, he was among the first and surely the most adamant and effective critics of the radicalism of the French Revolution in English politics.

Paine, an English-born immigrant to America, became one of the most eloquent and important voices championing the cause of independence for the colonies, and then, as revolution brewed in France, he became an influential advocate of the revolutionaries' cause as an essayist and activist in Paris and London. A master of the English language, Paine fervently believed in the potential of Enlightenment liberalism to advance the cause of justice and peace by uprooting corrupt and oppressive regimes and replacing them with governments answerable to the people. He was a brilliant and passionate advocate for liberty and equality.

Each was both a man of ideas and a man of action—a man of powerful political rhetoric and of deep and principled commitment to a cause. Each also saw in the debates of the age far more than the particulars of the events that launched them. The two men knew each other, met several times, exchanged letters, and publicly answered one another's published writings. Their private and public dispute over the French Revolution has been called "perhaps the most crucial ideological debate ever carried on in English."[1] But their profound disagreement extends well beyond their direct confrontations. Each voiced a worldview deeply at odds with the other over some of the most important questions of liberal-democratic political thought. While the capacious arguments of the time surely could not be fully captured in the debate between Burke and Paine, the important questions at stake can be far better understood by examining the two men's views with care. And yet the precise terms and subjects of their disagreement (especially as it relates to matters other than the French Revolution itself) remain to a surprising degree underexamined.

This book seeks to examine Burke and Paine's disagreement and to learn from it about both their era's politics and ours. Using not only their dispute about the French Revolution but also the two men's larger bodies of writing and correspondence, the book will explore the themes of the Burke-Paine dispute, taking apart each man's views of history, nature, society, reason, political institutions, freedom, equality, rights, and other key subjects, and seeking the premises informing each one's understanding of political life. It will argue that Burke and Paine each offers a coherent and, for the most part, internally consistent case about the character of society and politics, and that each man's case is greatly illuminated by contrasting it with the other's. It will demonstrate that Burke's and Paine's diverse arguments are tied together especially by a disagreement about the authority of the given past in political life—and that there is much more to this disagreement than a staid and simple dispute between tradition and progress.

Burke's reforming conservatism and Paine's restoring progressivism are both more complex and more coherent than they first appear. And a careful consideration of both can clarify the terms of our own debates, especially the fundamental dividing line of our politics. As Burke and Paine will show us, the line between progressives and conservatives really divides two kinds of liberals and two distinct visions of the liberal society.[2]

IT MAY SEEM STRANGE to seek philosophical arguments in the words of two men so deeply involved in day-to-day politics. We are not used to political actors who are also political theorists. Such actors were certainly a bit more common in Burke's and Paine's era—when in both Britain and America we encounter some politicians who wrote and thought like philosophers—but they were still very much a rare breed even then. And because nearly all of Burke's and Paine's pamphlets, speeches, letters, and books were written with some immediate political purpose in mind even as they made larger arguments, scholars of both men's views have battled over some very basic questions through the centuries.

In Burke's case, the leading question has been whether he had a consistent set of views throughout his life or whether the French Revolution transformed him somehow. As we will see, Burke spent the first two decades of his political career championing various sorts of reform: of the British government's finances, its treatment of religious minorities, its trade policy, and more. He spent much of this time pushing against the standing inertia of English politics. But after the revolution in France, which he was concerned might be imported to Britain, Burke was above all a staunch defender of Britain's political traditions. He strenuously opposed all efforts to weaken the power of the monarch and the aristocracy and warned against fundamental political reforms (like moves toward greater democratization) that might unmoor the nation from its long-standing traditions. He has sometimes been accused, therefore, of changing his most basic views and turning against his former co-partisans and friends. The charge could first be heard in his own lifetime (voiced by Paine, among others) and has been repeated by some of Burke's biographers and interpreters ever since.

But such a charge miscasts both Burke's earlier and later views, neglecting the arguments he offered both as a reformer and as a conserver of Britain's political tradition. Those arguments were always about finding a balance between stability and change—the quest that, as we will see, was at the core of Burke's ambitions. In the concluding words of his *Reflections on the Revolution in France*, clearly foreseeing the coming charge of inconsistency, Burke described himself as "one who wishes to preserve consistency, but who would preserve consistency by varying his means to secure the unity of his end, and, when the equipoise of the vessel in which he sails may be endangered by overloading it upon one side, is desirous of carrying the small weight of his reasons to that which may preserve its equipoise."[3]

This image of the man seeking to balance his ship—or to balance his country in a sea of troubles—against various threats to its cherished equipoise, is fitting, in light of Burke's varied causes and arguments throughout his eventful career. He was a reformer when some elements of the English constitution threatened to suffocate the whole. He was a preserver when it seemed to him, as David Bromwich has put it, "that revolution is the ultimate enemy of reform."[4] Equipoise, for Burke, is not stagnation, but rather a way of thinking about change and reform, and about political life more generally. As we will see, it was a central metaphor of his political thought.

Regarding Thomas Paine, meanwhile, the leading question that has divided scholars has run even deeper: Is Paine really a political thinker or just a particularly passionate pamphleteer and agitator? While his rhetorical skills are unquestionable, Paine's seriousness—his contention with genuine political ideas—has sometimes been brought into doubt. Critics in his own time sought to dismiss him as a rabid sloganeer or, as Burke himself put it, a man with "not even a moderate portion of learning of any kind."[5] And some scholars since then have repeated the charge that Paine brought more heat than light to the subjects he took up.

But such accusations have always been tinged with a revealing snobbery. They have been made by political opponents who considered Paine's philosophy unserious and who have therefore been inclined to see its champions—especially those who do not answer to the traditional description of the learned philosopher—as unserious as well. Certainly, Paine was not the erudite intellectual that Burke was. His formal education was minimal, and his engagement with the philosophical tradition of the West bore the telltale rough edges of the autodidact. One gets the sense that Paine took a sardonic pleasure in his peculiar, if plainly false, boast that in all his prolific years of writing, "I neither read books, nor studied other people's opinions; I thought for myself."[6] (Paine's friend Thomas Jefferson repeated a version of this backhanded praise when he noted that Paine always "thought more than he read.")[7] Paine's writing is indeed remarkably (though far from entirely) devoid of explicit references to great thinkers of the past. Nor did he have the intense and extended exposure to practical politics that Burke could boast of.

And yet, Paine's oversized role both in the American Revolution and in the English-speaking world's response to the French Revolution was no accident; nor was it a mere matter of fortunate timing or purely a function of great writing. On the contrary, Paine's great rhetorical power came from his ability to bring even modestly educated readers into contact with profound philosophical questions and to give those questions an immediacy and intensity that few political thinkers could match. Paine understood politics as moved by principles, and he thought that political systems had to answer to the right kinds of philosophical ideals—especially equality and liberty. However well established and grand they might be, however deep their roots might reach, all regimes had to be evaluated by how well they advanced these basic human goods. Thus, political principles and their instantiation in political actions are key to Paine's teaching and present themselves far more prominently in the foreground of his writing than even in Burke's. In an 1806 letter, Paine wrote this about himself: "My motive and object in all my political works, beginning with Common Sense, the first work I ever published, have been to rescue man from tyranny and false systems and false principles of government, and enable him to be free and establish government for himself."[8] Paine sought for the theories and ideas underlying political life, and argued that only a government that answers to the right theories and ideas can make any claim to legitimacy.

Precisely because Burke and Paine were both political thinkers and political actors, their dispute opens a window into the origins of our own political order. They help us to see how the kinds of arguments made in the heat of a policy debate relate to the kinds of arguments made in the calm of a philosopher's study. And they help us understand how the divisions on display in our everyday politics came to be.

Burke was always stung by the notion that he and Paine should be understood together, complaining in one letter to his friend William Elliott of that bothersome "Citizen Paine, who, they will have it, hunts with me in couples."[9] But bothered though they might have been by one another, Burke and Paine may truly be best understood as counterparts. Like the two broad parties to our own political disputes, they continue to this day to hunt in couples. So let us join them on the hunt and see what we can learn from them about both their time and our own.

ONE

Two Lives in the Arena

O N THE EVENING OF AUGUST 18, 1788, TWO OF THE fiercest combatants in the great political debates of the age of revolutions sat down together for a meal. Although they had given voice to deeply opposing political ideas for well over a decade, they had not yet quite grasped the degree of their profound dispute, and their time together, by all accounts, was pleasant and amicable. "I am just going to dine with the Duke of Portland, in company with the great American Paine," Edmund Burke had written to a friend earlier that day.[1] "From the part Mr. Burke took in the American Revolution," Thomas Paine would later write, "it was natural that I should consider him a friend to mankind; and . . . our acquaintance commenced on that ground."[2] Their acquaintance would end on very different ground, and their disagreement—which was soon to explode into the open around the French Revolution—would not only help to define the politics of their age but would also reverberate through the centuries and around the globe.

It is tempting now to think of those dinner companions that summer evening as embodiments of the ideas we have come to identify with them, and perhaps to wonder how they could have tolerated one another's company, given their differences. But human beings are more than the sum of their opinions, and before we can consider what Burke and Paine stood for, we must discover who they were and get a flavor of the age in which they lived. Doing both will help us understand how men with such deep differences could at first encounter one another as fellow travelers of a sort, if not indeed as kindred spirits.

Burke and Paine were both unusual figures in an unusual time. Each was a man of humble origins who became a celebrated luminary. Each was an outsider who transformed himself, by force of intellect and personality, into the great champion of a society in which he was not born. Each was a firebrand and master of political rhetoric yet was known as much for the force of his arguments as for the power of his words. And in every sense, Burke and Paine were men of their time— even if they disagreed vehemently about what their era represented and where its politics were headed.

In our political imagination, the late eighteenth century is often shrouded in an almost mystical aura. It was an age teeming with towering political figures who managed somehow to be simultaneously statesmen and philosophers. Among his close acquaintances and friends, Thomas Paine could count George Washington, Thomas Jefferson, James Madison, James Monroe, and many other legends of the American founding generation. He thought of Benjamin Franklin as a kind of patron, and Franklin once described Paine as his "adopted political son." Burke was well acquainted with Franklin too, having gotten to know him during Franklin's time as the representative of the American colonies in London. And Burke counted among his friends such leading lights of the British intellectual world as the great writer and moralist Samuel Johnson, the historian Edward Gibbon, the philosopher and economist Adam Smith, and essentially every prominent parliamentary and political figure of the day from King George III on down.

This profusion of philosophical and practical genius did not emerge all at once by accident. It arose in response to the profound social and political flux of the age. Even a century after England's Glorious Revolution had reestablished a stable Protestant monarchy in London, religious tensions continued to boil just below the surface throughout the Anglo-American world. And even before the American and French revolutions shattered the reigning order of Europe, it was clear to all that the challenge posed to the continent's political traditions by Enlightenment ideas about freedom and equality, combined with the challenge posed to its aristocratic economic arrangements by the gradual emergence of an industrial manufacturing system, would yield deep and lasting changes on both sides of the Atlantic.

The nature and character of those changes were at the heart of the debate in which Burke and Paine would take leading parts. But neither man was by any means a natural candidate for the part he turned out to play.

"A YOUNG MR. BURKE"

Edmund Burke was born in Dublin, Ireland, most likely in January 1729.[3] His father was a prominent (if never wealthy) attorney and a Protestant, and his mother was a Catholic from the Nagle family of County Cork. Such mixed marriages were not unheard of in Ireland in those days, but neither were they common. His Catholic wife meant that Burke's father, Richard, could never reach the pinnacle of Dublin society and that the religious divisions (which translated, as they still do, to economic and political divisions) in Ireland would never be far from Edmund's own view growing up. He was born the same year that Jonathan Swift described the miserable lot of Ireland's poor in his *Modest Proposal*. While Burke's family was always reasonably comfortable, he witnessed real poverty around him. At times, especially during extended visits with his mother's rural Catholic relatives, he even observed genuinely grinding deprivation of a degree barely imaginable to the English aristocrats he would come to know later in life.

As was the custom in mixed Irish marriages of the time, Burke and his two brothers were raised in their father's Anglican faith, while their sister was raised a Catholic. Burke's early education was in a Quaker boarding school, where he showed an early aptitude for poetry and philosophy. In an era of often bitter divisions (in both England and Ireland) between the official Anglican Church, Catholicism, and the dissenting Protestant sects (such as the Quakers), Burke managed in his first fifteen years to travel through all three circles. The experience of seeing differences of dogma made moot in practice by the bonds of family affection and neighborly respect was formative for him. It seemed to leave him with a lasting sense that life was more complicated in practice than in theory—and that this was a good thing. And his university education, at Dublin's renowned Trinity College, grounded this sense of the almost indescribable complexity of actual living communities in classical learning and a refined appreciation for philosophy and art.

Although he would spend the great bulk of the rest of his life in England, these early Irish lessons—along with his distinctive Irish accent—never left Burke. They helped him always mark a difference between abstract political ideals and actual life as lived. He retained a sense of how accommodations built up slowly from reserves of trust, warm sentiment, and moderation could enable people to live together even in the face of social tension, political oppression, and economic plight.

His Irish upbringing and education also left Burke with a deep love of language, the written word in particular. Upon graduation from Trinity, he left for London, ostensibly to study law at his father's urging, though he abandoned his legal studies in short order to pursue his dream of joining the ranks of the great city's intellectuals by becoming a writer on large public questions. London was a hotbed of philosophical and political debates, most often carried on through pamphlets—lengthy opinion essays (most of which would today qualify as short books), published and sold very cheaply, often answering one another and seeking to ground in deeper principles an immediate question of policy. These pamphlets would swiftly make the rounds of

London's burgeoning café culture and made for an exhilarating atmosphere of tense engagement with philosophy and politics.

From his earliest published writing—a lengthy pamphlet called *A Vindication of Natural Society* published in 1756—Burke tackled foundational questions of political life and revealed an inclination to recoil from potentially corrosive radicalism. The *Vindication* is a work of satire, lampooning the style of argument employed by Lord Bolingbroke—an important politician and thinker who had died a few years earlier, but whose final book, *Letters on the Study and Use of History*, had just been published posthumously. The book had been notable for its criticism of religion, including the official state religion. Bolingbroke had argued that all organized religions are essentially artificial and therefore unfounded and that only a simple, natural religion (or Deism) that does not claim access to revealed truth but merely expresses gratitude to God for the natural world could be legitimate. He drew a sharp distinction between "natural" and "artificial" beliefs, championing the former in the name of rational science and rejecting the latter as groundless dogma. Burke, in his critical satire, emulated Bolingbroke's style and case, but applied it to politics, suggesting that all artificial social institutions should be abandoned. He sought to show where such ways of arguing would lead if they were allowed to proceed to their logical conclusions, suggesting that arguments intended to undermine religion by appealing to a simple notion of nature in opposition to traditional institutions could also undermine all political authority and social allegiance, dissolving the bonds that hold societies together.

"What is remarkable in Burke's first performance," wrote his great nineteenth-century biographer John Morley, "is his discernment of the important fact that behind the intellectual disturbances in the sphere of philosophy, and the noisier agitations in the sphere of theology, there silently stalked a force that might shake the whole fabric of civil society itself."[4] A caustic and simplistic skepticism of all traditional institutions, supposedly grounded in a scientific rationality that took nothing for granted but in fact willfully ignored the true complexity of social life, seemed to Burke poorly suited for the study of society, and even dangerous when applied to it. Burke would warn of, and contend with, this force for the rest of his life.

The *Vindication* had displayed Burke's early tendency to write about philosophically serious subjects with political and social implications and yet to do so at some remove from daily politics. This was all the more evident the following year, 1757, when Burke published his most expressly theoretical work and his only real book: *A Philosophical Enquiry into the Origins of Our Ideas of the Sublime and the Beautiful*. It was an insightful if quirky work of aesthetics—the study of the human experience of beauty. Burke sought to explain the distinction between the beautiful (or well formed) and the sublime (or compelling) as grounded in the difference between love and fear. It was a surprisingly original contribution to a long-running debate among British philosophical thinkers about the sources of human perception and experience, and it opens a door to the young Burke's emerging political sensibilities. Burke argues that human nature relies on emotional, not only rational, edification and instruction—an idea that would become crucial to his insistence that government must function in accordance with the forms and traditions of a society's life and not only abstract principles of justice. "The influence of reason in producing our passions is nothing near so extensive as it is commonly believed," Burke writes.[5] We are moved by more than logic, and so politics must answer to more than cold arguments.

Both of Burke's works enjoyed moderate success and helped him make a name for himself in London's literary world. He was an early member of Samuel Johnson's lively circle—which included the famed painter Joshua Reynolds, Edward Gibbon, the actor David Garrick, the novelist Oliver Goldsmith, James Boswell (who later famously wrote a biography of Johnson), and other prominent intellectual figures of the era—and he thought of himself above all as a writer rather than a political thinker, though his writings always tended toward political and philosophical questions. The author and politician Horace Walpole ran across the still-precocious Burke at a dinner party in 1761 and offered a telling description. Among the guests, Walpole wrote in his private diary, was "a young Mr. Burke, who wrote a book in the style of Lord Bolingbroke, that is much admired. He is a sensible man, but has not worn off his authorism yet, and thinks there is nothing so charming as writers, and to be one. He will know better one of these days."[6]

Burke would come to know better as he ventured into politics, which he did largely for practical reasons at first. In late 1761, now married and a father of one, he needed a reliable livelihood and so put aside his writing ambitions. He took up a position as private secretary to William Gerard Hamilton, an ambitious member of Parliament who soon became the British government's chief secretary to Ireland (and took Burke with him). The post took Burke back to his birthplace for a time and gave him an even more direct view of the intense religious tensions that tore at Ireland's soul. In his many years in English politics, Burke would always be sensitive to being viewed as too immersed in the Irish question, given his roots, but he could never let go of it either. His religiously mixed family, combined with his experience at Hamilton's side, made him a devoted defender of the basic rights of Ireland's Catholics, often to his own political detriment.

After three years in the post, Burke left Hamilton's service and, through the help of mutual acquaintances, became private secretary to the Marquis of Rockingham, the great Whig leader who would serve briefly as prime minister and would be Burke's foremost political patron and friend. Rockingham immediately grasped Burke's immense talent and value—his erudition, his prudence, and his considerable rhetorical skills. He brought Burke into the inner circle of Whig politics and, in 1765, arranged for him to be elected to a seat in the House of Commons—Burke's great arena for the next three decades.

From that point until his death in 1797, Burke would be immersed in the political life of his country and would devote himself to seeing Britain through the staggering and seemingly endless succession of crises and other challenges of that period, taking passionate public views on the great questions of the day: Ireland's religious and political troubles, the American Revolution and its aftermath, Britain's management and mismanagement of India, contentious reforms of the British parliamentary and electoral system, the monumental challenge of the French Revolution, and the European war that followed. Though Burke would hold no prominent executive position and indeed would spend the great bulk of his time in Parliament in opposition, his voice would quickly become among the most prominent and recognizable in British politics, and his pen would prove crucial to the great events of the age.

As a counselor to the Whig Party's leaders, Burke established himself as a chief voice of the party and indeed soon became the leading advocate for the place of political parties in British public life. In a 1770 pamphlet, *Thoughts on the Causes of the Present Discontents*, written in the context of a scandal involving King George III's excessive involvement in government appointments and public jobs, Burke argued that political parties were not, as many people insisted, factions each contending for its own particular advantage, but rather were bodies of men each united by a vision of the common good of the whole nation. Partisanship, he insisted, was not only unavoidable but also beneficial, as it helped to organize politics into camps defined by different priorities about what was best for the country. This popular pamphlet, and others like it in that period, showed unmistakable early signs of Burke's distinctive political philosophy, as he argued for prudent statesmanship and an attention to the sentiments (and not just the material needs) of the people and to the venerated status of social and political institutions. Political reform, he suggested, must take account of these and proceed gradually and respectfully regarding them.

The pamphlet also revealed Burke's immense rhetorical skill—which expressed itself not only in a talent for captivating epigrams, but also in a sustained and coherent vision of political life and society laid out with impressive clarity and consistency. As Burke later put it in describing the talents required of a statesman, this vision combined "a disposition to preserve and an ability to improve."[7] And it was always reinforced by powerful and memorable written words that overwhelm the reader with images and ideas.

Burke also devoted a great deal of his time and energy to parliamentary and financial reform during this period. Frequent scandals around revelations of public mismanagement and corruption were undermining the nation's faith in its government, and Burke was concerned that an excessive response from his fellow members of Parliament to the scandals could threaten the integrity of Britain's mixed regime. Wasteful spending on the monarchy itself (especially the king's enormous staff and costly residences) was a particular concern, and Burke moved to stem that concern by reorganizing how the system was financed. He also sought to simplify Britain's immensely complex criminal law (which, he believed, assigned vastly excessive punishments for petty crimes) and to soften the punishment of debtors. Burke was keenly aware that society was always changing, and its laws needed to change too. But in every case, he advanced gradual and incremental rather than radical or fundamental reforms and he always called for respect for existing institutions and forms. Constructive change requires stability, so reformers always have to be careful. "I advance to it with a tremor that shakes me to the inmost fiber of my frame," he told the House of Commons in reference to his financial reforms. "I feel that I engage in a business . . . the most completely adverse that can be imagined to the natural turn and temper of my own mind."[8]

No eager democrat, Burke rejected the notion that a member of the Commons must simply express the views of those who sent him, even telling an audience of his own constituents in 1774 that he owed them his judgment rather than his obedience.[9] But for all the passionate expression he gave to the cause of preserving Britain's cherished institutions, Burke in these early years in Parliament was, above all, a reformer—of financial policy and trade policy, of laws restricting the freedom of Catholics and Protestant dissenters, and of the criminal law. He also opposed the slave trade as inhuman and unjust and resisted the undue intervention of the Crown in politics.

Burke approached the American crisis, which heated to a boil in the mid-1770s, with this mix of inclinations toward preservation and reform. As he saw it, the Tory administration of Lord North had acted imprudently in trying to pay Britain's war debts by levying new taxes on the Americans without consulting them. People who argued about whether Parliament had the right to tax the American colonies—the question essentially everyone on both sides of the debate took up—were focused on the wrong subject. Parliament certainly had that right, Burke suggested, because its legal prerogative to govern the empire was unquestionable. But having that right did not mean Parliament had to exercise it or that the government was wise to do so. The government of human beings, he argued, is a matter not of applying cold rules and principles, but of tending to warm sentiments and attachments to produce the strongest and best unified community possible. Surely London could work with the Americans to yield greater revenues rather than commanding their assent.

"Politics ought to be adjusted not to human reasonings but to human nature, of which the reason is but a part, and by no means the greatest part," Burke said.[10] The Americans, he argued in his *Speech on Conciliation with the Colonies,* had over time developed robust habits of freedom and an independent spirit, and if they were to be governed as Englishmen, some reasonable effort must be made to accommodate their character. In this way, Burke put himself at odds with the most passionate American advocates of independence (including Thomas Paine) by denying their most basic claims of rights and principles—claims he rejected not only as false in that instance but also as inappropriate for political judgment in general. Burke certainly believed in the central importance of political rights, but he thought that rights could not be disconnected from obligations in society and therefore could not quite be understood apart from the particular circumstances of particular societies in particular moments. The more radical liberals of his day treated politics as a kind of philosophical geometry, he thought, applying principles and postulates to come up with the right solution, but real societies did not work—or at least did not work well—that way. And yet he put himself on the radicals' side of the practical question, concluding finally that if North's administration could not govern the Americans prudently, it ought to set them free for the good of the empire.

In these speeches, we begin to get a sense of the richness of Burke's understanding of society and politics. Especially evident is his understanding of how to properly manage political change to balance the desire for justice and the need for social stability—a subject that, as we will see, was often foremost on his mind. In the years that followed the American war, these views continued to drive Burke to restrain and resist abuses of government power. "Government," he wrote, "is deeply interested in every thing which, even through the medium of some temporary uneasiness, may tend finally to compose the minds of the subjects, and to conciliate their affections."[11] Excessive and needlessly aggravating uses of power can undermine these affections, and this idea moved Burke to worry about the king's excessive involvement in politics in the early 1760s, the needless irritation of the Americans later in that decade and into the 1770s, and British abuses of the natives of India in the 1780s. Out of the latter concern, Burke in 1787 even launched a lengthy, albeit ultimately futile, impeachment effort against Warren Hastings, the chief British administrator of India. All of this made Burke a prominent reformer, though for reasons other than those of most of his fellows in that camp. He was never a radical modernizer, as some of his fellow Whigs were, but he worked with these more radical elements when he thought their efforts could counterbalance an abuse of power.

But the abuse of power was not the only solvent of the sentiments essential to a strong and happy people. The corrosion of public feelings, mutual attachments, and basic human dignity that resulted from reducing politics to abstract rights and principles could be no less caustic. Indeed, as Burke had seen in his earliest published work, such corrosion could be far more dangerous in the long run because it tended to encourage a radical disposition toward politics. Politics was first and foremost about particular people living together, rather than about general rules put into effect. This emphasis caused Burke to oppose the sort of liberalism expounded by many of the radical reformers of his day. They argued in the parlance of natural rights drawn from reflections on an individualist state of nature and sought to apply the principles of that approach directly to political life. "I do not enter into these metaphysical distinctions," Burke said in his *Speech on American Taxation*. "I hate the very sound of them."[12]

This way of thinking about politics made Burke a reformer of failing institutions who was wary of radical change and a preserver of venerated traditions who was wary of the abuse of power. To someone familiar only with his final positions on particular questions and not with the reasoning he offered to explain himself, Burke in the late 1780s—when Thomas Paine encountered him—would have been hard to read and easy to misunderstand. And Paine, thanks to his own unusual path to prominence, was himself not so easy to grasp.

"AN INGENIOUS WORTHY YOUNG MAN"

Thomas Paine was born in January 1737 in Thetford, in the south of England. His father, a corset maker by profession, was a Quaker, and his mother was an Anglican. Paine was baptized in his mother's church, his parents reasoning that this might open more doors for him in the future, but his father was the more religiously observant parent, and the young Thomas often accompanied him to the Quaker meeting house. Although as an adult Paine would criticize the austerity of the Quakers (once joking that if God had consulted the Quakers in the creation, then all the world's flowers would be gray), it is also clear that their stark moralism deeply shaped him. He had a lifelong ingrained sense that the laws of justice are clear and simple, that they embody a preference for the weak over the strong, and that there can be no excuse for disregarding them.

Whereas Burke's mixed parentage left him with a sense of the complexity of society, Paine's experience seems to have left him thinking that religious disputes were ultimately pointless, and that it was morality—which he thought could be distinguished from religion— that truly mattered. "My religion is to do good," he later wrote.[13]

Paine's father always had steady work, but only enough to keep the family on the precipice of poverty. Intelligent and bookish, Paine was admitted to a grammar school at the age of seven. His parents scrimped to keep their only child in school, but they did not have enough to take him past the five years of schooling he received there. These years would be his only formal education (though Paine was a devoted autodidact from then on).[14] After apprenticing in his father's craft, he spent a brief period in London—working in the trade by day and enjoying the city's literary café culture by night—and even made some extra money by serving for a few months as a privateer on a naval vessel in the Seven Years' War. Needing steadier work, he left London, first for Dover and then to start his own small stay-making business in the town of Sandwich, in the southeast of England. Paine did not much enjoy his work, but it offered him a living, and he used every spare moment to read, especially books of poetry, history, and science. In 1759, he was married to Mary Lambert—who had been working as a maid in the town.

Paine thus seemed to have begun his life's journey as a working-class Englishman. But in 1762, after the tragic death of his wife and child in childbirth, his world was turned upside down. Overcome with desperate grief, he abandoned his profession and his now empty home to become an excise officer—an itinerant collector of taxes on commodities like coffee, tea, and alcohol.

The excise trade was notoriously corrupt. The collectors were paid very poorly and were expected to carry out the thankless and challenging task of confronting popular shopkeepers for back taxes and even combatting smuggling and black-market profiteering. Many of his fellow excise officers took bribes (and Paine himself was accused of wrongdoing when he rented a room from a shopkeeper who was under his jurisdiction). The experience left Paine with an awareness of the potential for government corruption and for the abuse of workers—a sense that would stay with him.

He did begin to rebuild his life in this work—finding friends among his colleagues and in 1771 marrying a second time. But the difficult working conditions proved too much. In 1772, while working in East Sussex, Paine joined an effort launched by his fellow tax collectors to lobby Parliament for better pay and treatment. He had made a reputation for himself as an unusually well-read and well-spoken tax collector, and his fellow officers entrusted him to put their case in writing and press it before government officials. This was his first taste of the thrill of political action, and it led to his first political writing: A roughly twenty-page pamphlet titled *The Case of the Officers of Excise* was received with rapt enthusiasm by his colleagues.

Like his more famous later writings, this pamphlet contained a fascinating mix of careful lawyerly arguments, detailed facts and figures, and passages of passionate and at times powerfully beautiful rhetoric. It also clearly gave vent to Paine's own experience of poverty and even of grief at the loss of his first wife. Paine's response to the argument that the excise officers could find ways to make do with what the government paid them was thunderous: "He who never was hungered may argue finely on the subjection of his appetite; and he who never was distressed may harangue as beautifully on the power of principle. But poverty, like grief, has an incurable deafness, which never hears; the oration loses all its edge; and 'to be or not to be' becomes the only question."[15]

Here was the voice that would move history. But it would not move Parliament on this occasion. In the winter of 1773–1774, Paine spent all his time (taking leave from his work) in London distributing copies of his pamphlet and lobbying members of Parliament. The futile effort cost him his job, sent him deeply into debt, and ultimately became unbearable for his wife, who sought an end to their marriage.

But Paine's disastrous monomania did not altogether ruin him. Bankrupt and living in London, he was introduced by a friend to Benjamin Franklin, then the representative of the American colonies in Britain. Franklin, ever the talent scout for his home team, was impressed with Paine's intelligence and drive and advised him to seek a new start in America—providing him with a generous letter of introduction to ease his way. "The bearer," Franklin wrote, "is very well recommended to me as an ingenious worthy young man."[16] On November 30, 1774, Paine arrived in Philadelphia. For him, as for so many before and after him, America offered a new beginning. He was eager to start not where his working-class roots had placed him by birth but where his lengthy and deeply impressive philosophical and political self-education could enable him to operate. The reinvented Paine emerged very quickly into public prominence.

Within weeks he had found a job with Robert Aitken, a Philadelphia printer and publisher of the *Pennsylvania Magazine*, and by the spring of 1775, only half a year into his American journey, Paine was the magazine's editor and a regular voice in its pages. He wrote on a wide range of social and political subjects—from local scandals to international affairs—but always with a plainspoken moralism intent on protecting the needy and weak. One article in particular, a powerful denunciation of the slave trade, gained him the attention of Benjamin Rush—the great physician and statesman and the unofficial organizer of Philadelphia's small but deeply impressive intellectual community. Rush brought Paine into the inner circle of the city's political and literary elites, where Paine's writings gained ever greater prominence.

These early writings hint at both Paine's considerable rhetorical skills and his grasp of the reigning Enlightenment-liberal views of his time—a devotion to individual rights, a theory of government as guardian of these rights, righteous rage at every violation of them, and an unbending passion for justice for the weak suffering under the boot of the strong. His sheer rhetorical skill sometimes overwhelms the reader, just as in Burke's writing. But where Burke's considerable faculty for expression is most often employed to convey the complexity of social and political life, Paine's most often conveys a simplicity—a sense that the just and right way forward can be discerned by a proper application of key principles and that we are duty-bound to discern and to follow it. Paine's views, as they begin to emerge here, are not highly original, but they are fairly reliably representative of the Enlightenment-liberal (or radical) views of his day. In these early years, as in his later more prominent work, Paine spoke for many, but far more effectively than most.

Paine's magazine mostly steered clear of the great and growing political question of the day—the prospect of a break with Britain. His publisher feared antagonizing loyalist subscribers, and Paine himself was not initially sure where he stood on the question. But as events were giving shape to an American revolt, Paine came to believe that a reconciliation with Britain could no longer be had on just and honorable terms, and he began to employ his pen in the cause of independence. At first, he did so anonymously and outside the pages of the *Pennsylvania Magazine*. His first effort, an imagined dialogue between two British generals, was published in the *Pennsylvania Journal* in January 1775 and argued that the British were not interested in reconciliation.[17] He followed it with various essays, observations, and even poems intended to make the American case—at first gently and with an eye to possible rapprochement with Britain, but over time with increasing force and a growing emphasis on independence. In October 1775, he published a brief essay, "A Serious Thought," which laid out British violations of the rights of individuals around their empire, including in America. The piece concluded: "When I reflect on these, I hesitate not for a moment to believe that the Almighty will finally separate America from Britain. Call it independence or what you will, if it is the cause of God and humanity, it will go on."[18]

As he published these short writings, Paine had begun to work on a more extended and sustained case for independence. Spurred on by the early battles between American and British forces and the appointment of George Washington to command the army, Paine sought a means of persuading the people to fight and (perhaps even more so) persuading the colonial elites to support the move for independence. By the concluding days of 1775, he had composed an extended pamphlet for that purpose, which he aimed to title *Plain Truth*. Paine's friend Rush, upon reading the draft, encouraged its quick publication and suggested an improvement to the title—*Common Sense*.

The fifty-page pamphlet was an all-out assault on the British Crown and indeed on the notion of hereditary monarchy and the practices and premises of British politics. It laid out, too, the beginnings of a political philosophy. Paine's opening description of the work for his readers, on the title page of the original printed pamphlet, describes it as taking up four subjects: "The origin and design of government in general, with concise remarks on the English constitution; monarchy and hereditary succession; thoughts on the present state of American affairs; [and] the present ability of America, with some miscellaneous reflections." The pamphlet begins by establishing some principles for distinguishing legitimate from illegitimate rule: that government exists to secure the freedom and security of its equal citizens and that any government that fails to do so is not worthy of the name, regardless of its pedigree.

Paine's case for independence is grounded in these stark and fundamental principles, and *Common Sense* asserts that reasoning from such principles and rights is the only proper way to approach politics. In straightforward language accessible to every reader, Paine lays out a lengthy and logical case against the authority of Britain to command the colonies (since the colonists are not represented in the Parliament they answer to), against the legitimacy of Britain's own domestic political institutions (which give the king absolute power over the citizens his government is supposed to serve), and in favor of a republican government elected by the people and answerable to them.[19] He concludes that "however strange it may appear to some, or however unwilling they may be to think so, matters not, but many strong and striking reasons may be given to show that nothing can settle our affairs so expeditiously as an open and determined declaration for independence."[20]

Paine's earlier efforts had certainly been noticed, but *Common Sense* was simply a sensation. Within a few weeks, it had spread around the colonies, portions were reprinted in newspapers, and many tens of thousands of copies were sold.[21] It reached its readers at a moment when many thoughtful colonists were wondering if their leaders had carelessly marched them into a disastrous blunder by taking on the world's most powerful military force. Was this conflict with England all a tax revolt by wealthy elites? *Common Sense* answered powerfully in the negative: This was a righteous cause and well worth the struggle. The pamphlet offered bold, fiery declarations for those already inclined to independence as well as cool, logical arguments for those on the fence, and it seemed genuinely to persuade. "By private letters which I have lately received from Virginia," George Washington wrote to his friend Joseph Reed in April 1776, "I find that 'Common Sense' is working a powerful change there in the minds of many men."[22]

In the months that followed, Paine quickly became the leader of the rhetorical struggle for independence. He published a series of letters responding to critics of *Common Sense* and helped draft a new constitution for Pennsylvania, seeking to put into practice the principles held out as the impetus for revolution—a representative government that treated its citizens as free and equal. Paine also contributed directly to the war effort, working as a secretary for several officers and traveling with the army to memorialize its efforts. The fall of 1776 was a very difficult time for Washington's army, and morale among the advocates of independence was extremely low. In an effort to lift the spirits of the fighting men and their supporters, Paine, while traveling with the army in New Jersey, penned an essay that came to be known as "The American Crisis." The article would turn out to be the first of a line of *Crisis* papers. The first paper opens with what may be Paine's most famous lines: "These are the times that try men's souls. The summer soldier and the sunshine patriot will, in this crisis, shrink from the service of their country; but he that stands by it now, deserves the love and thanks of man and woman. Tyranny, like hell, is not easily conquered; yet we have this consolation with us, that the harder the conflict, the more glorious the triumph. What we obtain too cheap, we esteem too lightly: it is dearness only that gives every thing its value."[23]

Paine would publish sixteen *Crisis* papers over the subsequent seven years of war, each piece intended to address some particular exigency of the moment. Some of the papers were filled with facts and figures, others were simply pep talks for the troops, and yet others made large arguments in broad strokes about the illegitimacy of the British government's claim on the colonies. But all of the papers built on the arguments and worldview that Paine had laid out in *Common Sense*. Meanwhile, Paine was also actively involved in the administration of the war—serving as secretary to the Continental Congress's committee on foreign affairs and later as the clerk of the Pennsylvania legislature. He also continued to publish essays and pamphlets on public questions, including calls for a stronger central government to advance the war effort and arguments for an end to slavery.

At the end of the war, as compensation for his great service to the cause, the New York state legislature gave Paine a farm in New Rochelle, which had been confiscated from a loyalist family. There Paine lived until 1787, devoting himself largely to scientific pursuits and inventions and most notably to a new design for an iron bridge with a single large arch that might traverse the width of a river without obstructing the passage of the large commercial vessels increasingly found in American and European river traffic. He seemed to put politics behind him, though as it turned out, he could not keep away for long.

In the spring of 1787, Paine set out to find financing for his bridge design—financing that he knew could only come from Europe. He thus traveled to France and Britain in search of support, expecting to be gone for no more than a year. He did find some English funders, and eventually a bridge employing his design was built over the Wear River in the north of England. (Another, built decades later, still stands over the Dunlap Creek in Brownsville, Pennsylvania, to this day.) But as he surely must have known he would, Paine also encountered enormous political turmoil on his travels. The prospect of revolution was heavy in the air in France, and a sense of instability was palpable in Britain too.

As much as anyone on either side of the Atlantic, Paine had always believed the American Revolution was the beginning of a revolutionary chapter in world history. Universal principles of equality and liberty could not long be held back: "The independence of America, considered merely as a separation from England, would have been a matter but of little importance had it not been accompanied by a revolution in the principles and practice of governments. She made a stand not for herself only but for the world, and looked beyond the advantages herself could receive."[24] He fully expected the ideals of the revolution to spread to Britain and the continent.

Paine was in France—where his bridge design met with great interest (though not with financial backing) and where his reputation preceded him in radical and revolutionary circles—until the late summer of 1787. Paris in that period felt to him like Philadelphia in the year before the outbreak of war. He knew a great event was coming, and his hopes for it were high. In the fall, he traveled to Britain to seek support for his bridge and to meet some of those who had backed the American cause—among whose number Paine certainly counted Edmund Burke.

Paine thus approached his meeting with Burke with a sense that Burke and the other leading English Whigs were kindred spirits, persuaded as he was of the ideological foundation of the American Revolution and enthused by its potential to spark popular uprisings elsewhere. He could hardly have been more wrong about Burke's essential concerns and priorities. Burke himself, meanwhile, was certainly aware of Paine's role and resulting fame, though it is far from clear if Burke had read *Common Sense* before encountering its author. In his *Letter to the Sheriffs of Bristol*, in 1777, Burke had mentioned in passing "the author of the celebrated pamphlet which prepared the minds of the people for independence," and more or less justified that author as having been driven to his opinions by the excesses of the British government.[25] But he nowhere contends with the radical views of politics laid out in *Common Sense*, and it seems unlikely that Burke would have failed to react badly to those views had he encountered them.

FIRST ENCOUNTERS

Burke and Paine may have met for the first time, very briefly, in late 1787.[26] Then, in the summer of 1788, they not only met for a meal but also spent several days together at Burke's home. Burke wrote of hosting "the famous Mr. Paine, the author of Common Sense, the Crisis, etc. and Secretary to the congress for foreign affairs," noting that he "was not sorry to see a man who was active in such an important scene."[27] Paine was interested mainly in advancing his bridge, and apparently, the two steered largely away from politics, but got along reasonably well and remained in contact after the visit. In a January 1789 letter to Jefferson (who was then still in Paris), Paine wrote of being "in some intimacy with Mr. Burke."[28]

Paine's time in Paris had exposed him to the leaders of the radical wing of French politics. His reputation (in a culture that valued writers), his connections, and his politics made him a natural fit, and Paine was much taken with the spirit of the hour in Paris—with revolution threatening to erupt. He quickly abandoned his intention to return to America after a year, concluding that he might play some role on behalf of America, or of America's ideals, in France or Britain.

Burke, meanwhile, was much concerned with domestic affairs in Britain. In November 1788, King George III fell seriously ill, and his condition (which some modern researchers suggest might have been caused by long-term exposure to low doses of arsenic in his diet) expressed itself in, among other things, serious signs of mental imbalance. He would speak unceasingly in English and German at no one in particular for hours at a time, foaming at the mouth. And he was thoroughly unable to carry out his duties. Talk of a regency—or temporary substitute for the king—soon began and set off an explosive political crisis about the power of the regent.

The most plausible regent was the man who would succeed the king should his illness prove fatal: his son, the twenty-six-year old Prince George. The prince was known to harbor deep hostility to the Tory prime minister, William Pitt, and was indeed a personal friend of Whig leader Charles James Fox. Pitt, in an effort to prevent his government's dismissal, introduced a regency bill that would have placed far-reaching limits on the power of the regent, obliging the regent to keep the existing government in place and restraining him from exercising most of the powers of the monarch. Fox, meanwhile, asserted the prince's complete hereditary power to take over. The two thus found themselves in an odd reversal of roles, with the Tory (whose party normally defended the prerogatives of the monarch) insisting that the Crown must be answerable to Parliament and the Whig (whose party stood for the rights of Parliament in a limited monarchy) affirming the hereditary authority of the ruler. Pitt's bill, which would have forced a monumental constitutional crisis, was ready to be advanced when, in March 1788, the king recovered and the crisis was ended.

This Regency Crisis, as it came to be known, left Burke deeply shaken and alarmed. As described earlier, Burke was an unusual Whig. He was moved most fundamentally not by reforming inclinations (as most Whigs of his day were), but by a desire to sustain the stability and unity of his society. He was a Whig because the Whigs stood for the legacy of Britain's Glorious Revolution of 1688. But Burke valued that revolution (in which Parliament overthrew the Catholic king, James II, and installed William and Mary as joint monarchs to reassert a Protestant line of succession and avert a disastrous religious war) for preserving the regime, not, as some more radical Whigs argued, for introducing new principles of parliamentary supremacy that pointed toward a republican government. It had been, in Burke's words, "a revolution not made but prevented."[29] So although his great concern in the 1760s and early 1770s had been excessive royal authority, Burke now saw the monarch's role in the English system coming under threat, and he reacted with equal concern. That his party interests were also invested in the regency made him all the more tenacious, to be sure, but considering Burke's behavior in the crisis, he clearly began to feel profound apprehension for the essential stability of the British system. The sight of the Tories arguing against the authority of the Crown—and of many of his fellow Whigs being slowly convinced of the merits of their case—aroused a genuine concern about a ruinous republican revolution in Britain, which would in every way color his reaction to events in France soon after.

Thomas Paine, with whom Burke had exchanged a few brief and cordial letters since Paine's visit, did not help things. He wrote to Burke from France in the midst of the crisis to suggest that Burke "propose a national convention, to be fairly elected, for the purpose of taking the state of the nation into consideration" and essentially reorganizing the regime from scratch.[30] Such an idea could not have been further from Burke's preservationist inclinations, and while we have no evidence of a response from Burke, this was probably when Burke began to discern the true distance between his and Paine's views of politics.

Burke's passionate opposition to the Tory maneuver in the Regency Crisis had its costs, however. During a regency debate in the House of Commons, Burke, carried away by the heat of his own arguments, accused Pitt of setting himself up as a competitor for the

Crown against the Prince of Wales. Burke thereby effectively charged the prime minister with treason on the floor of the Commons. The remark drew a formal rebuke from the House of Commons and was a source of great frustration for Burke's own party leaders, who viewed it as weakening their position in a key moment. Their frustration was compounded, moreover, by what many in Burke's party saw as his excessive concentration on the impeachment trial of Warren Hastings—the British governor of India, who Burke believed had grossly abused the local population. Burke's concentration on the trial was entirely in keeping with his concern for the integrity of the British regime, but the trial dragged on longer than the party's leaders expected (in fact, it ultimately lasted far longer still, ending with acquittal only in 1794) and was, they feared, painting the party in a bad light, in no small part because of Burke's zeal in its prosecution.

In the summer of 1789, discouraged by these various setbacks and deeply worried about the commitment of his fellow Whigs to the maintenance of the English constitution, Burke seriously contemplated retirement from politics. He wrote to his friend the Earl of Charlemont: "There is a time of life in which, if a man cannot arrive at a certain degree of authority, derived from a confidence from the Prince or the people, which may aid him in his operations, and make him compass useful objects without a perpetual struggle, it becomes him to remit much of his activity."[31]

But retirement was not to be. The dispirited letter to Charlemont was dated July 10, 1789—four days before the storming of the Bastille and the beginning of the most celebrated and intense period of Burke's political life, and the period that would bring him most directly into conflict with Paine.

THE REVOLUTION IN FRANCE

Events in Paris began with an explosion of pent-up energy. In the course of a lengthy financial and political crisis, as the mass of the public fell into economic hardship, resentment against the king and his government had built up, and some release was inevitable. The second week of July 1789 saw unprecedented riots, looting, and public confrontations with the military and was capped by the capture of the Bastille—a prison and fortress that symbolized the power of the king. Less a paramilitary operation than a mob scene, the taking of the Bastille, which concluded with the prison's chief officer being publicly stabbed and decapitated and the crowd parading his head on a pike through Paris's main thoroughfares, set the tone for the early stages of the revolution. But these displays of rage were always accompanied by calls for justice and for a new system of government built on enlightened ideals of equality and liberty.

By late August, the leaders of the revolution had regained some control of events and published a statement of their principles (modeled in part on the American Declaration of Independence). The statement came to be known as the Declaration of the Rights of Man and of the Citizen and called for representative government and respect for human dignity. Throughout the West, the mystery of the character of this upheaval at the very heart of Europe quickly became the question of the day: Was Paris in the grip of a mad and violent terror or on the verge of an enlightened and rational new political order?

The British response to these early days of the revolution was overwhelmingly positive, and Burke's fellow Whigs in particular believed that the French were moving to liberalize their government on the model of English liberty. Charles James Fox, the party's leader, responded to the storming of the Bastille with enthusiasm and glee: "How much the greatest event it is that ever happened in the world! And how much the best!"[32] From the outset, Burke's own response was far more guarded. He recognized the injustice of the old regime, but worried about the violent zeal of the revolutionaries. "England is gazing with astonishment at a French struggle for liberty, and not knowing whether to blame or to applaud," he wrote to a friend on August 9:

> The spirit it is impossible not to admire; but the old Parisian ferocity has broken out in a shocking manner. It is true that this may be no more than a sudden explosion; if so, no indication can be taken

from it; but if it should be *character* rather than accident, then the people are not fit for liberty and must have a strong hand, like that of their former masters, to coerce them. Men must have a certain fund of natural moderation to qualify them for freedom, else it becomes noxious to themselves and a perfect nuisance to every body else. What will be the event it is hard I think still to say.[33]

These sentiments would turn out to be Burke's least negative judgment of the revolution. With time, as the character (and especially the philosophical ambitions) of the revolutionaries became clearer, Burke would turn from skeptic to adamant opponent. The October 1789 assault on Versailles, in which a mob attacked the young queen and nearly killed her, convinced Burke that the revolution was not only out of control but also intent on undermining the deep sentiments and social attachments essential to holding a people together. He feared that the revolution had become a profound threat not only to France but to its neighbors as well. This incident would later draw some of the most famous and eloquent rhetoric in Burke's writings about the revolution, as we will see, but his letters of that October clearly show that the emotion expressed later was not manufactured for effect but genuinely felt. On October 10, Burke wrote to his son of the latest news from France and concluded that "the elements which compose human society seem all to be dissolved, and a world of monsters to be produced in the place of it."[34] On the heels of the Regency Crisis, Burke watched the French combine mob rule with precisely the kind of stark and cold political philosophy he had worried about since his earliest public writings. These observations left him concerned for the fate of the political stability that he believed was essential to liberty.

Where Burke saw chaos and terror, however, Thomas Paine saw the natural extension of both America's own revolution and the empire of rights and legitimate government. Dispirited by the Regency Crisis, which he believed revealed that the Whigs, and British society more generally, simply had no stomach for radical democratization, Paine had turned his ambitions and hopes to France, where he returned a few months before the outbreak of the French Revolution.

He was by then acquainted with the early leaders of the revolution (including especially the Marquis de Lafayette, who had taken a crucial part in the American Revolution), took part in some of their deliberations, and even played a minor part in drafting the Declaration of the Rights of Man and of the Citizen. The events of that summer exhilarated Paine, who took it upon himself to build support for the revolutionaries in the Anglo-American world.

Unaware that Burke's view of the revolution was very different from his own, Paine wrote his erstwhile host several letters from France describing the situation in the hope of gaining in Burke an important friend for the revolutionaries' cause in London. In the process, Paine reported all manner of news that must have greatly alarmed Burke. Most notable was Paine's final missive, written January 17, 1790, and passing along a report from Thomas Jefferson (who had just returned to America, but remained extremely well informed about events in Paris). The national assembly, Jefferson had written with enthusiasm, was willing "to set fire to the four Corners of the Kingdom and to perish with it themselves rather than relinquish one iota from their plan of a total change of government." To Jefferson's evocative description Paine added that "the assembly is now fixing the boundaries of the division of the nation into 83 parts, latitudinally and longitudinally. It is intended by this arrangement to lose entirely the name of provinces and consequently of provincial distinction."[35] Paine clearly believed that this assertive effort to overcome long-standing local prejudices and attachments and rationally establish a new French national identity from scratch was both wise and encouraging. It was a sign of the new government's commitment to reestablish French society on new and better principles.

Paine expected this report to please Burke or encourage him to support the revolutionary cause. But nothing could have been more upsetting to Burke than news of such extremism and of an intentional effort to erase well-established local attachments, except perhaps Paine's ominous promise, delivered in a tenor of hope, that "the revolution in France is certainly a fore-runner to other revolutions in Europe."[36] This letter surely played a role in confirming Burke's concerns and inciting his worst fears about the revolution in France. What worried him above all was the combination of philosophical pretensions and applied savagery of the revolution—mob rule making its case in metaphysical abstractions. Paine was no advocate of mob rule, to be sure, but his case for the revolution—that it directly applied the political philosophy of the Enlightenment, seeking to instantiate the ideals of an individualist egalitarianism—was precisely the sort Burke feared most for its corrosive effect on people's reverence for their society's political institutions and traditions.

And the prospect of a contagion of such philosophies—of the spread of revolutionary sentiment into Britain in particular—loomed large in Burke's mind after he read a November 1789 speech by Richard Price, a prominent and respected Unitarian dissenter. Price addressed the Society for Commemorating the Revolution (that is, the Glorious Revolution, or the English Revolution of 1688) and pointed to the French Revolution as confirming English principles. He argued that inherent in the English constitution was the people's right to overturn their regime if their individual rights—understood in Enlightenment-liberal terms—were not respected, and that English politics had fallen behind the French in putting into practice its own principles. In a rush of enthusiasm he told his audience:

> What an eventful period this is! I am thankful that I have lived to see it. . . . I have lived to see 30 MILLIONS of people, indignant and resolute, spurning at slavery, and demanding liberty with an irresistible voice; their king led in triumph, and an arbitrary monarch surrendering himself to his subjects.—After sharing in the benefits of one revolution, I have been spared to be witness to two other revolutions, both glorious. And now methinks I see the love for liberty catching and spreading.[37]

The society published Price's speech as a pamphlet and sent a copy to the French National Assembly with a letter building on his themes, noting especially "the glorious example given in France to encourage other nations to assert the unalienable rights of Mankind, and thereby to introduce a general reformation in the government of Europe, and to make the world free and happy."[38]

Burke would later write, with great understatement, that reading Price's sermon and the accompanying letter left him with "a considerable degree of uneasiness."[39] He was alarmed not only about the celebration of events in France but especially about Price's attempt to recast English history in the mold of the French Revolution. Price had argued that the Glorious Revolution itself had established the principle that the monarchy was subject to popular choice (exactly the view Burke opposed in the Regency Crisis) and indeed that the Glorious Revolution was fought over "unalienable rights." It was this effort to commandeer the English constitution for the revolutionary cause that Burke could see creeping into the thought of his fellow Whigs; he would oppose this effort most adamantly in his writings about France.

Burke resolved to reply to Price's lecture and to begin to make the case against the French Revolution at every opportunity, despite the reigning sentiment in his own party and in the country at large. A House of Commons debate about military spending in February 1790 would provide his first opportunity. The annual debate always involved a general discussion of world affairs (since the state of world politics would determine the government's expectations of its military needs), and Burke knew France would loom large. The revolution had been proceeding apace, with the government increasingly moving to confiscate private property and collapse the structures and institutions of the old regime.

As the debate opened, the Tory prime minister, William Pitt, as well as Fox and several other fellow Whigs, expressed measured but firm support for the revolution. Burke's views were known to his close friends, but were not yet widely known in Parliament, and as he rose to speak, he knew that his remarks would cause a stir. By uprooting the foundations of their existing regime and by confiscating the property of the church, the French had undone both the balance of their politics and the freedom of their people, Burke argued, and they were headed for disaster. The trouble, moreover, was not just a matter of bungled administration and execution—it was rooted in the fundamental ideals of the revolution. The Declaration of the Rights of Man and of the Citizen, he said, was filled with a foolish "abuse of elementary principles as would have disgraced a schoolboy." It was "a sort of institute and digest of anarchy" and contained the seeds of political catastrophe. "This mad declaration," Burke said, had caused France to inflict wounds upon itself normally suffered only by nations at war, and indeed the declaration "may in the end produce such a war, and perhaps many such."[40] The revolution was a mortal threat to liberty, and no friend of liberty should be warm to it.

Burke had laid down his marker and from this point—at great cost to his standing in his party and to the immense ire of many of his friends—would be an unbending and very public opponent of the French Revolution. He criticized it in exceedingly harsh terms on almost every imaginable ground and offered a stern defense of the English regime against the onslaught of a theoretical politics intent on uprooting all long-standing social institutions and practices.

After the House of Commons debate, Burke also realized that he needed to complete his formal response to Price, so that a counterargument could be fully expounded on Burke's terms. As he thought about how best to do this, he remembered a letter he had received in 1789 from a young Frenchman named Charles-Jean-François Depont seeking his views on the revolution. Depont clearly expected praise for the revolution, but he instead received a brief, early version of Burke's case against it. In his response to Depont, Burke laid out an argument against radical individualism, arbitrary power, the decimation of social institutions, and a politics of metaphysical theory: "I must delay my congratulations on your acquisition of liberty. You may have made a revolution, but not a reformation. You may have subverted monarchy, but not recovered freedom."[41]

In mid-1790, Burke decided that the best response to Price would take the form of a second letter to Depont (though, since it would be published, he would keep his addressee anonymous). The form of a letter would allow him more freedom in organizing his case and require less formality in presenting it. Burke spent months composing and editing the letter, which he had decided would be published and distributed as a long pamphlet under the title *Reflections on the Revolution in France and on the Proceedings of Certain Societies in London Relative to that Event: In a Letter Intended to Have Been Sent to a Gentleman in Paris*. After numerous drafts and revisions, the pamphlet ever since known simply as *Reflections on the Revolution in France* finally emerged on November 1, 1790.

The *Reflections* was a masterwork of rhetoric. In its style, cadences, images, and evocative metaphors it was perhaps the best of Burke's writing. But it was also a deep and serious work of political thought and the first sustained assessment and dissection of the claims of liberal radicalism in the age of revolutions. Burke begins with a defense of the English system from what he takes to be the distortions of Price and his fellows. By suggesting that the Glorious Revolution made the British government legitimate because it had put in place an "elective monarchy," Burke says Price and others delegitimize all prior English history.[42]

He warns his French correspondent that the effort to present the French Revolution as an extension of English liberalism seeks to deceive both the French and the English to each accept a dangerous radical novelty as a gift from the other: "We ought not, on either side of the water, to suffer ourselves to be imposed upon by the counterfeit wares which some persons, by a double fraud, export to you in illicit bottoms as raw commodities of British growth, though wholly alien to our soil."[43]

Burke articulates the significance of the hereditary principle in the English system not only in sustaining the monarchy but in securing the people's liberties and allegiance to the laws. And he provides a stirring portrait of Britain's mixed regime as justified by the enormous success it has achieved in providing for a stable and successful national life while gradually evolving to meet the people's changing needs. The radicals are angry, he argues, and so they speak more loudly and forcefully than the rest of the otherwise contented British nation— but no one should assume therefore that they speak for all: "Because half a dozen grasshoppers under a fern make the field ring with their importunate chink, whilst thousands of great cattle, reposed beneath the shadow of the British oak, chew the cud and are silent, pray do not imagine that those who make the noise are the only inhabitants of the field."[44]

This image of Britain as well served by a kind of deeply rooted calm is everywhere in Burke's rhetoric in the *Reflections*. And he bluntly derides the attempts of the French to uproot their long-standing social institutions under the influence of childish theories of social life unworthy of their own great nation. He dissents from the dominant individualism and state-of-nature theorizing of the day. And he lays out his own political theory—the theory taken up in this book—as an answer to the theories of natural rights underlying the revolution. Burke concludes with an extended comparison of the French and English systems of government, economies, and social orders. His comparison reflects very poorly on the wisdom of the French revolutionaries and seeks to highlight Britain's relative stability, prosperity, and comfort in an effort to suggest to his countrymen that emulating France would be disastrous. Praising the gradualism of the English constitution while mocking the supposedly enlightened radicalism of the revolutionary French, Burke sums up his sense of the limits of human reason and power:

> A politic caution, a guarded circumspection, a moral rather than a complexional timidity were among the ruling principles of our forefathers in their most decided conduct. Not being illuminated with the light of which the gentlemen of France tell us they have got so abundant a share, they acted under a strong impression of the ignorance and fallibility of mankind. . . . Let us imitate their caution if we wish to deserve their fortune or to retain their bequests. . . . [L]et us be satisfied to admire rather than attempt to follow in their desperate flights the aeronauts of France.[45]

Burke's audience in the *Reflections* was clearly British and not, as his epistolary mode would have it, a French gentleman. If it were actually a letter to a Frenchman, the *Reflections* would have been grossly inappropriate, boasting and mocking as it does. But as a letter to his countrymen, it sought as much to remind (or persuade) them of the origins and principles of their own social and political institutions—to show them what they ought to be by insisting it was what they already were—as to argue against the French, and all in the cause of building up a resistance to revolutionary appeals.

The publication of Burke's missive drew an enormous amount of interest and debate. "Within our remembrance no publication has excited more anxious curiosity," noted the *London Chronicle* a few days after its release.[46] And it appears to have sold about seven thousand copies in a week, which made it a massive best-seller for the time.[47] It also quickly drew a series of responses from English radicals, who were aghast at its substance and tone and especially surprised to see it coming from Burke, whom they had thought of as something of a fellow traveler.

News of Burke's vehement opposition to the revolution had reached Paine in France soon after Burke's fiery speech in Parliament in February 1790, and Paine immediately understood that a response was essential. In the heated debate culture of the era, an attack from so prominent and effective a critic could not be left to simmer. When he then also heard that Burke would publish a pamphlet against the revolution, Paine promised his French friends he would write a response to make their case to the English-speaking world. He planned to turn an essay he was already writing about the revolution into such a reply once Burke's missive arrived.

The resulting book, which Paine titled, with his usual flair, *Rights of Man*, is part answer to Burke, part stand-alone defense of the principles of the French Revolution. It offers a logical, sustained, focused, passionate, and powerful argument, delivered with often astonishing rhetorical force. Certainly among the most complete and most widely read elucidations of the basic worldview underlying the revolution, it is Paine's most expressly theoretical work. Here, Paine's political teaching—the set of views that will pervade the rest of this book—is most fully put forward. Standing as it did as an answer to Burke's *Reflections*, the book marks the moment when these two giants of the age of revolutions were set clearly against one another and when the great debate they launched had truly come into its own.

Published in March 1791, *Rights of Man* launches vehement attacks against Burke and his views, even referring to rumors about supposed financial misconduct by Burke, and describing the *Reflections* and particularly its epistolary style as a "wild unsystematical display of paradoxical rhapsodies."[48] Burke completely misunderstood both the causes and the nature of the revolution, Paine suggests, because he displays no real grasp of French society and politics: "As wise men are astonished at foolish things and other people at wise ones, I know not on which ground to account for Mr. Burke's astonishment; but certain it is that he does not understand the French Revolution."[49]

Paine's case for the revolution is strikingly philosophical. He spends very little time on the suffering of the French lower classes under the old regime or the abuses and excesses of the French aristocracy. Leading with a systematic attempt to refute or dismiss Burke's key points, it quickly turns to an enthusiastic case for human liberty. Paine writes with resolute confidence in the efficacy of reason in political life. He argues that the revolution is the working out of inescapable principles of politics and that its success and extension are therefore essentially inevitable. The objections of its opponents, including Burke's, merely mark the alarm of those who see that their old and unjust systems of privilege and oppression are in danger:

> What are the present Governments of Europe but a scene of iniquity and oppression? What is that of England? Do not its own inhabitants say it is a market where every man has his price, and where corruption is common traffic at the expense of a deluded people? No wonder, then, that the French Revolution is traduced. Had it confined itself merely to the destruction of flagrant despotism perhaps Mr. Burke and some others had been silent. Their cry now is, "It has gone too far"—that is, it has gone too far for them.[50]

Paine's is a politics of applied principle, and he believes the only way to rescue polities constructed on the wrong principles is to tear them down and rebuild from scratch. He clearly believes, as he had written in *Common Sense* years earlier, that "we have it in our power to begin the world over again."[51] In *Rights of Man*, he indeed suggests that this is the only way to construct a just society. He also offers a thorough and vigorous case against hereditary rule and aristocracy (a "mere animal system" unsuited to a rational politics) and against the right of one generation to impose its notions and arrangements on those that follow. The age of hereditary government has come and gone, he insists:

> It is not difficult to perceive, from the enlightened state of mankind, that hereditary Governments are verging to their decline, and that Revolutions on the broad basis of national sovereignty and Government by representation, are making their way in Europe.[52]

Paine lays out his political vision in greater detail in *Rights of Man* than in any of his earlier writings: a vision of individualism, natural rights, and equal justice for all made possible by a government that lives up to true republican ideals. He is persuaded that all this has become possible in his time. "From what we now see, nothing of reform on the political world ought to be held improbable. . . . It is an age of revolutions in which every thing may be looked for."[53]

What emerges is a set of principles consistent with Paine's writings during the American war but worked out more thoroughly and philosophically and therefore now more clearly at odds with Burke's view of the world. Like Burke, however, Paine addressed himself to an English audience and used the question of France to raise the question of the English regime—its past and especially its future. And Paine certainly succeeded in reaching an English readership. *Rights of Man* likely sold tens of thousands of copies and reached a wide audience well beyond London's elite (and well beyond Burke's readership).[54]

The Battle of the Books

The battle lines were now drawn, and the English reading public was very much engaged in the debate. In America, too, the exchange drew intense attention and began to sketch political battle lines that would last. John Quincy Adams, son of the sitting vice president (and himself of course a future president) published a series of essays in a Boston newspaper under the pen name Publicola, which offered a kind of running narrative of the Burke-Paine debate (siding far more with Burke than Paine). In Virginia, Senator James Monroe (a champion of Paine's and another future president) noted in a letter to Thomas Jefferson that "the contest of Burke and Paine . . . is much the subject of discussion in all parts of this state."[55]

Paine's book was the most significant reply to Burke's *Reflections on the Revolution in France*, though it was by no means the only one. Indeed, dozens of counter-pamphlets soon appeared, mostly from English radicals and dissenters accusing Burke of abandoning both Whig principles and his own principles. They charged him with a profound inconsistency, given his support for the American Revolution and his earlier assertion (in his 1770 pamphlet *Thoughts on the Causes of the Present Discontents*) that the deep disgruntlement of an entire population is proof that the state requires serious reform. Thomas Jefferson spoke for many when, upon reading the *Reflections*, he remarked that "the Revolution in France does not astonish me so much as the revolution in Mr. Burke."[56] This theme of inconsistency would follow Burke for the rest of his life and indeed well beyond his life, among historians.

Burke was stung by such accusations and well aware of the spread of Paine's *Rights of Man*. He was also alert to the growing rift he was causing among the Whigs by his sharp break with Fox. He therefore decided to make his case in writing again. In August 1791, he published *An Appeal from the New to the Old Whigs* to try to address all these varied challenges at once. The *Appeal* articulates many of the same ideas found in the *Reflections* and earlier writings, but with more light and less heat, and it grounds them in a deeper contention with some basic political and philosophical questions. Burke claims for himself the mantle of the great Whig tradition and describes his opponents in the party as hungry for radical democracy. He directly addresses a number of Paine's claims, using long quotes from *Rights of Man* and yet never mentioning Paine by name. Like the *Reflections*, the *Appeal* is deeply concerned with the relations among generations, though, as David Bromwich has astutely noted, it emphasizes the essential connection between the present and the future, while the *Reflections*, in a far more conservative mood, addressed mostly the link between the past and the present—a subtle but important difference, as we will see.[57] More than any of Burke's other works, the *Appeal* presents a robust view of the kind of social and political life he seeks to defend.

Paine, meanwhile, returned to Britain in July 1791 and was hard at work spreading his ideas. After the publication of Burke's *Appeal*, which Paine perceived (correctly) as largely a response to him, he set about writing a further reply, in the form of a second part of *Rights of Man*, published in February 1792. This sequel was in many ways more ambitious than the original and in every way more radical. Burke and Paine had forced one another to get to the core of their differences: a dispute about what makes a government legitimate, what the individual's place is in the larger society, and how each generation should think about those who came before and those who will come after.

This second part of *Rights of Man* was, to begin with, an all-out assault on monarchical government, including quite expressly the British monarchy. It was also a reflection on the causes of poverty and the plight of the lower classes and in this sense offers an extremely useful model of how the essential ideas of the Enlightenment-liberal theorists point to and connect with some later forms of radical politics. Paine begins to take the next steps on liberalism's path: He advocates for a public pension system for the poor, free public education, public benefits for parents, more parliamentary representation for the lower classes, and a progressive income tax. He even offers a plan for world peace through the extension of reason and knowledge: "If men will permit themselves to think as rational beings ought to think, nothing can appear more ridiculous and absurd" than to waste public funds on military expenditures.[58] Paine denies Burke's every premise and raises the stakes of the argument.

But by the time Paine's second volume was published in February 1792, the situation in France had begun to look far more ominous to many Englishmen. The attempt to sustain a constitutional monarchy had failed, and the king had been imprisoned, while the National Assembly had manifestly failed to keep order in Paris and to get the country's finances under control. Its hold on power was increasingly uncertain as factionalism among the revolutionaries grew. Paine's outright calls for overturning the British regime—a risky move in any climate—turned out to be especially unwise in this moment of growing concern. In May 1792, Pitt's Tory government, with significant Whig support (including Burke's, although he was notably silent in the debate on the bill, since his fellow members were well aware of his personal animosity toward Paine), enacted a proclamation against seditious writings—a move aimed expressly at Paine. The bill did not mention him by name, but the prime minister was not shy about its purpose. "Principles had been laid down by Mr. Paine," Pitt told the House of Commons, "which struck at the hereditary nobility, and which went to the destruction of monarchy and religion."[59] Paine, who was in London, was charged under the new law, and in September he left again for France rather than face a trial. He was tried and found guilty in absentia and would never again return to Britain.

As more extreme factions took control in Paris, British public opinion continued steadily to shift against the French and in favor of Burke's critical view of the revolution, which he continued to express in pamphlets and speeches. The European powers had begun to array themselves against the revolutionary regime, and war seemed increasingly likely on the continent, while in France the revolution turned to terror. The execution of the French king in January 1793 wrought a decisive change of attitudes in London, and the British public and political leadership alike soon turned sharply anti-French. By the end of that year, England was officially at war with France, and the reversal of public sentiment Burke had sought was largely (though, of course, not simply or entirely) achieved—with much help from the disastrous course of the revolution itself.

This turn against the French did not, however, resolve the profound questions brought to the surface by the revolution and taken up with such passion by Burke and Paine. Was the philosophy of the revolution misguided at its core, or did the French Revolutionaries merely fail to live up to it? The question of that philosophy—the question of the character of modern liberal government—was pressed with special force in the early days of the revolution, but it neither began with the upheaval in Paris nor ended with it. In the wake of the French Revolution, this question had clearly become a crucial dividing line of modern political life.

In a 1796 pamphlet titled *Letters on a Regicide Peace*, Burke argued that the old division between a party of royal prerogative and a party of parliamentary power in British politics was falling away: "These parties, which by their dissensions have so often distracted the Kingdom, which by their union have once saved it, and which by their collision and mutual resistance, have preserved the variety of this Constitution in its unity, [are] nearly extinct by the growth of new ones."[60] These new parties, which he termed the party of conservation and the party of Jacobins (the name of the most radical faction in Paris), would be divided along the new axis revealed in the French Revolution—they would be, in effect, the parties of Burke and Paine.

In America, too, the French Revolution had sharpened a set of differences that the American Revolution had tended to blur, and by the mid-1790s, the politics of the American republic were clearly split into two factions with two very different views of events in France. With these two views came corresponding differences on a variety of domestic and international questions. Here, too, a left and a right were beginning to show themselves, very much along the lines that Burke and Paine had sketched.

While their ideas gave rise to followers and factions, Burke and Paine did not remain active on the scene long after this final chapter of their confrontation. Paine stayed in France through much of the rest of the revolution—all the way until the fall of 1802. But as the movement's leaders grew increasingly radical and his own friends fell increasingly into the background, Paine became estranged from those in power (even spending several months in prison for affiliating with moderate rebels deemed insufficiently zealous). He devoted himself to what he took to be the logical next chapter of his intellectual project: a book in defense of Deism—the view that God's existence and work are accessible to reason without need for revelation or organized religion—and so against most established religions. This final book of Paine's made precisely the argument that Burke's very first published writing had risen to oppose decades earlier.

Paine believed that an age of enlightened liberal government would carry with it an enlightened liberal religious outlook that would discourage the kind of sectarian conflict that had so long torn Europe apart: "A revolution in the system of government would be followed by a revolution in the system of religion."[61] But because his book, which he titled *The Age of Reason*, criticized the traditional forms of organized religion with the same zealous passion for justice he had brought to his political writing, it set itself so adamantly in opposition to Christianity that it was bound to spark controversy and would cast a shadow over Paine's reputation, especially in America. "Of all the systems of religion that ever were invented," he wrote, "there is none more derogatory to the Almighty, more unedifying to man, more repugnant to reason, and more contradictory to itself than this thing called Christianity."[62] Having composed such lines, how could he have expected anything but the hostile reception his book swiftly received on both sides of the Atlantic?

When he returned to America in 1802 at the invitation of its new president, his dear friend Thomas Jefferson, Paine found that his attack on Christianity and his political radicalism made him something of a lightning rod. He continued to write, but he was not active in politics and only occasionally offered advice to Jefferson and his allies. With his health and his finances failing him in time, Paine spent his last days in relative poverty at a boarding house in New York City. He died on June 8, 1809, and was buried in New Rochelle, New York.

Burke, too, was completing his political projects by the mid-1790s as his confrontation with Paine reached its height. The trial of Hastings, which had dragged on for seven years, came to an end in 1794 with a disappointing acquittal. Burke had earlier declared his intention to leave Parliament upon the trial's completion, and now, sixty-four years old and largely vindicated in his crusade against the revolution, he did so.

His hopes turned to his son, Richard, who Burke thought might take up his vacated seat in the Commons. The scene seemed set for this plan to succeed when, in the summer of 1794, Richard Burke fell seriously ill. He died in August of that year, leaving his father suddenly broken and despondent. Edmund Burke's remaining three years were lived in mourning and were taken up with a defense of his honor from spurious charges of corruption surrounding his pension, and a firming up of England's resolve against the French. Burke died on July 9, 1797, actively engaged to the last in the war of ideas over England's future. Parliament was prepared to have him laid to rest among Britain's celebrated men at Westminster Abbey, but in accordance with his will, Burke was buried near his home at Beaconsfield.

BEYOND BIOGRAPHY

Reviewing these two intensely eventful political and intellectual careers, we might find it hard not to be struck by the scope and the variety of challenges confronting the Anglo-American politics of the time. And yet, if we consider the substance of Burke's and Paine's views, what stands out is not the diversity of subjects taken up, but the consistency of key themes and arguments within each man's life work and the overarching unity of their extended disagreement. Their core concerns, convictions, and arguments remained remarkably stable over three decades of turmoil. And each contended with essentially the same set of questions as the other, arriving at starkly different conclusions.

In this respect the historical chronology of their dispute, while crucial to any understanding of the issues at stake, does not finally reveal the true shape of the argument. The philosophical contours of the great debate are not fully captured by its historical contours. We must pursue them instead by carefully drawing the two men's deepest arguments out of the intense staccato of day-to-day intellectual and political combat, putting them into order in a way that allows their assumptions and reasoning to be considered, and then applying what we learn back onto the patterns of political life. This is the work not quite of history but of political philosophy—which allows us to look beneath the mad rush of events and consider how ideas move politics.

The chapters that follow apply this method to Burke's and Paine's profound debate and seek to peel back the layers of the arguments that still shape our times. We will begin where Burke and Paine both did: with the question of what idea of nature and human nature should serve as the backdrop against which political reasoning and judgment occur, and what place history is to have in such judgments. We will then consider the two men's very different ideas about natural and political right, and then analyze each man's view of social and political relations. We will then take up their treatment of the place of reason in political thought and their views of the proper means and the appropriate ends of such thought. Only after examining these facets of their deep disagreement will we approach the subject that generally comes up first in discussions of Burke and Paine: their views of political change, reform, and revolution. And finally, looking over these facets of the argument, we will highlight a crucial common thread in the large and varied debates between Burke and Paine: a dispute about the status of the past and the meaning of the future in political life—an unusual and unfamiliar question that to this day often sits silently at the heart of our politics.

TWO

Nature and History

To uncover the philosophical underpinnings of political debates, we have to first assume that what goes on in politics answers to more than just people's passing preferences and material interests. If political ideas are applications of philosophical ideas—of some understanding of what is true and good in life—then serious political debates must be rooted in different philosophical assumptions. And because such differences involve what lies beneath the level of events and arguments, they often come down to disputes about what we take to be true by nature about human beings. That is why debates about political philosophy often begin from debates about nature and human nature. But the meanings of these terms—nature and human nature—are not simple or self-evident. They are themselves subject to intense debate, and that prior debate about what we mean by the natural is often an indicator of the assumptions that guide our political thinking.

Such differences are powerfully evident in the Burke-Paine debate, and both men were exceptionally well aware of them. Burke and

Paine each sought to base his arguments—from his very earliest writings on—on an idea of what nature and human nature were and what they should mean for political life. Their dispute begins, in effect, with a debate about nature and its relation to history, so our examination of their views should begin there too.

PAINE'S NATURAL SOCIETY

For the modern-day reader of Thomas Paine's *Common Sense*, the pamphlet's opening sections cannot help but come as a surprise. Given the immense influence of Paine's case for American independence and the author's reputation for brilliant and fiery rhetoric, we expect to be greeted with a passionate call to arms and a catalog of British offenses. But Paine takes his time getting to the American crisis (which does not really appear until the pamphlet's third section) and instead launches into a thought experiment he insists is essential to grounding any theory of politics: "In order to gain a clear and just idea of the design and end of government, let us suppose a small number of persons settled in some sequestered part of the earth, unconnected with the rest, they will then represent the first peopling of any country, or of the world. In this state of natural liberty, society will be their first thought."[1]

Paine argues for a just resolution of the Anglo-American dispute—as he will argue for a variety of political causes throughout the long career begun by this pamphlet—by starting from first and fundamental political principles. When seeking to understand political and social institutions, he suggests, we must seek for their earliest origins and deepest roots; we can only truly understand them by seeing where they came from. "The error of those who reason by precedents drawn from antiquity respecting the rights of man," Paine explains in *Rights of Man*, "is that they do not go far enough into antiquity. They do not go the whole way."[2]

This "whole way," as Paine repeatedly makes clear, involves looking not to history, but beyond history to nature. And by "nature," he means the condition that preceded all social and political arrangements and therefore the facts regarding what every human being is, regardless of social or political circumstances. Our nature remains just as it was at the beginning of the human race, since our various social arrangements don't change what we are by nature—what every human being always has been and will be. And so our basic nature must remain the foundation of our political thinking—of our understanding of what human beings are and how they ought to live together.

Paine begins nearly all of his major writings by restating this basic case, the key features of which come from Thomas Hobbes, John Locke, and other political thinkers of the Enlightenment. It is the essential starting point of his political philosophy: that reflection on politics must begin from permanent natural facts about human beings, which means it must begin from man himself, apart from society (and therefore, in essence, before society).[3] The only reliable source of authority is the original source: "If a dispute about the rights of man had arisen at the distance of an hundred years from the creation, it is to this source of authority they must have referred, and it is to this same source of authority that we must now refer."[4] Paine argues that when we look at politics in this way—as if all of human history had never happened—"we are brought at once to the point of seeing government begin, as if we had lived in the beginning of time. The real volume, not of history, but of facts, is directly before us, unmutilated by contrivance, or the errors of tradition."[5]

And just what are these facts that nature offers up? What does Paine see when he looks past history to our natural beginnings? The very method of searching after the natural human condition in this way suggests to Paine one inescapable fact about man first and foremost: At his origin, man is an individual. And because he has no social relations to start with, he is burdened by no social distinctions and therefore is equal to all other men. Social hierarchies have no natural foundation:

Every history of the creation, . . . however they may vary in their opinion or belief of certain particulars, all agree in establishing one point, the unity of man; by which I mean that men are all of one

degree, and consequently that all men are born equal, and with
equal natural right, in the same manner as if posterity had been
continued by creation instead of generation, the latter being only
the mode by which the former is carried forward; and consequently
every child born into the world must be considered as deriving its
existence from God. The world is as new to him as it was to the first
man that existed, and his natural right in it is of the same kind.[6]

Here Paine makes explicit something that other liberal theorists
tended not to. To imagine that we are unchanged since the beginning
of time is to believe that the means of human generation and the pro-
cession of generations through time tell us nothing of great importance about human life. That is, social relations and distinctions built
up over generations have no inherent authority.

And it means, also, that human beings are always most fully understood as distinct and equal individuals. Society and government
involve collections of such individuals—organized by those individuals for their benefit—but these groupings of people never fully
overwhelm the essentially solitary character of the human person.
"A nation," Paine writes, "is composed of distinct, unconnected individuals, [and] . . . public good is not a term opposed to the good
of individuals; on the contrary, it is the good of every individual
collected."[7]

In pursuit of that good, moreover, individuals begin to assemble
into groups. Just as man is best understood by his origins, so too are
society and government, and for that reason, Paine takes society and
government to be two distinct things. Men originally join together
out of necessity and a desire for company. "No one man is capable,"
he writes, "without the aid of society, of supplying his own wants, and
those wants, acting upon every individual, impel the whole of them
into society, as naturally as gravitation acts to a center." And just as
it supplies the need, nature also supplies the desire for society: "She
has not only forced man into society by a diversity of wants which the
reciprocal aid of each other can supply, but she has implanted in him

a system of social affections, which, though not necessary to his existence, are essential to his happiness."[8] Human beings are therefore social creatures with needs and wants that reach beyond themselves. But even for the purpose of assessing their sociality, humans are best understood as equal and separate individuals.

In his description of this natural human condition, Paine certainly sounds a lot like the Enlightenment-liberal theorists of his day and like John Locke, on whom they drew. To make the case for individual rights and social equality, these thinkers built on theories of how individuals first formed societies. But more than most, and certainly more than Locke, Paine emphasizes the difference between the gathering of human beings into society—driven by the need to meet necessities and by the desire for company—and the establishment of governments over these societies.

For Paine, there is a crucial middle step between the state of nature and the political community: the natural society that exists at first without a government. When humans first gathered into society, the motives and needs that drew them together naturally governed their cooperation, and they achieved a relatively sophisticated degree of social life without a need for government as such. But over time, as they succeeded in overcoming necessity, they relaxed in their duties, and some form of government became necessary to restrain their vices.

Paine makes more of this distinction between society and government than do many liberal theorists before him, because it is crucial to his case for revolution, both in America and in France.[9] To the charge (made by Edmund Burke, among others) that an all-out revolution would bring the dissolution of society itself and so make any government that followed illegitimate, Paine has an answer. First, he says, society is older and more important than government. Second, a revolution consists of a reversion to the natural society for the purpose of establishing a new government from the same origins as the old one, but better and more justly formed and organized. "A great part of that order which reigns among mankind is not the effect of government," Paine argues in *Rights of Man*. "It has its origin in the principles of society and the natural constitution of man. It existed prior to government, and would exist if the formality of government was abolished."[10] Paine considers the original society a function of human nature, while government is an artifice created by human will and therefore subject to imperfect judgment and especially to corruption by power and greed.

This natural society, however, remains permanently accessible. Because it is essentially a function of human nature, we can always revert to it when the conventional government has failed to carry out its functions or has violated the rights of its citizens. Such a reversion allows a society to, as Paine puts it, "go back to nature for information" and "regenerate" itself.[11] Thus, as Paine famously declares, "we have it in our power to begin the world over again."[12] By throwing off our government, we can regenerate our original society and can "see government begin as if we lived at the beginning of time."[13]

This is what a revolution means for Paine—it is, at its core, a return to the distant past to begin again, and better. "What were formerly called Revolutions," he tells us in *Rights of Man*, "were little more than a change of persons, or an alteration of local circumstances. . . . But what we now see in the world, from the Revolutions of America and France, are a renovation of the natural order of things, a system of principles as universal as truth and the existence of man, and combining moral with political happiness and national prosperity."[14]

The recovery Paine has in mind, however, is not a return to some earlier period of recorded human history. Rather he seeks a return to the purity of nature, which, although it ought to inform our political life, has never been properly put into practice as the organizing principle of a government. In this respect, Paine's revolutionary ethic is indeed progressive, even though it looks back to the very beginning of politics. It understands itself as innovative because it begins from a knowledge of nature that has never before been achieved. Nature itself has always been as it is, but Paine believed that it was only becoming understood for the first time in his own day: "Though it might be proved that the system of government now called the new is the most ancient in principle of all that have existed, being founded on the original, inherent Rights of Man: yet, as tyranny and the sword have suspended the exercise of those rights for many centuries past, it serves better the purpose of distinction to call it the new, than to claim the right of calling it the old."[15]

Paine considers most of human history until his own enlightened age a diversion from the effort to understand the proper principles of government: "[People] have had so few opportunities of making the necessary trials on modes and principles of government, in order to discover the best, that government is but now beginning to be known."[16]

Government was only in his day beginning to be known, Paine believed, because nature itself was only then beginning to be properly known. Like most of his late-Enlightenment contemporaries, Paine drew heavily on the worldview of the new natural science in formulating his idea of nature. Just half a century after Isaac Newton's death, the age in which Paine lived was still very much in thrall of the revolution in physics—a revolution that seemed to open endless possibilities for the conquest of nature and the empowerment of man. And the fundamental principle of this new science was the understanding of nature as consisting of distinct and separable forces acting on distinct and separable objects according to rational rules—rather than (as in the ancient science of Aristotle that it displaced) of organic wholes defined by the ends they were meant to achieve.

Like many of his contemporaries, Paine considered his political philosophy an application of this new way of understanding nature. This is one reason he places such emphasis on tracing things back to their origins, and why when he speaks of the "facts" of nature, he appears to have in mind principles—rational laws and rules—that set the boundaries for action, rather than an organic model of complex wholes interacting. "I draw my idea of the form of government from a principle in nature which no art can overturn," Paine writes, "viz. that the more simple any thing is, the less liable it is to be disordered; and the easier repaired when disordered."[17]

The distinction between nature and "art," or intentional human action, is crucial and firm for Paine: Nature is that which is inherent about man, absent all effort and will, while art is the product of man's work. Nature is there to be understood, and the understanding of nature produces a set of rules to guide our choices. Presenting itself as a set of generalizable laws, nature is thus in most respects an abstraction.

Nature, in Paine's view, is therefore the set of facts and axioms about both man and his world that describes all that man has not himself created. It is orderly, rational, and governed by abstract rules with general application. We can best understand nature by breaking it down into its simplest possible parts and tracing it back to the earliest possible beginnings, where the parts are most readily discerned.

As Paine defines it, then, society is a function of nature, while government is a product of art. But the purposes of government are defined by man's natural rights and natural limits, so although men create government, they must create it with the facts of nature in mind, and in such a way as to protect each man's natural prerogatives and rights and to secure the natural freedom and best interest of all. The science of government, therefore, begins from a knowledge of nature through reason, and government can be judged by how effectively it respects man's individual freedom and equality.

Paine believes that the failure to form governments in accordance with this understanding is responsible for the failures of politics up to his day. "Can we possibly suppose," he wonders, "that if governments had originated in a right principle, and had not an interest in pursuing a wrong one, the world could have been in the wretched and quarrelsome condition we have seen it?"[18]

To assess the legitimacy of existing governments, therefore, Paine argues that we must look to the precepts of nature—the principles especially of human equality and individuality, which give each man an equal right with every other to determine the course of government. That means that only power willingly granted is legitimate, and only a government by consent is just. "All power exercised over a nation must have some beginning," Paine writes. "It must either be delegated or assumed. There are no other sources. All delegated power is trust, and all assumed power is usurpation. Time does not alter the nature and quality of either."[19] However far we might be from it, we must look back to the beginning of our society to determine which sort of society it is, and those who refuse to look cannot make judgments regarding legitimacy.

At its source, a legitimate government is established by the choice of the people. When moved by the necessity of creating a regime, they all meet together, forming a kind of parliament in which every citizen has his own seat "by natural right." But over time, as the community grows, it will be impossible for everyone to attend to public matters personally all the time, so they appoint representatives "who will act in the same manner as the whole body would were they present."[20] This representative democracy is the form of government best in line with nature, according to Paine.

But it was, of course, not the form most commonly found in the world in Paine's time. He believed that the more common form at the time, the monarchy, traced its origins in every instance to some usurper who had established himself over others by force. There could be no justification in nature for such unequal power, and so there was no justification in practice. "When men are spoken of as kings and subjects, or when government is mentioned under the distinct or combined heads of monarchy, aristocracy, and democracy, what is it that reasoning man is to understand by these terms?" Paine asks. "If there really existed in the world two or more distinct and separate elements of human power, we should then see the several origins to which those terms would descriptively apply; but as there is but one species of man, there can be but one element of human power, and that element is man himself."[21] Of kings, he therefore asserts with plain derision in *Common Sense*, "as nature knows them not, they know not her, and although they are beings of our own creating, they know not us and are become the gods of their creators."[22]

Kings and nobles commonly seek to portray themselves as possessed of elevated origins deep in the mists of history, but Paine will have none of it: "It is more than probable that, could we take off the dark covering of antiquity, and trace them to their first rise, we should find the first of them nothing better than the principal ruffian of some restless gang, whose savage manners, or pre-eminence in subtlety, obtained him the title of chief among the plunderers."[23] And worse yet, monarchs pass their illegitimate power on to their children, denying their people's natural rights beyond their own lives. Because of Paine's insistence on the importance of origins, he considers the hereditary principle near the root of all evil. By compelling men to accept the decisions of prior generations, it denies them their natural right to self-determination and is therefore a profoundly unnatural principle of government.

Paine thus consistently asserts the supremacy of nature (understood in terms of principles accessible to reason) over history (understood as a catalog of human failures to apply the proper principles to politics). The facts that nature teaches us about human beings explain why society came to be, and the natural imperfection of human beings explains why legitimate government is necessary, while the existence of illegitimate government explains why wars, poverty, and endless other troubles have occurred. The solution is to replace illegitimate governments with ones more in line with the emerging understanding of man's nature and thereby to advance the cause of natural peace. And the end of a political revolution, properly understood, is a return to natural society with this purpose in mind. The great bulk of Paine's political ideas begin from these reflections on nature and pursue their implications.

BURKE'S HISTORICAL SOCIETY

Edmund Burke began his own public career by rejecting precisely the view of nature and its relation to politics that we have just seen Paine lay out. His first major work, *The Vindication of Natural Society*, published in 1756, argues in essence that looking past all conventional institutions and accepting only nature (narrowly understood as an abstract set of rules) as a source of authority or insight about human affairs would be deeply corrosive of political and social life.

In the satirical voice of the *Vindication*, Burke mocks the idea that people can make any progress by assuming that all of human history has in essence been a failure because all existing governments have been corruptions of our original natural condition. While Paine would employ this method to attack monarchy and aristocracy, Burke in the *Vindication* and other publications suggests such a method could just as easily undermine any other form of government and indeed any other human institution.

Burke believes, first of all, that this method is wrong because it makes far too much of social and political beginnings. He considers the exposure of origins a misguided, needless, and potentially destructive enterprise. A government does not derive its legitimacy by beginning from the proper principles, drawn from nature. Instead, government develops through time along lines that serve the needs and well-being of the people and therefore point toward some natural idea of the good.

The beginnings of any society, Burke writes, are almost certain to involve some form of barbarism (not to say crime). But over time, by slowly responding to circumstantial exigencies, societies develop more mature forms—a process that, as Burke puts it in the *Reflections on the Revolution in France*, "mellows into legality governments that were violent in their commencement."[24] A return to beginnings would thus not offer an opportunity to start anew on proper principles, but would rather risk a reversion to barbarism. "There is a sacred veil to be drawn over the beginnings of all governments," Burke argues, because there is little to be learned by exposing them, and there is a very real risk of harm in the exposure itself—especially the risk of weakening the allegiance of the people to their regime by exposing its imperfect origins.[25]

This rejection of the importance of beginnings separates Burke from the vast majority of political thinkers in the Western tradition—from Plato and Aristotle through Hobbes and Locke and their modern successors. These thinkers have argued that a founding is a crucial political moment, when the character of a regime is decisively given shape.[26] As detailed in later chapters, Burke argues instead that a regime takes shape over time and is never in fact "the effect of a single instantaneous regulation." Thus, its original shape (let alone the origin of all political society) is not so crucial as its current shape and function and its development to this point.[27]

Paine roundly criticized Burke's denigration of beginnings, arguing that it is simply an effort to avoid confronting Britain's particular illegitimate origins: "A certain something forbids him to look back to a beginning, lest some robber, or some Robin Hood, should rise from the long obscurity of time and say, 'I am the origin.'"[28] Burke does acknowledge a concern of this sort, noting that an intimate familiarity with the barbarous origins of their regime may undermine the people's patriotism. But his greater concern is that in looking past history in search of nature, people would look past the best available source of wisdom and instruction to a source of little if any useful knowledge about political life.

Burke never quite bothers to dispute the particular assertions that Paine and other liberal theorists make about what man's presocial nature might tell us, because he thinks it is absurd to think about a presocial man to begin with.[29] This does not mean that an understanding of man's nature is not crucial to an understanding of society and politics, but Burke argues that to learn about man's nature, we need to understand man as he is and, to our knowledge at least, has always been: a social creature, living together with others in an organized society with a government. To imagine him as solitary and asocial is to ignore man himself in pursuit of an abstraction with little to teach us. "I have in my contemplation the civil social man, and no other," Burke writes.[30]

The institutions of society are certainly conventional, he argues. They "are often the contrivances of deep human wisdom (not the rights of men, as some people in my opinion not very wisely talk of them)."[31] But it is man's nature to affect such conventions, and we make a serious mistake if we draw a sharp distinction between the natural and the artificial in human affairs and thereby ignore everything that man does in the world as we seek to understand his nature. "Art is man's nature," Burke argues. "We are as much, at least, in a state of nature in formed manhood, as in immature and helpless infancy . . . the state of civil society . . . is a state of nature, and much more truly so than a savage and incoherent mode of life."[32] This blurring of the distinction between nature and artifice is a crucial move for Burke, distinguishing him sharply from Paine and other Enlightenment-liberal theorists of his day. Burke shows, in David Bromwich's apt phrase, "respect for society and nature as elements of a single human environment."[33]

As we have seen, the distinction between artifice and nature is crucial for Thomas Paine's view of the world because he accuses the corrupt regimes—the aristocracies and monarchies—most especially of raising artificial barriers between nature and man and therefore denying individual human beings the rights to which they are entitled by nature. A revolution, as Paine sees it, throws off all convention and reverts to the original conditions from which regimes emerge, to regenerate and begin again from the start. By denying the stark distinction between the natural and artificial or conventional, therefore, Burke closes off the possibility of such reversion. Regimes, he says, are built primarily on conventions and are natural in the sense that artistry and artifice are natural to man. A society cannot be grounded in rights that exist only outside of society.

"The pretended *rights of man*, which have made this havoc," Burke writes regarding the French Revolution in direct response to Paine in 1791, "cannot be the rights of the people. For to be a people, and to have these rights, are things incompatible. The one supposes the presence, the other the absence of a state of civil society."[34] A people therefore cannot revert to a presocial state in which such rights are in effect, because in doing so, they would cease to be a people. Burke continues:

> The idea of a people is the idea of a corporation. It is wholly artificial; and made like all other legal fictions by common agreement. . . . When men, therefore, break up the original compact or agreement which gives its corporate form and capacity to a state, they are no longer a people; they have no longer a corporate existence; they have no longer a legal coactive force to bind within, nor a claim to be recognized abroad. They are a number of vague loose individuals, and nothing more.[35]

Paine's idea of revolution, therefore, seems to Burke a recipe for societal suicide, because it relies on the presumption—which Burke takes to be false—that by the nature of things, the society will persist when its regime has been dissolved. In the wake of such a dissolution, Burke argues, there will be no rules or methods by which a new regime could form: no protections of property or persons, no reason to follow a leader or adhere to majority rule, no means for "regenerating."

In fact, Burke considers the very desire for such a regeneration of one's own society appalling. "I cannot conceive how any man can have brought himself to consider his country as nothing but *carte blanche*, upon which he may scribble whatever he pleases," Burke writes. "A man full of warm speculative benevolence may wish his society otherwise constituted than he finds it; but a good patriot, and a true politician, always considers how he shall make the most of the existing materials of his country."[36] We do not have it in our power to begin the world over again, Burke suggests.

Building on existing forms using existing materials requires not an abstract study of nature but a very particular understanding of the history and character of one's society. Because the state is conventional, and because the abstract rights of man do not provide explicit rules for political life directly, statesmanship is almost always a matter of prudence, an "experimental science," as Burke puts it.[37] The results of such experiments do not become evident immediately, so that to learn from them takes time—often more than any single lifetime. For this reason, history, and not only nature, must inform political life, and existing political forms should not be abandoned lightly.[38] This does not mean that history is always an honor roll of great and wise accomplishments. Human history, Burke writes in the *Reflections on the Revolution in France*, "consists for the most part of the miseries brought upon the world by pride, ambition, avarice, revenge, lust, sedition, hypocrisy, ungoverned zeal, and all the train of disorderly appetites," but it also consists of efforts to address these vices, and in both its best and worst manifestations, history offers lessons no statesman can afford to ignore.[39]

Burke thus disagrees profoundly with the method of argument and the notion of nature that informs Paine and the more radical liberal philosophers. But his inclination to present his views as a critique of others tends to mask the positive teaching about nature that underlies Burke's arguments. His sharp rejection of Paine's idea of nature begins to point toward his own very different idea.

The Enlightenment philosophers, Burke worries, "are so taken up with their theories about the rights of man, that they have totally forgotten his nature."[40] Burke is fairly specific as to what they miss about that nature: the part that is not simply matter in motion or reason in action. A politics oriented to man's nature understands man as an animal being, a rational being, and a creature of sympathies and sentiments.[41] Paine and other radical liberal thinkers leave the human sentiments and the role of the imagination out of their understanding of human nature. By overemphasizing both the animal and the rational elements of man, Burke worries, they not only disregard but also undermine the sentiments that are in fact key to human nature and political order.

The revolutionaries imagined that man was basically a rational animal, so that if his simple needs (for food and safety) were met, his reason would govern him.[42] Those he disagreed with, including Paine, did not of course deny that there were other parts to human nature, but Burke believed they had far too much faith in the ability of reason alone to govern those other elements—and especially the passions and sentiments.

From a young age, Burke had concerned himself with the place of the passions in human affairs, and his *Philosophical Enquiry into the Origin of Our Ideas of the Sublime and the Beautiful*, written just a year after the *Vindication of Natural Society* when Burke was only twenty-eight, was devoted to the subject. He argued especially that the sublime, which draws on man's simultaneous fear of and fascination with death, exercises enormous power over the human imagination. That power can unleash violent torrents of energy into social life if it is not properly managed by an appeal to man's simultaneous (if often weaker) attraction to order and social peace (that is, to the beautiful). The common life of a community depends a great deal on sentimental attachments and implicit appeals to this love of the beautiful and the orderly, and in Burke's view, these play a vital but generally underappreciated role in the prevention of political violence and the maintenance of warm and peaceful relations in society. This is one reason why, for Burke, the stable order of society should not be needlessly disrupted, and the importance of the rituals, ceremonies, and outright pomp that often accompany social and political life should not be dismissed.

Burke was not a sentimentalist, however.[43] "Leave a man to his passions," he wrote, "and you leave a wild beast to a savage and capricious nature."[44] Rather, he argued that while politics does answer to reason, human reason does not interact directly with the world but is always mediated by our imagination, which helps us to give order and shape to the data we derive from our senses. One way or another, reason applies through the sentiments and passions, so it is crucial to tend to what he calls our "moral imagination" because left untended, it will direct our reason toward violence and disorder.[45]

The dark side of our sentiments is mitigated not by pure reason, but by more beneficent sentiments. We cannot be simply argued out of our vices, but we can be deterred from indulging them by the trust and love that develops among neighbors, by deeply established habits of order and peace, and by pride in our community or country. And part of the statesman's difficult charge is keeping this balance together, acting rationally on this understanding of the limits of reason. "The temper of the people amongst whom he presides ought therefore to be the first study of a statesman," Burke asserts.[46] It is for Burke another reason why politics can never be reduced to a simple application of logical axioms. As Burke's contemporary William Hazlitt put it: "[Burke] knew that man had affections and passions and powers of imagination, as well as hunger and thirst and the sense of heat and cold. . . . He knew that the rules that form the basis of private morality are not founded in reason, that is, in the abstract properties of those things which are the subjects of them, but in the nature of man, and his capacity of being affected by certain things from habit, from imagination, and sentiment, as well as from reason."[47]

This lifelong interest in the natural passions made Burke acutely attuned to the role of habits and sentiments in political life and to the risks of either breaking the habits of peace or creating habits of unchecked terror or power. He thus objected to British actions in America as an affront to the habits and sentiments of the Americans, even if the actions were not a violation of Americans' rights. The same concern caused him to worry about how the young British men sent to India would be influenced by the unlimited authority they were given over the locals there. It caused him to fear far earlier than most that the French revolutionaries, by exploding all the myths that beautified social life, would unleash a wave of mesmerizing horror that could unmoor everyone involved from their habits and restraints.

In this respect, Burke argued that the actions of the revolutionaries—by denying the sentimental aspect of human nature—were profoundly unnatural and anti-natural. He refused to cede the language of nature in politics to Paine and the French and English radicals, because he grounded his case for resisting radical political disruption in a notion of nature quite different from that of the radicals. In his writings on the French Revolution, Burke repeatedly argued that the revolutionaries were "at war with nature" or overturning "the order of nature."[48] But he did not suggest that the particular institutions or arrangements of prerevolutionary France were themselves natural. That was not the order being overturned. Rather, the revolutionaries were warring against human nature. By ignoring or failing to restrain popular passions, they threatened to unleash the darkest of those passions upon society, utterly desensitizing the people to acts of terror and violence and so making orderly social life after the revolution impossible.

This is why Burke placed such heavy emphasis on what he argued was a natural revulsion to some of the particular actions that characterized the revolution. The natural revulsion to terrible power is absolutely essential to Burke's vision of the functional society. The revolutionaries' lack of any such natural reaction had a great deal to do with Burke's vehemence in opposing them. He explains what he found so off-putting about Richard Price's celebration of the mob violence of the revolution (which was what first moved him to write the *Reflections*):

> Why do I feel so differently from the Reverend Dr. Price, and those of his lay flock, who will choose to adopt the sentiments of his discourse? For this plain reason—because it is *natural* I should; because we are so made as to be affected at such spectacles with melancholy sentiments upon the unstable condition of mortal prosperity, and the tremendous uncertainty of human greatness; because in those natural feelings we learn great lessons; because in events like these our passions instruct our reason. . . . Some tears might be drawn from me, if such a spectacle were exhibited on the stage. I should be truly ashamed of finding in myself that superficial, theatric sense of painted distress, whilst I could exult over it in real life.[49]

Burke saw in the absence of such a natural reaction to the spectacles of the revolution a sure sign of trouble—a lack of restraint that could only end in disaster. This radically unnatural lack of restraint, in his view, had to be taught. A product of a political theory at odds with nature, it justified violence and threatened to desensitize the public to violence. "Such must be the consequences of losing, in the splendor of these triumphs of the rights of men, all *natural* sense of wrong and right," Burke worries.[50] A sophisticated theory in the service of mob violence was nearly the most dangerous thing in the world.

Burke believed that most Englishmen, by contrast, had not yet been educated out of their habits of peace. His countrymen, he writes, are "generally men of untaught feelings," which speak more truly of human nature than the radicalism of the revolutionaries. In one of the most famous passages of the *Reflections*, Burke expounds on the peaceful habits of the English:

> In England, we . . . have not yet been completely emboweled of our natural entrails; we still feel within us, and we cherish and cultivate, . . . those inbred sentiments which are the faithful guard-

ians, the active monitors of our duty, the true supporters of all liberal and manly morals. We have not been drawn and trussed, in order that we may be filled, like stuffed birds in a museum, with chaff and rags, and paltry blurred shreds of paper about the rights of man. . . . We have real hearts of flesh and blood beating in our bosoms. We fear God; we look up with awe to kings; with affection to parliaments; with duty to magistrates; with reverence to priests; and with respect to nobility. Why? Because when such ideas are brought before our minds, it is natural to be so affected; because all other feelings are false and spurious, and tend to corrupt our minds, to vitiate our primary morals, to render us unfit for rational liberty.[51]

In his description, an entire system of morals, habits, and practices had arisen to support the sentiments friendly to society, and the attempt to overthrow that system threatens to eviscerate those sentiments and thereby endanger social peace and individual security.

The system, Burke argues, has generally gone by the old-fashioned name of "chivalry." It is the collection of habits intended to pacify and to beautify two crucial and often dangerous sets of relationships: those between men and women on the one hand, and those between ruler and ruled on the other. The system of chivalry ennobled both sets of connections by elevating them with high sentiments and feelings (gentleness, devotion, and faithfulness in the one case; obligation, duty, and loyalty in the other).[52] But this tradition, which Burke believed had given its character to modern Europe, was under attack by the revolutionaries:

All is to be changed. All the pleasing illusions, which made power gentle and obedience liberal, which harmonized the different shades of life, and which, by a bland assimilation, incorporated into politics the sentiments which beautify and soften private society, are to be dissolved by this new conquering empire of light and reason. All the decent drapery of life is to be rudely torn off. All the superadded ideas, furnished from the wardrobe of a moral imagination, which the heart owns, and the understanding ratifies, as necessary to cover the defects of our naked, shivering nature, and to raise it to dignity in our own estimation, are to be exploded as ridiculous, absurd, and antiquated fashion.[53]

The radicals' idea of nature, Burke argues, is only our naked animal nature and the naked reason that reveals it, and by stripping away the appeal to beauty, this stark philosophy eradicates every obstacle to radicalism and violence: "On this scheme of things, a king is but a man; a queen is but a woman; a woman is but an animal; and an animal not of the highest order."[54] In this sense, radicalism is truly dehumanizing.

And the absence of chivalry—the failure to respond with outrage to grievous violations and abuses—has terrible implications for society. This is the context for one of the most famous and most highly criticized flourishes in Burke's writings on France: his grand romantic paean to Marie Antoinette, written in reaction to the events of October 6, 1789, when a mob attacked the palace of Louis XVI and nearly killed the queen. Burke begins his reflection by recalling his once having met the queen while on a semi-official visit to Versailles:

> It is now sixteen or seventeen years since I saw the queen of France, then the dauphiness, at Versailles, and surely never lighted on this orb, which she hardly seemed to touch, a more delightful vision. I saw her just above the horizon, decorating and cheering the elevated sphere she just began to move in—glittering like the morning star, full of life and splendor and joy. Oh! what a revolution! and what a heart must I have to contemplate without emotion that elevation and that fall! Little did I dream when she added titles of veneration to those of enthusiastic, distant, respectful love, that she should ever be obliged to carry the sharp antidote against disgrace concealed in that bosom.

Burke is deeply disturbed that the people of France would not rise to the defense of their queen when her life was threatened and that they did not even seem particularly moved by the attack. As he notes in a famously (and almost painfully) flowery passage of the *Reflections*:

> Little did I dream that I should have lived to see such disasters fallen upon her in a nation of gallant men, in a nation of men of honor and of cavaliers. I thought ten thousand swords must have leaped from their scabbards to avenge even a look that threatened her with insult. But the age of chivalry is gone. That of sophisters, economists, and calculators has succeeded; and the glory of Europe is extinguished forever. Never, never more shall we behold that generous loyalty to rank and sex, that proud submission, that dignified obedience, that subordination of the heart which kept alive, even in servitude itself, the spirit of an exalted freedom. The unbought grace of life, the cheap defense of nations, the nurse of manly sentiment and heroic enterprise, is gone! It is gone, that sensibility of principle, that chastity of honor which felt a stain like a wound, which inspired courage whilst it mitigated ferocity, which ennobled whatever it touched, and under which vice itself lost half its evil by losing all its grossness.[55]

The sheer floridity of this passage was bound to draw scorn, and it immediately did. The very first reader of the *Reflections*, Burke's good friend Philip Francis, was sent an early draft for comment. He wrote to Burke that while the essay as a whole was very powerful, "in my opinion all that you say of the queen is pure foppery. If she be a perfect female character you ought to take your ground upon her virtues. If she be the reverse it is ridiculous in any but a lover to place her personal charms in opposition to her crimes."[56]

Paine's critique was even more severe, accusing Burke of sketching "tragic paintings" for his readers to mask the horrors committed by the old regime in France and describing him as a kind of quixotic knight chasing windmills in search of a lost age of chivalry.[57] And in a sense, this critique is more accurate than Francis's. As Burke made clear in his response to Francis, the notion that a thousand swords should have leaped to protect the queen was not a reflection on the queen's character. It reflected on the character of those who lived under a chivalrous system and who would not let a woman be mistreated. Men should be so cultured that their natural reaction of pity and reverence is allowed to govern their actions, rather than being replaced by a sophisticated cynicism. A political system that gives up on the effort to educate man's natural sentiments to good ends would quickly degenerate into despotism, because it would have no hold on its people's allegiance except the threat of force. "On the scheme of this barbarous philosophy," Burke wrote in the *Reflections*, "which is the offspring of cold hearts and muddy understandings, and which is as void of solid wisdom as it is destitute of all taste and elegance, laws are to be supported only by their own terrors. . . . In the groves of *their* academy, at the end of every vista, you see nothing but the gallows. Nothing is left which engages the affections on the part of the commonwealth."[58]

Burke thus first rejects the radical appeal to nature as potentially ruinous and then offers the beginning of a positive description of man's nature by reference to what exactly he believes might be ruined by the radicals. Man's reliance on his imagination to guide even his reason is a natural fact crucially relevant to political life. A successful political order must protect and sustain the "wardrobe of our moral imagination" and never lose sight of its importance.

But just how could such a political order be constructed and sustained over time? Thomas Paine's model of nature, after all, offered both means and ends for political action by holding up a particular understanding of nature—taken to be a set of rational rules that begin from individualism and equality—as the standard of legitimacy that should give shape to change over time. Burke's understanding of human nature offers reasons, including reasons grounded in a positive teaching about human nature, to worry about the actual consequences of applying Paine's model. But what does Burke's own alternative view have to say about political change? Here Burke turns most explicitly to nature for an answer.

While he denies that any particular political system is somehow natural to man, he believes that in thinking about how best to manage and guide political change over time, we would be wise to look to the *model* of how change happens in nature and to follow that model by choice. His model of nature is not Paine's system of rational rules akin to modern physics but something more like the example of biological organisms transmitting their traits through the generations: a system of inheritance. In an extraordinary passage in the *Reflections*, Burke lays out how the natural example is crucial to his larger view of political life:

> By a constitutional policy, working after the pattern of nature, we receive, we hold, we transmit our government and our privileges, in the same manner in which we enjoy and transmit our property and our lives. The institutions of policy, the goods of fortune, the gifts of providence, are handed down to us, and from us, in the same course and order. Our political system is placed in a just correspondence and symmetry with the order of the world, and with the mode of existence decreed to a permanent body composed of transitory parts; wherein, by the disposition of a stupendous wisdom, molding together the great mysterious incorporation of the human race, the whole at one time is never old, or middle-aged, or young, but in a condition of unchangeable constancy, moves on through the varied tenor of perpetual decay, fall, renovation, and progression. Thus, by preserving the method of nature in the conduct of the state, in what we improve, we are never wholly new; in what we retain, we are never wholly obsolete.[59]

This analogy teaches us a great deal about Burke's view of nature. It points to his focus on the facts of birth and death and the need to manage change, decay, renovation, and progress. He has in mind, too, a kind of model of species, rather than individuals, so that his appeal to nature, quite unlike Paine's, does not yield in individualism but in a case for the implicit and inescapable embeddedness of every individual in a larger context.

But Burke also clearly asserts that he sees this interpretation only as a model. This approach to politics is a kind of choice, not a natural fact. Parallels between nature and politics "rather furnish similitudes to illustrate or adorn, than supply analogies from which to reason."[60] The English, Burke argues, *choose* to adhere to a model of nature—a model of transmission and inheritance that enables gentle, gradual change—in their political life. They might well have chosen otherwise. But they wisely follow the model of nature because it draws on some of the advantages apparent in the natural world for dealing with certain complicated and inescapable natural obstacles to progress. First and foremost among these obstacles, people are born and die, and so the human race is always threatened by discontinuities. By connecting the generations to one another, rather than sending each all the way back to the first origins of man for information, Burke's model secures a means of cultural transmission that takes account of the life cycle, about which we human beings have no choice.

It also enables responsible change. By always seeing ourselves as carrying forward and improving on an inheritance, Burke reasons, we need not feel like the first to do anything, and even new ideas can be fitted into the patterns of old ones—so that gradual innovations might bring improvements without the usual impudence of innovators. A sense of age and long-standing also breeds respect and encourages peaceful and benevolent sentimental attachments to one's society: "By this means, our liberty becomes a noble freedom. It carries an imposing and majestic aspect. It has a pedigree and illustrating ancestors."[61]

By treating existing political institutions and practices as an entailed inheritance, citizens learn to think of them as a kind of charge—a gift from the past that, preserved and suitably improved upon, is owed to the future—and therefore learn not to dismiss them lightly. Men are by nature drawn to novelty and excitement, Burke worries, and only by being stirred by the beauty of the given can they see its advantages and so be appropriately skeptical and cautious about overturning it.[62] The old and tried model will not always work, of course, but when it fails, societies would be wise to fix it by gradually building on what does work about it rather than by starting fresh with an untried idea.

Burke thus offers a model of gradual change—of evolution rather than revolution. In a sense, he sees tradition as a process with something of the character that modern biology ascribes to natural evolution. The products of that process are valuable not because they are old, but because they are advanced—having developed through years of trial and error and adapted to their circumstances. The approach to political life built on this model, which Burke often dubs "prescription," is a way of adapting well-established practices and institutions to changing times, rather than starting over and losing the advantages of age and experience. This model of nature is by no means the whole of Burke's idea of prescription, as we will see, but is the foundation of it.

Burke, however, is not arguing for static adherence to past practices. On the contrary, he believes that contending with constant change is one of the greatest strengths of the natural world, in ways that human communities would do well to learn from. "We must all obey the great law of change," Burke writes. "It is the most powerful law of nature, and the means perhaps of its conservation. All we can do, and that human wisdom can do, is to provide that the change shall proceed by insensible degrees. This has all the benefits which may be in change, without any of the inconveniences of mutation."[63] And this is achieved by investing people in the given world, on the model of nature. For Burke, therefore, nature offers not a source of principles and axioms, but a living model of change, and one especially well suited to human nature, with its reliance on imagination and the sentiments, and to the natural facts of man's life and death.

But Burke's imperative that change must be made gradual raises a vexing question that points to another deep division between him and Paine: Is the *pace* of change all that matters for social peace and political legitimacy? Does the substance or direction not matter as well? Is one kind of change as good as another as long as it is carried out gradually and with respect for precedent?

Paine's emphasis on nature over history is an appeal to principles of proper action and therefore an appeal to justice. Burke's invocation of nature understood through history calls for a model of thoughtful and gradual change and is therefore an appeal to order. But does the appeal to justice require a means of political and social change that is so radical and revolutionary that it must undermine all hope for political and social order? And does the appeal to order leave any room for principles of justice as the proper guides to action in the world? Burke and Paine's disagreement about the proper model of nature for politics therefore leads inexorably to a dispute about justice and order.

THREE

JUSTICE AND ORDER

OTH BURKE AND PAINE APPEAL TO MODELS OF NATURE
to ground their political thought and especially their understanding of political change. But the differences between their
models have huge implications for how they distinguish good change
from bad.

For Paine, the appeal to nature is primarily an appeal to justice. Despite his rather abstract and theoretical mode of expression,
Paine's passion always comes from outrage against injustice and
human suffering. He detects a moral vacuum in Burke's denial of
the natural roots of political principle and a marked lack of compassion for the low and the weak in Burke's romantic celebration
of the noble and the mighty. It may be easier to paint great tragic
pictures when a queen is threatened by a mob, Paine says, but it is
more important to offer help when an entire people is crushed by a
corrupt regime. "He pities the plumage, but forgets the dying bird,"
Paine famously writes of Burke.[1] And Paine believes Burke has been
blinded to the injustice done to the French people by precisely his

(in Paine's view, quite excessive) emphasis on the place of the moral imagination in politics.

All of Burke's appeals to beauty and order, to the imposing majesty of the deeply rooted practices we inherit, strike Paine as excuses for inequality, indifference, and injustice. He does not think men are innately so vicious as to require beautiful illusions to restrain them. The illusions, Paine argues, are necessary only to keep the people from seeing that they have been denied their rights. In a sense, then, Burke and Paine accuse each other of the same vice: Each says the other is made cold to human suffering by his theories of nature and of politics.

In his writings on France, Burke undeniably makes far more of the suffering of the powerful at the hands of the mob than the suffering of the people at the hands of their rulers. He insists he does this out of concern not for the property of the nobles or the priests but for the moral degradation of the mob, which he takes to be driven to violent radicalism by misguided theories.[2] But Burke only rarely acknowledges the suffering of the French people themselves, and even then, only when he argues that the leveling philosophies of the revolution will do the people more harm still and that there were means of addressing their condition without overturning their society. Burke does not quite defend the old regime, but he thinks the new one is not an improvement. The revolution, he writes, involved "the change of one piece of barbarism for another, and a worse."[3] His concerns are not expressly humanitarian, and the model of nature he defends is not a model of justice but a model of gradual change.

There is no question, too, that Paine is not only cold to the suffering of those forcibly deposed from power, but sometimes downright giddy at their downfall and mistreatment. To Paine, the mob's actions, which so distress Burke, are not only justified but also expressly caused by the regime's extreme despotism and injustice.[4]

Each man is therefore partially right to accuse the other of letting his theories of politics (and, really, his theories of nature) blind him to certain kinds of injustice. But each also has an answer to the charge. Paine's answer is loud and clear: For him, justice is embodied in the rational principles of liberal politics. Anything short of a government chosen and consented to by the people—a government that respects their rights and represents their interests—is an unjust regime and can only survive through brazen crimes. Paine's politics is firmly anchored in a moral standard. But the moral grounding of Burke's politics is a far more complicated problem.

Moral Order and Moral Law

What might we say of Burke's idea of justice, especially given his understanding of nature? He appeals to a model of nature to guide social and political organization, but does he also appeal to a *standard* of nature in judging political action? Does he have a standard of justice at all, or does his emphasis on the conventional character of political societies mean that he sees no external measure but the law itself? Burke offers no simple answer to this crucial question, and scholars of his work have been divided over his view of it for two centuries.

On one side are those who read Burke as a kind of sophisticated utilitarian or "procedural conservative," concerned for social peace and effective government, worried about the dangers of poorly managed political change, but lacking any strong moral code to define political life.[5] Burke's vehement objections to the direct application of abstract theories in political life; his emphasis on prescription (in which practices and institutions are judged by their effects), prudence, and expedience in political judgment; and his assertion that political communities are essentially conventional lead these readers of Burke to see him as concerned with means to the exclusion of ends and so as a practitioner of almost pure expediency in political judgment.[6] He worries about the pace of change, but not about its direction.

Some have gone as far as to argue that Burke did not fundamentally disagree with the substantive aims underlying the rationalism of the French Revolution—that "he merely wants to further its ends less precipitously."[7] As these readers see it, his reasons for defending liberty and opposing violations of human dignity (reasons evident, for instance, in his views of the American conflict and of British misbehavior in India) have to do with the integrity of Britain's governing institutions and social cohesion, not with moral principles that define political life. He is thus not simply a defender of the given, but he is a defender of the successful and effective, and his definition of success is highly procedural.

But these readers of Burke face some serious difficulties in his own writing. Of the idea that the conventional origins of political institutions mean that any laws made according to a society's usual procedures are inherently morally legitimate, Burke offers an unwavering condemnation:

> It would be hard to point out any error more truly subversive of all the order and beauty, of all the peace and happiness, of human society than the position that the body of men have a right to make what laws they please; or that laws can derive any authority from their institution merely and independent of the quality of the subject-matter. No arguments of policy, reason of state, or preservation of the constitution can be pleaded in favor of such a practice. They may in deed impeach the frame of that constitution; but can never touch this immovable principle. This seems to be, indeed, the principle which Hobbes broached in the last century, and which was then so frequently and so ably refuted.[8]

Clearly, Burke believed there could be unjust laws, and that being effective doesn't make a particular policy moral or right. He explicitly denied seeking "to make the success of villainy the standard of innocence," and his writings support this denial.[9] "All human laws are, properly speaking, only declaratory; they may alter the mode and application, but have no power over the substance of original justice," he writes.[10] Nor does he refute the notion that political life fulfills some inclinations impressed upon man by his nature, or his maker. Although Burke could be exceedingly vague when taking up these questions, he clearly sees himself vindicating a moral vision in his political crusades.

Indeed, his (at least tonal) moralism has led some Burke scholars to argue that not only was Burke not a utilitarian or pure proceduralist, but he was in fact a natural-law philosopher—that is, a believer in a clear moral standard, made evident in nature or made accessible through revelation, that serves as a model and standard for human life.[11] Burke, they insist, "conceived of statecraft as the practical application in concrete human affairs of primary moral principles, clearly evident to man's right reason."[12] To support this view, they point to Burke's repeated references to God, religion, and the order of nature, especially in his writings on India and Ireland.

And it is true that in taking up those last two subjects, Burke most explicitly asserts that the standards of judgment in politics must go beyond efficacy to some idea of justice. In 1787, after word had reached London of gross mistreatment of the natives of India by the East India Company (which represented the government's interests in that important part of the empire), Burke launched an impeachment proceeding against Warren Hastings—the British governor general of India. Burke considered the case crucial to setting the character of the growing empire, and although Hastings was ultimately acquitted by the House of Lords, Burke later described his own part in the trial as among his most significant accomplishments.[13] Because he had very little positive law to appeal to in making his case, he grounded his passionate and powerful appeal in a higher law. "I impeach him," Burke told the lords regarding Hastings, "in the name and by virtue of those eternal laws of justice which he has violated. I impeach him in the name of human nature itself, which he has cruelly outraged, injured, and oppressed, in both sexes, at every age, rank, situation, and condition of life."[14]

Similarly, in the case of laws restricting the rights and privileges of Catholics in his native Ireland, Burke argued that the policy amounted to "a deprivation of all the rights of human nature."[15] In a private letter, he described a bill to outlaw intermarriage between Irish Catholics and Protestants (a subject that was, of course, quite personal for Burke) as filled with "outrages on the rights of humanity and laws of nature."[16] And in the Irish context, in fact, he comes closest to defining his understanding of the explicit purpose of government and political life: "Everybody is satisfied that a conservation and secure enjoyment of our natural rights is the great and ultimate purpose of civil society; and that therefore all forms whatsoever of government are only good as they are subservient to that purpose to which they are entirely subordinate."[17]

This language sounds a lot like Paine's and that of the French Revolutionaries and seems on its face to contradict Burke's frequent denial of the direct relevance of natural rights to life in civil society. It is not hard to see why some readers would take such declarations as evidence that Burke sees an accessible natural law above the positive law. But this view is no less problematic than the charge that Burke is a utilitarian. It falls apart especially when we consider the very subject that the natural-law readers of Burke point to above all: his frequent references to religion.

Burke's view of the appropriate place of religion in public life, made most extensively in the *Reflections on the Revolution in France*, is in fact strikingly utilitarian. In his first take on the subject—in the *Vindication of Natural Society*—Burke worried that people who attacked religious institutions and practices as merely "artificial" or conventional risked undermining civil society. The case against organized religion, he argues, could easily become a case against all social institutions grounded in tradition. In the *Reflections*, he offers much the same point in a positive sense: Just as attacks on religion could be harmful to social peace, so could the public elevation and endorsement of religious practice and belief reinforce social harmony and civil society. Religion, then, is an element in the larger system of chivalry, ennobling the use of political power and moderating its users. "When they are habitually convinced that no evil can be acceptable, either in the act or the permission, to him whose essence is good," Burke writes of citizens living under an established church, "they will be better able to extirpate out of the minds of all magistrates, civil, ecclesiastical, or military, any thing that bears the least resemblance to a proud and lawless domination."[18]

Moreover, religion, by "consecrating" the state, gives the people an added impetus to respect and regard their regime.[19] Religion, and especially an established church, helps to give people the kind of sen-

timental attachments and peaceful habits necessary to sustain a political order grounded in generational continuity and prescription.[20]
Covering the state in sacred garb also helps to shield its origins and
protect it from rash and extreme reform or revolution.[21] And finally,
religion also helps the poor deal with their condition. To deprive them
of this source of consolation is to make oneself "the cruel oppressor,
the merciless enemy of the poor and wretched."[22]

Burke therefore writes about religion almost exclusively in terms
of its use to society and the state rather than as a path to divine truth.
He invokes the power and beauty of religious ceremony as means of
building popular allegiance and solidarity.[23] The majesty and pomp of
a great cathedral, in this view, can strengthen social bonds, whether
or not they celebrate a true revealed divine justice. "We know and it
is our pride to know," Burke writes, "that man is by his constitution a
religious animal," and for this reason, atheism seems to him a recipe
for social unrest, and religion a necessary prop for peace.[24] But it is as
such a prop, and not explicitly as the particular and ultimate standard
of judgment, that religion is accorded a central place in Burke's political thought. He does not deny the truth of Christianity—and in his
private life and letters offers reason to think he was a relatively ortho-
dox believer—but he does not think politics can be directly grounded
in Christian moral claims. Instead, he says, politics can be based only
on the piety these claims yield in the believer.

Indeed, Burke is remarkably forthright in denying a necessary
connection between the social value of religious piety and the theological truth underlying it. Of French Catholics, he writes that some
of their beliefs are surely simple superstition, but that this being their
ancient religion, it nonetheless plays a crucial role in sustaining social
and political life.[25] Even in England, he argues, it makes sense for
statesmen to follow the code and the forms of the established religion
regardless of their own sense of its ultimate truth: "If by their conduct
(the only language that rarely lies) they seemed to regard the great
ruling principle of the moral and the natural world as a mere invention to keep the vulgar in obedience, they apprehend that by such a
conduct they would defeat the politic purpose they have in view. They

would find it difficult to make others to believe in a system to which they manifestly gave no credit themselves."[26]

This is a case for a consecrated state religion, but not truly for a politics that answers finally to a divine standard. Indeed, another element of Burke's larger political teaching undermines even further the case for natural law as the essence of his philosophy. Although he does insist on a standard outside the positive law by which political action should be measured, his rejection of beginnings as the ultimate source of authority and understanding suggests he would not search for that standard at the beginning of human history, where natural law ultimately points. As we have seen, Burke argues that beginnings should be shrouded in a veil, and that the results of the long chain of tradition and practice—results like stability, prosperity, allegiance, patriotism, and nobility—are what we must seek to protect. Thus, the long chain itself is to be guarded, but not because its origins were perfect; he says plainly that he does not believe they were. This is not Christian traditionalism. It is prescription, a very different and quite innovative way of thinking about social development.

Burke turns out, therefore, to be neither a utilitarian proceduralist nor a natural-law philosopher. He does not believe that man-made law is the final authority and that only consequences matter. Nor does he believe that political life is an expression of unchanging Christian truths. The regime, he suggests, does not owe its legitimacy directly to God, and neither is every whim of the sovereign legitimate. He proposes, rather, a novel notion of political change that emerges from precisely his model of nature and his (again, rather novel) idea of prescription. And yet over time, this idea points us toward a standard of justice and judgment beyond pure utility.

Burke does not differ with Paine's or the natural-law school's view that a standard of justice must guide political life. He differs, rather, in his view of our ability to *know* and discover that standard. Paine argues that we can know the standard by rational deduction from the premises of our understanding of nature. So, for instance, our knowledge of presocial man tells us that all men are equal—an understanding that must define political life. The natural-law tradition argues that we can know the standard through philosophical reflection on theological or philosophical premises (many of them evident in the functioning of nature). Burke, however, is far more skeptical of our ability to discover and apply directly this higher standard of justice in politics. The higher standard is not directly accessible to reason, he argues, because human beings generally cannot reason directly about abstract ideas without some imaginative context, and because social life is not the simple playing out of presocial natural premises. Burke's view of nature and of human nature suggests to him that the standards of justice that are to guide political life are rather discoverable—to the extent we can know them at all—implicitly through the experience of political life itself.

Burke believes, therefore, that the traditions embodied in England's social and political institutions (what he describes as "the English constitution"), built as they are on the model of natural generation, are the best means available for his countrymen to reach a transcendent standard for government. He acknowledges that the constitutional tradition does not speak with one voice and cannot be traced back to a simple set of original principles that rely on man's beginnings to define his rights. But it does offer, in the norms it builds up, though always with exceptions, an approach by degrees to a real standard beyond mere convention. This view is neither natural-law philosophy nor a standard-less utilitarianism. Grounded in Burke's natural model of change, this approach respects traditional practices not because they began a long time ago but because they have survived and evolved, through a process of trial and error, for a long time.

Prescription—which improves society by building upon its strengths—with its analogy of nature, makes this trial and error possible and helps us distinguish error from success. It is indeed a model of change, but one suited to help us discern the general shape of some permanent underlying principles of justice. The historical experience of social and political life consists in essence of a kind of rubbing up against the principles of natural justice, and the institutions and practices that survive the experience thereby take on something of the shape of those principles, because only those that have this shape do survive. Over time, therefore, provided they develop in accordance with the model of prescription, societies come to express in their institutions, their charters, their traditions, and their habits a simulacrum of the standard of justice. Society, as it exists after such long experience, therefore offers an approximation of society as it should exist. Social and political change can help to bring a society slowly closer to the standard, if only by degrees. But such progress is likely to happen only if the change is in keeping with the spirit of society's preexisting modes and orders, since they offer the only real sense we can have of what the sought-after standard looks like. We should seek to emulate our ancestors, Burke argues, "who, by looking backward as well as forward . . . went on, insensibly drawing this constitution nearer and nearer to its perfection by never departing from its fundamental principles, nor introducing any amendment which had not a subsisting root in the laws, constitution, and usages of the kingdom."[27] Burke in this sense is not a backward-looking but a forward-looking traditionalist; he believes that the present is better than the past, and he is committed to sustaining the means by which it has become better, to facilitate further improvement.

The best kind of political change, in Burke's view, builds on what is best about the given world to improve what is worst about it, and leaves society as it was but more so. This is the best sort of change not because our conventional institutions define the standards of our politics, but because the conventions that have survived the test of time are those that somehow answer to that standard. "This great law does not arise from our conventions or compacts; on the contrary, it gives to our conventions and compacts all the force and sanction they can have."[28] This is the reason prescription is such an effective model of change; over time, it "mellows into legality governments that were violent in their commencement."[29]

Social change can thus be generally ameliorative if it is properly managed, though it is not simply progressive: it does not move in only one direction. Burke's idea of a just society is not an end state that is the ultimate goal of all political change. Rather, a just society provides space for thriving private lives and a thriving national life within the bounds of the constitution by allowing for some balance of order and freedom. Political life occurs within that space, and political change sustains and defends that space and therefore moves in various directions as events warrant—sometimes restraining or strengthening one element of the constitution, and sometimes another. Political change helps to slowly draw the constitution toward its perfection, but the change is far from linear and never simple. Precisely because of the generational character of human societies, political change cannot achieve a genuine perfection. Thus, societies are always contending with the most basic flaws of human nature. Those cannot be overcome, because we humans are always human, even as our social institutions improve with time as we learn from experience.[30] The statesman's task is therefore not to drive society toward some particular ultimate and just condition but to create and constantly sustain a space in which the people may exercise their freedom and enjoy the benefits of life in society.

Successful political change in Burke's view is thus utterly continuous with a society's past and character. To plan, manage, judge, and carry off such successful change therefore requires a profound understanding of the history, the spirit, the norms, the practices, and the traditions of one's society, and a successful politics is guided by this kind of understanding—which goes by the name of prudence. Prudence is not the opposite of either principle or theory. Prudence, rather, is the application of general experience to particular practical problems. In Burke's view, the prudent person believes that the experience of our society generally points to underlying principles of justice (and of nature) and so offers more reliable, if less specific, guidance than do abstract theories like the natural-rights liberalism that Paine would import wholesale into practical politics.

"History is a preceptor of prudence, not of principles," Burke writes; it does not offer us direct knowledge of precise or abstract rules.[31] But it does give us general rules, which are certainly good enough most of the time. In an early pamphlet, Burke argues that there are no exact formulas for civil or political wisdom:

They are a matter incapable of exact definition. But, though no man can draw a stroke between the confines of day and night, yet light and darkness are upon the whole tolerably distinguishable. Nor will it be impossible for a Prince to find out such a mode of government, and such persons to administer it, as will give a great degree of content to his people, without any curious and anxious research for that abstract, universal, perfect harmony, which, while he is seeking, he abandons those means of ordinary tranquility which are in his power without any research at all.[32]

That well-functioning societies approach the standard of justice over time does not mean that all societies will gravitate toward the same institutions and forms, however. Precisely because we can never access it directly and in full, there are many ways to approach the standard of justice by degrees. "Liberty inheres in some sensible object," Burke writes, "and every nation has formed to itself some favorite point, which by way of eminence becomes the criterion of their happiness."[33] Not only do different nations in Europe approach this ideal in different ways, but even distinct communities of Englishmen take different approaches. Burke points to the American colonists as examples. Living apart from Britain for several generations, the Americans, he says, have developed a powerful attachment to personal liberty and an insatiable entrepreneurialism, which their political institutions will inevitably reflect, while the British at home are more attached to firm and stable authority.[34]

But each of these criteria of happiness, if it has resulted in societies that allow for liberty, dignity, prosperity, and honor, makes for a legitimate standard of judgment and change for the nation in question, and each is expressed in that nation's political tradition. "If the people are happy, united, wealthy, and powerful, we presume the rest," Burke writes. "We conclude that to be good from whence good is derived. In old establishments various correctives have been found for their aberrations from theory. Indeed they are the results of various necessities and expediencies. They are not often constructed after any theory; theories are rather drawn from them."[35]

Most political questions present themselves *within* the bounds established by the constitution and so do not raise essential questions of natural justice but rather challenges to prudence. They ought therefore to be settled by expedient judgment guided by constitutional precedent, and if they are found to have been made incorrectly, they can be corrected, again by prudent statesmanship. Most of the political life of a reasonably functional society, therefore, is a matter of straightforward prudence, which is "in politics, the first of virtues," Burke writes.[36] But there are two crucial exceptions to this expediency.

First, sometimes a particular policy is so starkly at odds with the constitutional tradition and therefore so likely to be at odds with the standards of justice that guide political life, it must be opposed by direct recourse to justice and right, and not only on prudential grounds. "Justice is itself the great standing policy of civil society; and any eminent departure from it, under any circumstances, lies under the suspicion of being no policy at all," Burke writes.[37] Most policy questions do not rise to the level of fundamental matters of justice. But those that do will require special attention and urgency because they present something of an unprecedented challenge, for which the constitutional tradition is not well suited. British conduct in India and Ireland so obviously violated the pattern of English history, in Burke's view, that it was equally clear that they violated natural justice. Burke contrasts the East India Company's charter with what he calls the great charters of English history, starting with the Magna Carta, which laid out the rights of Englishmen in 1215. "*Magna Carta* is a charter to restrain power, and to destroy monopoly," he writes. "The East India charter is a charter to establish monopoly, and to create power. Political power and commercial monopoly are *not* the rights of men."[38] Burke opposed the slave trade on similar grounds.

The second exception to the reign of pure prudence challenges not the traditions of the constitution but the mode of change that has made the development of the constitution possible. The prospect of total revolution, which is the prospect Burke perceived in France, threatens to throw off all that has been laboriously built up over generations by prescription and start over from scratch. It is the deepest and most dangerous threat to Burke's nature-inspired model of change. He believed that the French Revolution threatened to cut society off not only from the institutions it had built up over countless generations but (as a result) from the standard of justice itself, leaving no other standard by which to judge politics than naked power masquerading as philosophy. This is what he perceived in the mobs of Paris. The intensity and the very early awakening of Burke's opposition to the revolution are much easier to understand when we realize just what he believed was threatened and why.

For Burke therefore, nature, history, justice, and order are inextricably connected. In his view, we can know the standard of nature only generally and only through the experience of history, whereas in Paine's view we can know it precisely but only by liberating ourselves from the burdens of history and seeking for direct rational understanding of natural principles. For Burke the resort to history *is* the model of nature. For Paine, nature waits for us behind the distractions of history, which is merely a sorry tale of errors, crimes, and misunderstandings. Paine's model of nature is a model of permanent justice that offers us principles for the proper arrangement of political life; Burke's model of nature is a model of gradual change that stands a chance of pointing society in the right direction.

Natural Equality and the Order of Society

Only now, having gotten a sense of what both Paine and Burke mean by nature and its consequences for justice and political life, can we begin to understand the deep differences that divide them. As we have begun to see, their disagreements about nature, history, and justice bear heavily on their other, more prominent disagreements about political change. But the most direct implications of their views of nature and justice have to do with Burke's and Paine's understanding of social relations and connections—and perhaps most notably the two men's very different notions of equality.

Burke's model of nature does not point to social equality. In a society sustained by inheritance, social eminence and great wealth will tend to stay in certain families and beyond the reach of others. Not that change and reform cannot happen, or that those who are able to rise in society are somehow unworthy of it, but equality itself should not be a primary goal of politics. Social peace, prosperity, and stability are more important for everyone, and are often not well served by the pursuit of equality—especially because true social equality is ultimately an unachievable goal.

"The idea of forcing every thing to an artificial equality has something, at first view, very captivating in it," Burke writes. "It has all the appearance imaginable of justice and good order; and very many persons, without any sort of partial purposes, have been led to adopt such schemes and to pursue them with great earnestness and warmth."[39] But it is ultimately both misguided and impractical. "Believe me, sir," he writes in the *Reflections*, "those who attempt to level never equalize. In all societies consisting of various descriptions of citizens, some description must be uppermost."[40] The only question is which element will predominate, and in a society that makes leveling and equalizing its central principle, the great middle will tend to predominate, overpowering both the rich and the poor. But this middle, especially in a society focused on equalizing, will tend to be badly suited to rule. "The levelers therefore only change and pervert the natural order of things. They load the edifice of society by setting up in the air what the solidity of the structure requires to be on the ground. The association of tailors and carpenters, of which the republic (of Paris, for instance) is composed, cannot be equal to the situation into which, by the worst usurpations, an usurpation of the prerogatives of nature, you attempt to force them."[41]

As this passage demonstrates, for Burke the question of political equality—or of who has the right to rule—is even more important than that of social or economic equality. In a society with an egalitarian idea of rule, there will not be true equality, but rather a disorderly rule by the unfit. Because it will organize itself around an idea of equality that it can never truly achieve, such a society will also always be in disarray and flux. The idea of eliminating all social distinctions in society, Burke argues, is a "monstrous fiction, which by inspiring false ideas and vain expectations into men destined to travel in the obscure walk of laborious life, serves only to aggravate and embitter that real inequality, which it can never remove; and which the order of civil life establishes as much for the benefit of those whom it must leave in an humble state as those whom it is able to exalt to a condition more splendid, but not more happy."[42]

Burke certainly isn't defending a simple social status quo, where those born to privilege and those born to toil must remain where they are. He makes clear that he does not intend "to confine power, authority, and distinction to blood and names and titles."[43] Rather, distinction should go to those who are best suited for power, and Burke believes one important component of that suitability has to do with property and leisure, which tend to be inherited. It should be possible, but not too easy, for others to break in to the ruling class if they prove themselves (as indeed Burke himself had done). But as a general matter, he writes, "some decent, regulated preeminence, some preference (not exclusive appropriation) given to birth is neither unnatural, nor unjust, nor impolitic."[44]

Why should this preference be given, if (as Burke asserts) natural ability is not itself inherited? One chief reason has to do with the importance Burke attributes to prudence in political life. Put simply, governing is very difficult, and not everyone can do it. And in a society shaped by prescription, governing requires not so much raw intelligence as knowledge of history and tradition, a sense of the people, and clear-eyed prudence in making decisions. Because it is more than the expression of public preferences or the application of geometrical principles, governing requires quality more than quantity—a quality that is developed through experience and study that build judgment and so is harder to come by for people in some professions and ways of life than others.[45] "Rational and experienced men tolerably well know, and have always known, how to distinguish between true and false liberty and between the genuine adherence and the false pretence to what is true," Burke writes in *An Appeal from the New to the Old Whigs*. "But none, except those who are profoundly studied, can comprehend the elaborate contrivance of a fabric fitted to unite private and public liberty with public force, with order, with peace, with justice, and, above all, with the institutions formed for bestowing permanence and stability through ages, upon this invaluable whole."[46]

Men have these abilities in differing degrees not because some are born more prudent than others but because prudence is a function of experience and education. Indeed, this case for political inequality seems motivated precisely by a belief in natural equality. "The savage hath within him the seeds of the logician, of the man of taste and breeding, the orator, the statesman, the man of virtue, and the saint," Burke writes, "which seeds, though planted in his mind by nature, yet, through want of culture, and exercise, must lie for ever buried, and be hardly perceivable by himself or others."[47] To cultivate these seeds requires a certain type of life. Those who live it and who benefit by it are a kind of natural aristocracy, entitled to rule because they possess the requisite judgment. In an extraordinary passage in the *Appeal*, Burke sets forth a list of more than fifteen qualities or abilities (e.g., "To see nothing low and sordid from one's infancy"; "To be taught to despise danger in the pursuit of honor and duty"; "To have leisure to read, to reflect, to converse"; "To be a professor of high science, or of liberal and ingenuous art") that might help constitute a member of the natural aristocracy.[48]

Such people, of course, can be formed only under particular social conditions. And there is no shame or injustice in preferring for rule those who are better formed for making judgments, Burke argues. Societies should seek to be well governed, rather than to merely play out the implications of an abstract ideal of political equality, and to be well governed requires giving more authority to those better able to govern.[49] Societies whose core concern is social equality not only will tend to fail to elevate the worthy, but will even tend to elevate and celebrate those most poorly qualified to govern.[50]

For this reason, as society sustains itself through inheritance, it will sustain certain social and political inequalities, too, for its own good. And these inequalities have a crucial added benefit, beyond elevating the best qualified. They also offer means for containing and resisting abuses of power, by requiring power to flow through the deep-cut channels that compose the uneven social topography. The division of citizens into distinct groups and classes, Burke writes, "composes a strong barrier against the excesses of despotism," by establishing habits and obligations of restraint in ruler and ruled alike grounded in the relations of groups or classes in society.[51] To remove these traditional restraints, which hold in check both the individual and the state, would mean empowering only the state to restrain the individual, and in turn restraining the state with only principles and rules, or parchment barriers. Neither, Burke thought, could be stronger or more effective than the restraints of habit and custom that grow out of group identity and loyalty. Burke's famous reference to the little platoon—"To be attached to the subdivision, to love the little platoon we belong to in society, is the first principle (the germ as it were) of public affections"—is often cited as an example of a case for local government or allegiance to place, but in its context in the *Reflections*, the passage is very clearly a reference to social class.[52]

Breaking apart all the connections that stand between the individual and the state and leaving equal but separate individuals alone would expose them all to the raw power of the state directly. The people would also have no protection from one another or from the mass of citizens, in such a situation. Burke worries that this would leave them unable to defend their freedoms and subject to even more brutal and dangerous abuses of power than the ancient despotisms could have been capable of. The social institutions that stand between the individual and the government are crucial barriers to the ruthlessness of public officials and the occasional cruelty of majorities. They are essential to liberty.[53]

Meanwhile, Burke believes that the very process of stripping the high and the mighty of power and stature threatens to unleash forces that could easily destroy the structured peace of society. He attributes the disloyalty and mutiny of French soldiers, for instance, to their having seen the nobles humiliated.[54] The effect of the experience of leveling, Burke worries, is to eliminate all sense of respect and obligation and leave the people ill suited for peace and order, even in civil society, let alone in political life. As noted in Chapter 2, Burke famously lamented that "on this scheme of things, a king is but a man;

a queen is but a woman; a woman is but an animal; and an animal not of the highest order."[55] The descent to barbarism begins by demoting kings and queens to mere men and women.

And yet, for all his opposition to social and political leveling, Burke does not deny the natural equality of man.[56] It is precisely because he thinks human beings are more or less equal in natural abilities that he wants only those who have been properly formed and trained to govern. Thus, natural equality not only does not necessitate social equality (as Paine would insist it does), but also makes necessary some social inequality. Society is natural to man, and the people living in it are inevitably unequal in some material and social respects. But society makes possible a deeper kind of equality, which is one of the ideals toward which he sees the model of nature pointing. "The inequality which grows out of the nature of things by time, custom, succession, accumulation, permutation, and improvement of property, is much nearer that true equality, which is the foundation of equity and just policy, than any thing which can be contrived by the tricks and devices of human skill," Burke writes.[57] This "true equality," which he describes as a "moral equality," does not take the form of an equal right to rule but is something more like an equal right to one's station in life: "All men have equal rights, but not to equal things."[58]

This moral equality, derived from ancient chivalry and its appeal to the peaceful sentiments, distinguishes modern European civilization from all others and even from the greatest civilizations of the past. "It was this," Burke writes, "which without confounding ranks had produced a noble equality, and handed it down through all the gradations of social life."[59] A mode of politics ordered to support the sentiments of social peace and sustained by a prescriptive model of change will tend to elevate the low and bring the high to submission without actually eradicating all social distinctions or atomizing society into mere disparate individuals. It composes a whole of which all are equally parts, even if not equal parts. And through it, all are better able, Burke writes, "to seek and to recognize the happiness that is to be found by virtue in all conditions; in which consists the true moral equality of mankind."[60] Such happiness is only possible in a well-governed society, and such a society in turn is made possible only by certain kinds of social and political inequalities.

Thomas Paine, of course, could hardly disagree more with Burke than he did on this point. Paine's work was the very embodiment of the radical egalitarianism that Burke feared. Paine believed that every man stands in an equal relation to his origin with every other, and therefore that none is somehow entitled to reign supreme. "Where there are not distinctions there can be no superiority," Paine writes in *Common Sense*.[61] And since "all men [are] originally equals, no one by birth could have a right to set up his own family in perpetual preference to all others for ever."[62] Because it violates the rights of every new generation, inherited social status is a recipe for an unjust society that could never be well governed. There is "no truly natural or religious reason" for the distinction between kings and subjects, he argues. "Male and female are distinctions of nature, good and bad the distinctions of heaven, but how a race of men came into the world so exalted above the rest and distinguished like some new species, is worth inquiring into, and whether they are the means of happiness or misery to mankind."[63] In other words, a king quite obviously *is* but a man. The idea that social standing or the right to rule, like property, should somehow be transmitted through the generations therefore strikes Paine as a profound misunderstanding of the nature of man and of political life.

"What is government more than the management of the affairs of a Nation?" Paine asks in *Rights of Man*. "It is not, and from its nature cannot be, the property of any particular man or family, but of the whole community, at whose expense it is supported; and though by force and contrivance it has been usurped into an inheritance, the usurpation cannot alter the right of things."[64]

Paine well understood Burke's contention that noble families' ruling privilege stemmed not from any natural right to rule but from the education in prudence and statesmanship that their inherited access to leisure allowed. But Paine's very different view of the relation of politics to nature and human nature persuaded him that government is not as complicated as Burke suggests, and therefore does not require a life of leisure and learning. "Notwithstanding the mystery with which the science of government has been enveloped for the purpose of enslaving, plundering, and imposing upon mankind, it is of all things the least mysterious and the most easy to be understood," he writes in his *Dissertation on First Principles in Government*.[65] Those who call it complicated do so only to protect their interests, like magicians sheltering their tricks. In the *Rights of Man*, he accuses the old regime in France of this dishonest tactic. "In all cases they took care to represent government as a thing made up of mysteries, which only themselves understood; and they hid from the understanding of the nation the only thing that was beneficial to know, namely, that government is nothing more than a national association acting on the principles of society."[66] These principles, accessible by reflection upon nature, do not require a deep study of history and do not change from one time and place to another.[67]

Paine argues that government is ultimately a kind of intellectual exercise requiring raw intelligence, not a knowledge of history or philosophy, and raw intelligence is more or less randomly distributed by nature. Interestingly, Burke bases his case against social equality on the roughly equal natural distribution of abilities, which require leisure and education—advantages not equally available—if they are to be honed and developed, whereas Paine bases his case for social equality on the unequal but random distribution of natural abilities. "It is impossible to control Nature in her distribution of mental powers," Paine writes. "She gives them as she pleases. I smile to myself when I contemplate the ridiculous insignificance into which literature and all the sciences would sink, were they made hereditary; and I carry the same idea into governments."[68]

Political rule, according to Paine, is thus like artistic or scientific achievement—it takes a natural talent, in this case, "mental powers," which enable the possessor to best understand the laws and rights of nature and apply them. No class of men is uniquely gifted with such abilities, and those who have them will not necessarily pass them down to their children. Only an egalitarian society could allow them to emerge and serve the interests of the polity. The equal right to rule is thus essential to the success and prosperity of society. Paine is not a leveler of property, as Burke sometimes accuses him of being, but he is a leveler of authority.[69]

ALTHOUGH THEIR DIFFERING VIEWS about nature and justice do not finally explain their larger dispute in full, both Burke and Paine begin from these questions, and their views of the subject begin to lay open their larger political philosophies. Paine argues for revolution in the cause of recovering natural liberties (which he believes have been trampled by governments). Burke argues against revolution in the cause of defending the natural order of things (which he believes is expressed in political life). Part of their dispute is about whether nature provides underlying principles for judging political institutions or provides the order and structure that those institutions constitute. Both men point to something permanent about nature, but for Burke, what is permanent is change (birth, growth, and death, as well as their political counterparts), while for Paine, what is permanent is unchanging principle. In this sense, Burke operates from an expectation of constant change, and Paine's radical liberalism is timeless. But from his reflections on change, Burke concludes that stability and continuity are essential to a sustainable society. Paine, in contrast, concludes from his reflections on timelessness that total and radical transformation is always an option.

Burke also draws from his reflections a sense that human beings are connected in the midst of change, that some links bind us inescapably across society and time; while for Paine the encounter with timeless principles is individual and direct. In considering the Burke-Paine dispute as a whole, therefore, the question of nature and its consequences for order and justice points us inevitably toward the question of social and political relations and commitments—that is, toward the question of choice and obligation.

FOUR

CHOICE AND OBLIGATION

URKE AND PAINE'S DISPUTE ABOUT NATURE AND justice sets the scene for a profound disagreement about the very purpose of politics. For Paine, the natural equality of all human beings translates to complete political equality and therefore to a right to self-determination. The formation of society was itself a choice made by free individuals, so the natural rights that people bring with them into society are rights to act as one chooses, free of coercion. Each person should have the right to do as he chooses unless his choices interfere with the equal rights and freedoms of others. And when that happens—when society as a whole must act through its government to restrict the freedom of some of its members—government can only act in accordance with the wishes of the majority, aggregated through a political process. Politics, in this view, is fundamentally an arena for the exercise of choice, and our only real political obligations are to respect the freedoms and choices of others.

For Burke, human nature can only be understood within society and therefore within the complex web of relations in which every person is embedded. None of us chooses the nation, community, or family into which we are born, and while we can choose to change our circumstances to some degree as we get older, we are always defined by some crucial obligations and relationships not of our own choosing. A just and healthy politics must recognize these obligations and relationships and respond to society as it exists, before politics can enable us to make changes for the better. In this view, politics must reinforce the bonds that hold people together, enabling us to be free within society rather than defining freedom to the exclusion of society and allowing us to meet our obligations to past and future generations, too. Meeting obligations is as essential to our happiness and our nature as making choices.

Paine's formulation of the purpose of politics is, on the surface, much more familiar to us Americans today. It is perhaps the most familiar of all the elements of Enlightenment liberalism's view of the world—but we rarely think about its premises and consequences. Burke's notion, while barely known to us at all as a theory of government, speaks in some important ways to how we actually live. Both views are more complex and problematic than we might expect—and take us toward the heart of the debate that defines modern liberal democracy.

A Politics of Choice

The idea of rights sits at the core of Thomas Paine's political philosophy. Rights are the organizing principle of his thought and the prime concern of all his writings about government. But the clearest and most accessible elucidation of Paine's idea of rights comes not in any of his essays on political questions, which all take a certain notion of political and natural rights for granted, but in an extraordinary letter he wrote to Thomas Jefferson in the momentous year 1789.

The note, apparently a follow-up to a discussion between the two men, summarizes Paine's own views on the question of rights in the midst of the chaos and excitement of the revolution in France. The revolutionaries said they were dedicated to the "rights of man," but what exactly did that mean? Paine begins, in the great Enlighten-ment-liberal tradition, by imagining a founding:

> Suppose twenty persons, strangers to each other, to meet in a coun-try not before inhabited. Each would be a Sovereign in his own natural right. His will would be his law, but his power, in many cases, inadequate to his right; and the consequence would be that each might be exposed, not only to each other, but to the other nineteen. It would then occur to them that their condition would be much improved if a way could be devised to exchange that quantity of danger into so much protection; so that each individual should possess the strength of the whole number.

In this situation, he suggests, the people would trade freedom for protection, but they would not quite give up their basic presocial rights. Instead, they would build on them:

> As all their rights in the first case are natural rights, and the exer-cise of those rights supported only by their own natural individual power, they would begin by distinguishing between those rights they could individually exercise, fully and perfectly, and those they could not. Of the first kind are the rights of thinking, speaking, forming and giving opinions, and perhaps are those which can be fully exer-cised by the individual without the aid of exterior assistance; or in other words, rights of personal competency. Of the second kind are those of personal protection, of acquiring and possessing property, in the exercise of which the individual power is less than the natural right. . . . These I consider to be civil rights, or rights of compact, and are distinguishable from natural rights because in the one we act wholly in our own person, in the other we agree not to do so, but act under the guarantee of society.[1]

This cogent description grounds rights in a highly individualistic understanding of the citizen. It sees social and political bonds as the products of individual choices driven by calculations of utility and need. Every citizen has the right to freedom of action, and when an individual right cannot be exercised individually, citizens draw on the power of the state to put their rights into practice. This power is not a gift of society; it is an entitlement—access to it is the reason we enter into society. We form societies to protect and vindicate preexisting natural rights, and what we call our civil rights are means of drawing upon the common capital of society so that natural rights can be given effect. As Paine puts it in *Rights of Man*, "society grants [the citizen] nothing. Every man is a proprietor in society, and draws on the capital as a matter of right."[2]

This means that the rights we have in society and the rights we have by nature are in essence rights to the same things—and especially to freedom of choice. "Man did not enter into society to become worse than he was before, nor to have fewer rights than he had before, but to have those rights better secured," Paine writes. He thus sees men in their natural state transformed into citizens for the protection of their rights, and he describes society explicitly as the product of this utilitarian arrangement. In *Rights of Man*, he offers this description in the form of three essential premises of his political thought:

> First, That every civil right grows out of a natural right; or, in other words, is a natural right exchanged. Secondly, That civil power properly considered as such is made up of the aggregate of that class of the natural rights of man, which becomes defective in the individual in point of power, and answers not his purpose, but when collected to a focus becomes competent to the Purpose of every one. Thirdly, That the power produced from the aggregate of natural rights, imperfect in power in the individual, cannot be applied to invade the natural rights which are retained in the individual, and in which the power to execute is as perfect as the right itself. We have now, in a few words, traced man from a natural individual to a member of society, and shown, or endeavored to show, the quality of the natural rights retained, and of those which are exchanged for civil rights.[3]

Society is therefore a means to accomplish what each individual has the right but not the ability to accomplish. For Paine, this means it is above all a means to enable *choice*, or the freedom to shape our own future uncoerced—a means to the radical liberation of the individual from the burdens of his circumstances, his given nature, and his fellow man. Equality, individualism, and natural rights (some transformed into civil rights) are descriptive and prescriptive facts regarding the human condition, but personal liberty—the right to choose—is the end toward which we aim in politics. Societies exist to protect acts of choice, by meeting animal necessities on the one hand and by protecting individuals from coercion on the other. This means that government itself, in protecting and giving effect to the rights of individuals, must be understood as a chosen arrangement defined by clear contractual rules.

Like most political thinkers of his day, Paine often refers to society as a contract, though he is always sure to insist that he means a contract not between the people and the sovereign power, but rather among the people themselves. "It has been thought a considerable advance towards establishing the principles of Freedom to say that Government is a compact between those who govern and those who are governed," Paine notes in *Rights of Man*, "but this cannot be true, because it is putting the effect before the cause; for as man must have existed before governments existed, there necessarily was a time when governments did not exist, and consequently there could originally exist no governors to form such a compact with."[4] Reaching back as always to beginnings for his reasoning, Paine thus describes the social contract in starkly individualist terms: "The fact therefore must be that the individuals themselves, each in his own personal and sovereign right, entered into a compact with each other to produce a government: and this is the only mode in which governments have a right to arise, and the only principle on which they have a right to exist."[5]

Only the founding generation of any regime can truly exercise consent in this explicit sense, but Paine argues that implicit consent, as expressed in the decisions of subsequent generations to refrain from overturning the laws, is the only source of legitimacy any regime ever possesses.[6] Every legitimate political society, therefore, is a contract among its living members, and not an agreement between them and their government or an agreement among their forefathers that somehow binds them.

As a contract, society not only provides benefits to its members but also requires of them certain obligations in return. Yet even these obligations come down to making room for choice. Paine puts it succinctly: "The right which I enjoy becomes my duty to guarantee it to another, and he to me, and those who violate the duty justly incur a forfeiture of the right."[7] Our social duties, therefore, amount to respecting the rights of others as they respect our own, so that the obligations that define society are obligations to the freedom of choice of its individual members. They are chosen obligations intended to protect choice.

And how is this society to be led? Paine's answer—that popular sovereignty and the election of leaders are essential features of any legitimate regime—flows directly from his belief in individual choice. Hereditary government violates the rights of the governed, even if at its origin, generations ago, such a government was installed by the choice of the public. People can choose to be governed by a king with broad powers, but they cannot choose to empower that king's children and grandchildren permanently over their own. "If the present generation, or any other, are disposed to be slaves, it does not lessen the right of the succeeding generation to be free," Paine argues.[8]

Paine spends a great deal of time in *Rights of Man* arguing this point, and he does so in direct response to Edmund Burke's writings on the French Revolution. Burke argued not only that the French had removed their government in an illegitimate way but also that the very notion that people always have a right to remove their government and select their own rulers was in error. The idea that choice sits at the center of all political thought struck him as a mistake. It is upon this matter of the rights of the people to choose their own regime and their own rulers, more than upon any other subject, that Paine addresses himself squarely to Burke, and upon this matter, too, that Burke most expressly offers an answer to Paine in his own subsequent writings. Their very different views about the nature of social obligation and individual rights come to a head on the question of consent—of just how central choice really is in political life.

AN ETHIC OF OBLIGATION

Burke's views on consent were bound to be provocative for Paine. Any modern friend of democracy reading the *Reflections on the Revolution in France* must be struck by the vehemence with which Burke rejects the general proposition that the people have a fundamental right to choose their own rulers. The *Reflections* is known as an anti-revolutionary work, an attack on the extremism Burke believed was on display in France, and a defense of established practices and forms. But the work in fact begins with a concerted assault against claims made by the prominent dissenting Protestant minister Richard Price regarding the English Revolution of 1688. Price had insisted that the Glorious Revolution had established the English regime upon three fundamental rights: "to choose our own governors, to cashier them for misconduct, [and] to frame a government for ourselves."[9] What was happening in France, Price contended, was an effort to catch up with these English liberties. Burke devotes the opening portion of his essay to a savage attack against these claims: "This new and hitherto unheard-of bill of rights, though made in the name of the whole people, belongs to those gentlemen and their faction only. The body of the people of England have no share in it. They utterly disclaim it. They will resist the practical assertion of it with their lives and fortunes."[10] Burke thus fears not just the specter of the frenzied Paris mob but also the theory of rule by consent at the heart of Enlightenment liberalism.

This stark denial of the people's right to choose their leaders appears at first to be primarily a defense of the English constitution, since if Price's (and Paine's) principles are valid, then most of English history has consisted of illegitimate rule. "Do they mean to invalidate, annul, or to call into question, together with the titles of the whole line of our kings, that great body of our statute law which passed under those whom they now treat as usurpers?" Burke asks.[11] In 1784, in a speech on parliamentary reform, Burke had argued that the principles of the radical reformers simply could not coexist with the British system of government: "It is ridiculous to talk to them of the British Constitution upon any or all of its bases; for they lay it down that every man ought to govern himself, and that where he cannot go himself he must send his representative; that all other government is usurpation. . . . If this claim be founded, it is clear to what it goes."[12] It goes, Burke worried, to a complete rejection of the English constitution, and it opens the door to sedition and revolution.

English champions of republican principles, like Richard Price, answered this charge of sedition by pointing precisely to the revolution of 1688, which, they argued, established the monarchy by the choice of the people. Though most monarchs around the world were indeed illegitimate, as they governed without the consent of their people, the English monarchy had been reestablished as an act of choice by the 1688 Parliament and so governed in accordance with the principle that the people could establish and remove their rulers at will. Burke adamantly rejects this defense: The Glorious Revolution, he argues, was a moment of extreme crisis, but the Englishmen who saw their country through it (the "old Whigs" to whom Burke appeals) chose precisely to avoid turning that crisis into an opportunity to establish an English republic, by finding a monarch descended from their ancient line and continuing their regime on its established foundations. "The Revolution was made to preserve our *ancient* indisputable laws and liberties, and that *ancient* constitution of government which is our only security for law and liberty," Burke argues. "The very idea of the fabrication of a new government is enough to fill us with disgust and horror. We wished at the period of the Revolution, and do now wish, to derive all we possess as *an inheritance from our forefathers*."[13]

This inheritance surely does contain an element of choice and popular sovereignty, along with other elements. Even in his day, Burke's treasured House of Commons was, after all, a relatively democratic element in a mixed regime, and Burke does not object to popular elections and democratic politics. He has often been accused, by critics from

Paine himself to scholars in the twenty-first century, of being just that: an antidemocratic defender of old privileges. But this charge requires a rather crude reading of his views on consent, elections, and representation. He frequently defends representative institutions, which he argues are necessary counterweights to the excesses of the monarch and the aristocracy. But representative institutions are not the purpose of the regime, only one of its parts. A good government should take its cue from the proclivities of its people. "In effect, to follow, not to force the public inclination; to give a direction, a form, a technical dress, and a specific sanction, to the general sense of the community, is the true end of legislature," he writes, and this requires both a means of letting the people have a voice and a means of subjecting the public will to prudent leadership and wise restraint.[14] The problem comes, Burke argues, in thinking of consent as the essential defining principle of a regime. "I reprobate no form of government merely upon abstract principles," Burke writes, and democracy certainly can be part of a legitimate government. But pure democracy, a regime formed to serve choice above all, seems to him a recipe for disaster, in theory and in practice, as it carries no clear principle of restraint.[15]

A long philosophical tradition, from Plato to Montesquieu and right to Burke's own day, had noted the dangerous excesses of absolute democracy, and in pointing to these dangers, Burke makes an unusually explicit appeal to philosophy: "Not being wholly unread in the authors who had seen the most of [democratic] constitutions, and who best understood them, I cannot help concurring with their opinion, that an absolute democracy, no more than absolute monarchy, is to be reckoned among the legitimate forms of government. . . . If I recollect rightly, Aristotle observes that a democracy has many striking points of resemblance with a tyranny."[16] This notion of tyranny, a tyranny of the unchecked majority over the minority, much alive in Burke's mind at the time of the French Revolution, would underlie his critique of unchecked democracy. As he put it in the *Reflections:*

Of this I am certain, that in a democracy, the majority of the citizens is capable of exercising the most cruel oppressions upon the minority, whenever strong divisions prevail in that kind of polity, as they often must; and that oppression of the minority will extend to far greater numbers, and will be carried on with much greater fury, than can almost ever be apprehended from the dominion of a single scepter. In such a popular persecution, individual sufferers are in a much more deplorable condition than in any other.

Under a cruel king, Burke argues, members of an oppressed minority "have the balmy compassion of mankind to assuage the smart of their wounds." But under a tyrannical democracy, the public as a whole is against them. "They seem deserted by mankind, overpowered by a conspiracy of their whole species."[17] Their oppression seems somehow legitimated.

On top of this tyranny of the majority, and perhaps an even greater threat to legitimate government, is the danger of arbitrary rule in a democracy—of the government never having to answer for its actions, because they are carried out in the name of the people. In his *Appeal from the New Whigs to the Old*, Burke quotes at length Paine's case that election is the only legitimate source of authority, and then paraphrases the attitude he sees in it: "Discuss any of their schemes—their answer is—It is the act of the *people*, and that is sufficient. Are we to deny to a *majority* of the people the right of altering even the whole frame of their society, if such should be their pleasure? They may change it, say they, from a monarchy to a republic to-day, and to-morrow back again from a republic to a monarchy; and so backward and forward as often as they like."[18]

If there is no source of authority but this moment's popular will, then no arrangements or institutions of society can be expected to remain in place one moment longer than the majority wishes them there. This, Burke argues, is not only impractical (as it would lead to a debilitating uncertainty and make it impossible for any citizen to plan his future), but also an error in principle. "Neither the few nor the many have a right to act merely by their will, in any matter connected with duty, trust, engagement, or obligation." It makes no difference if a majority chooses it or not, "as no one of us men can dispense with public or private faith, or with any other tie of moral obligation, so neither can any number of us."[19] There are crucial instances when choice is simply not an option.

And here we come to the heart of Burke's trouble with consent. While the threats to the English constitution and the risk of majority tyranny worry him, the more profound and fundamental problem, Burke argues, is that the focus on choice amounts to a fundamental misunderstanding of the human condition. A politics of choice begins in error.

As Burke sees it, each man is in society not by choice but by birth. And the facts of his birth—the family, the station, and the nation he is born into—exert inescapable demands on him, while also granting him some privileges and protections that the newborn has, of course, done nothing to earn. Men can change their circumstances and can garner or lose privileges and obligations in the course of their lives, but even when they do so, they take on in their new stations new obligations that are not simply chosen and cannot simply be discarded at will: "The place of every man determines his duty."[20] The most essential human obligations and relations—especially those involving the family but also many of those involving community, the nation, and one's religious faith—are not chosen and could never really be chosen, and political and social life begins from these, not from an act of will. "We have obligations to mankind at large, which are not in consequence of any special voluntary pact," Burke writes. "They arise from the relation of man to man, and the relation of man to God, which relations are not matters of choice. On the contrary, the force of all the pacts which we enter into with any particular person or number of persons amongst mankind, depends upon those prior obligations. In some cases the subordinate relations are voluntary, in others they are necessary—but the duties are all compulsive."[21] Only by beginning one's theory of politics from a highly implausible thought experiment about perfectly independent people founding a society by choice can one imagine a society in which choice is utterly central. When one looks at how human beings actually live, it is impossible to ignore the centrality and the value of compulsory obligations.

Perhaps the most perfectly inescapable fact about how we live is that all human beings enter a world that already exists—a world in which they belong to a particular family and community that are responsible for them and toward which they in turn have obligations. Paine's error, Burke suggests, begins with a flawed notion of original freedom and independence. In the *Appeal from the New to the Old Whigs*, in direct response to Paine, Burke reveals the heart of his own anthropology with an extraordinary depiction of human relations. It is quite possibly the most important paragraph in Burke's decades of writing, and so is worth quoting at length:

> Dark and inscrutable are the ways by which we come into the world. The instincts which give rise to this mysterious process of nature are not of our making. But out of physical causes, unknown to us, perhaps unknowable, arise moral duties, which, as we are able perfectly to comprehend, we are bound indispensably to perform. Parents may not be consenting to their moral relation; but consenting or not, they are bound to a long train of burthensome duties towards those with whom they have never made a convention of any sort. Children are not consenting to their relation, but their relation, without their actual consent, binds them to its duties; or rather it implies their consent because the presumed consent of every rational creature is in unison with the predisposed order of things. Men come in that manner into a community with the social state of their parents, endowed with all the benefits, loaded with all the duties of their situation. If the social ties and ligaments, spun out of those physical relations which are the elements of the commonwealth, in most cases begin, and always continue, independently of our will, so without any stipulation, on our part, are we bound by that relation called our country, which comprehends (as it has been well said) "all the charities of all." Nor are we left without powerful instincts to make this duty as dear and grateful to us, as it is awful and coercive.[22]

Just as Paine's understanding of rights and choice sits at the heart of his political thought, so this vision of obligations not chosen but nevertheless binding forms the very core of Edmund Burke's moral and political philosophy. An enormous portion of Burke's (and the conservative) worldview becomes clearer in light of the importance he places on the basic facts and character of human procreation, and an enormous portion of Paine's (and the progressive) worldview becomes clearer in light of the desire he evinces to be liberated from the implications of those facts and that character. Almost all of what we loosely call the "the social issues" have to do with the dispute about whether such liberation is possible and desirable and, because it raises the question of the relation between generations (as we will see in Chapter 7), that dispute also shapes a surprising portion of our other prominent debates. Burke takes the human person to be embedded in a web of obligations that give shape to our lives.

The role of consent in this view of society is secondary at best. Social relations flow out of natural relations, and consent is assumed where it cannot be expressed, not because the individual chooses to accept his obligations, but because the consent of every rational creature is assumed to be in line with "the predisposed order of things." This vision of society begins with the family—not the individual—and moves up toward society.

Burke believes that the French revolutionaries deliberately and explicitly wanted to weaken these bonds of obligation—to weaken the family, to begin with, and so to weaken the deepest source of resistance to the revolutionary ethic. In his *Letter to a Member of the National Assembly*, written in 1791, Burke argues that the revolutionaries, following Rousseau, seek to reject the duties of the family "as not founded in the social compact, and not binding according to the rights of men; because the relation is not, of course, the result of free election—never on the side of the children, not always on the part of the parents."[23] The family is the primary obstacle to an ethic of choice and so a primary target of genuinely radical liberal revolutionaries.

If Paine saw government's primary obligation as the protection of individual choice and the enabling of popular will, the obligations that emerge from Burke's natural relations are those of the care and protection of the web of social relations and of society's patrimony. Occasionally, choice will be the best means of meeting these obligations, as when the elected House of Commons restrains the king's excessive intrusion into local affairs, but choice is, for Burke, never the essence of the obligation itself or the end being served. The ends are defined by the social relations and duties created by the nature and the shape of the social order and can be better understood and better served by a political system grounded in prescription—one modeled on the nature of society itself and so best suited for continual and gradual improvement. Prescription, Burke argues, is a type of cross-genera-tional choice preferable to individual choice. It is what allows him, he believes, to deny the principle of consent without abiding despotism:

> This is a choice not of one day, or one set of people, not a tumultuary and giddy choice; it is a deliberate election of ages and of generations; it is a constitution made by what is ten thousand times better than choice, it is made by the peculiar circumstances, occasions, tempers, dispositions, and moral, civil, and social habitudes of the people, which disclose themselves only in a long space of time. It is a vestment which accommodates itself to the body. Nor is prescription of government formed upon blind, unmeaning prejudices—for man is a most unwise and a most wise being. The individual is foolish; the multitude, for the moment, is foolish, when they act without deliberation; but the species is wise, and when time is given to it, as a species it always acts right.[24]

While Burke acknowledges that a particular civil order may begin historically in a voluntary act and that some constitutions may be ex-plicit compacts between rulers and ruled, he believes that such origins are not nearly as important as the Enlightenment liberals assumed. Society does not depend for its legitimacy on such a source, and polit-ical life cannot make everything a matter of choice, because the most important facts about human societies are not the result of anyone's choice and cannot be changed by anyone's choice.

A great many of the deepest differences between Burke and Paine become apparent in the light of this very different idea of how social relations work. Burke's view begins from the "dark and inscrutable" biological origins of every new generation and so assumes a limit to our ability to explicitly understand and articulate the character of political life. Because politics does not begin in choice, it is not entirely ours to make. We have to build our politics around our society rather than building society on the principles of our theory of politics. As the great Burke biographer John Morley put it, "To Burke there was an element of mystery in the cohesion of men in societies, in political obedience, in the sanctity of contract; in all that fabric of law and charter and obligation, whether written or unwritten, which is the sheltering bulwark between civilization and barbarism. When reason and history had contributed all they could to the explanation, it seemed to him as if the vital force, the secret of organization, the binding framework, must still come from the impenetrable regions beyond reasoning and beyond history."[25]

In other words, Burke's description of society can never make for the kind of hard and total explanation that Paine and other radicals believed could be had through their theories of rights and liberties. No calculation of individual rights, interests, obligations, choices, and actions adds up to a sum of the whole in Burke's politics, but only a kind of picture of relations. His social relations flow and roll out of personal ones and are sustained by sentimental attachments and habits of affection. "We begin our public affections in our families," Burke writes. "We pass on to our neighbourhoods, and our habitual provincial connections. These are inns and resting-places. Such divisions of our country as have been formed by habit, and not by a sudden jerk of authority, were so many little images of the great country in which the heart found something which it could fill."[26]

From Burke's *Reflections*, Paine well understood that this notion of society as an array of layered obligations marked a critical difference between his view and Burke's. To Paine's mind, social relations were best understood by studying individuals (as society was the sum of its parts), and the layers of social relations that Burke put between individual men and mankind's original rights were needless distractions or intentional obstructions used to justify oppressive traditions. In the *Rights of Man*, Paine puts it this way:

It is not among the least of the evils of the present existing governments in all parts of Europe that man, considered as man, is thrown
back to a vast distance from his Maker, and the artificial chasm filled
up with a succession of barriers, or sort of turnpike gates, through
which he has to pass. I will quote Mr. Burke's catalogue of barriers
that he has set up between man and his Maker. Putting himself in
the character of a herald, he says, "We fear God; we look with awe
to kings; with affection to Parliaments with duty to magistrates; with
reverence to priests; and with respect to nobility." Mr. Burke has forgotten to put in "chivalry." He has also forgotten to put in Peter. The
duty of man is not a wilderness of turnpike gates, through which he
is to pass by tickets from one to the other. It is plain and simple, and
consists but of two points: His duty to God, which every man must
feel; and with respect to his neighbor, to do as he would be done by. [27]

But to Burke's mind, these barriers and "turnpike gates"—the layers of relations and institutions between the individual and the state—
are the social order. There is thus more to society than the "regime" or
the formal institutions of government, and a political and social order
cannot be undone and redone at will without badly damaging society.

For Burke, therefore, the "social contract" is not an *agreement* made
among the people—an agreement that prescribes the shape of their political arrangements—but rather a *description* of binding relations. In
his writings of the 1790s, Burke was increasingly clear on this point.
Spurred especially by Paine's critique and others, he came to see that
this dispute about the meaning of consent, contract, and social relations
was among the deepest points of separation between him and his adversaries on the question of France. "I cannot too often recommend it to
the serious consideration of all men who think civil society to be within
the province of moral jurisdiction," he wrote in 1791,

that if we owe to it any duty, it is not subject to our will. Duties are not
voluntary. Duty and will are even contradictory terms. Now though
civil society might be at first a voluntary act (which in many cases
it undoubtedly was) its continuance is under a permanent standing

covenant, coexisting with the society; and it attaches upon every individual of that society, without any formal act of his own. . . . Men without their choice derive benefits from that association; without their choice they are subjected to duties in consequence of these benefits; and without their choice they enter into a virtual obligation as binding as any that is actual. Look through the whole of life and the whole system of duties. Much the strongest moral obligations are such as were never the results of our option.[28]

Burke thus seeks to redefine the concept of the social contract to suit it to his own picture of politics.

His contract is not a set of quid pro quos, with rights exchanged for obligations by free people making choices about what is best for them, but a description of relations that are inescapable and binding. Society is not an agreement, but an arrangement (a "great arrangement of mankind," as he puts it), and the contract lays it out for us to see, not to choose.[29] Burke's notion of the social contract is thus distinct from Paine's and from the common Enlightenment-liberal social-contract teaching. He puts it most clearly in a justifiably famous passage in the *Reflections*:

Society is indeed a contract. Subordinate contracts, for objects of mere occasional interest, may be dissolved at pleasure; but the state ought not to be considered as nothing better than a partnership agreement in a trade of pepper and coffee . . . or some other such low concern, . . . to be dissolved by the fancy of the parties. It is to be looked on with other reverence. . . . It is a partnership in all science; a partnership in all art; a partnership in every virtue, and in all perfection. As the ends of such a partnership cannot be obtained in many generations, it becomes a partnership not only between those who are living, but between those who are living, those who are dead, and those who are to be born. . . . The municipal corporations of that universal kingdom are not morally at liberty . . . to dissolve it into an unsocial, uncivil, unconnected chaos of elementary principles. It is the first and supreme necessity only, a necessity that is not chosen but chooses, a necessity paramount to deliberation, that admits no discussion, and demands no evidence, which alone can justify a resort to anarchy.[30]

Burke thus employs the concept of the social contract to a purpose almost the opposite of Paine's. And Burke's discussions of contract almost never touch on the subject generally of greatest interest to Enlightenment-liberal contract theorists (and, for that matter, to political philosophers in general): the structure of the regime and its institutions. He lays out the proper functions of government in terms of the services it ought to render to society, but he contends that "the circumstances and habits of every country . . . decide upon the form of its government," and this form can gradually change with time as circumstances require.[31]

Nor does Burke think that describing the nature of society means describing the history of society—as the usual modern (perhaps scientific) approach to political life would seek to do. He is instead seeking something more like the essential character of social life and so looks at society as he believes it is, rather than trying to understand the chronology of its development. And because Burke's contract is a description, the contract does not establish the grounds on which society may be dissolved or may continue, but rather presents the relation between its parts. Burke argues that the Enlightenment-liberal social-contract theorists apply their contract only to extreme situations, grounding it in the moment of founding and drawing from it rules for when revolution may be appropriate. "But the very habit of stating these extreme cases is not very laudable or safe," he writes, "because in general it is not right to turn our duties into doubts. They are imposed to govern our conduct, not to exercise our ingenuity; and therefore, our opinions about them ought not to be in a state of fluctuation, but steady, sure, and resolved."[32] Burke's contract describes the everyday life of his society.

To deny the centrality of consent is surely to deny as well the importance of rights, as Enlightenment-liberal theory understands them.

And Thomas Paine argues fervently that Burke's unusual twist on the social contract leaves him incapable of any case for rights. "Does Mr. Burke mean to deny that man has any rights?" he asks in *Rights of Man*. "If he does, then he must mean that there are no such things as rights anywhere, and that he has none himself; for who is there in the world but man? But if Mr. Burke means to admit that man has rights, the question then will be: What are those rights, and how man came by them originally?"[33]

But Burke refuses to allow his opponents to own the idea of rights. As he does with the concept of the social contract (and as we will see him do as well with the idea of liberty), he invokes the vocabulary of the Enlightenment radicals, but with different meanings in mind: "In denying their false claims of right, I do not mean to injure those which are real, and are such as their pretended rights would totally destroy."[34] And just what are these real claims of right? Burke offers his fullest answer in the *Reflections*:

> If civil society be made for the advantage of man, all the advantages for which it is made become his right. It is an institution of benefi-cence; and law itself is only beneficence acting by a rule. Men have a right to live by that rule; they have a right to justice; as between their fellows, whether their fellows are in politic function or in or-dinary occupation. They have a right to the fruits of their industry; and to the means of making their industry fruitful. They have a right to the acquisitions of their parents; to the nourishment and improvement of their offspring; to instruction in life, and to con-solation in death. Whatever each man can separately do, without trespassing upon others, he has a right to do for himself; and he has a right to a fair portion of all which society, with all its combinations of skill and force, can do in his favor.[35]

Burke essentially denies the relevance (though not necessarily the existence) of abstract, individual, natural rights. He defines instead some practical rights to the benefits of society. And these benefits do not amount to freedom or power. In fact, some of the benefits of society to which men have a right involve restraints on their freedoms and their passions. Burke writes:

> Government is not made in virtue of natural rights, which may and do exist in total independence of it; and exist in much greater clearness, and in a much greater degree of abstract perfection: but their abstract perfection is their practical defect. By having a right to every thing they want every thing. Government is a contrivance of human wisdom to provide for human *wants*. Men have a right that these wants should be provided for by this wisdom. Among these wants is to be reckoned the want, out of civil society, of a sufficient restraint upon their passions.

Society's ability to limit the range of our choices is thus an important advantage:

> Society requires not only that the passions of individuals should be subjected, but that even in the mass and body as well as in the individuals, the inclinations of men should frequently be thwarted, their will controlled, and their passions brought into subjection. This can only be done *by a power out of themselves*; and not, in the exercise of its function, subject to that will and to those passions which it is its office to bridle and subdue. In this sense the restraints on men, as well as their liberties, are to be reckoned among their rights. But as the liberties and the restrictions vary with times and circumstances, and admit of infinite modifications, they cannot be settled upon any abstract rule; and nothing is so foolish as to discuss them upon that principle.[36]

Human beings cannot live in society if they follow their wants and passions unrestrained, and so one of the rights of citizens is to have their passions brought under some control. Thus society guarantees some liberties and some restraints, and precisely how these are balanced is in normal times a matter of prudence, not absolute principle.

The calculus of prudence aims not to maximize choice, but to meet the true wants of the people, as these emerge from the complex and layered society that Burke describes. His rights are therefore relations, not individual entitlements—they describe a person's place in the large scheme of obligations and privileges and offer the protection and benefits of that scheme and that place.

Since choice is not central to Burke's understanding of rights, he rather readily dismisses the right to self-government—that "share of power, authority, and direction which each individual ought to have in the management of the state."[37] The state, as Burke sees it, owes certain advantages to its people, and whatever means can best achieve these while retaining the loyalty of the people ought to be pursued. The key is not that each man should have his views expressed through the actions of the state, but that each man should have his needs served by the actions of the state. The people's desires and their interests can conflict, Burke says, and the able statesman must seek to serve their true interests. The nation, therefore, ought to be understood as guided by a purpose, and not by a duty to its origins or to man's natural rights. The state proves itself by achieving its purpose, which is the benefit of its citizens.

Even in the democratic element of the British regime, Burke believes, the role of each member of Parliament was not to stand in for his constituents but to apply his wisdom to advance their interests and needs and those of the entire nation. In 1774, just after winning election to the House of Commons from Bristol—England's second largest city at the time—Burke told his new constituents that he would not see his role as merely the representative of their views: "Your representative owes you, not his industry only, but his judgment; and he betrays, instead of serving you, if he sacrifices it to your opinion."[38] Even the Commons, in other words, is not a fully representative institution, and Burke acknowledges no inherent right to take part in self-government. Government is not the counting of heads, but an application of prudence to circumstances, and in Burke's view, there is no reason to imagine that every man is entitled to a part in it—direct or indirect. Under some circumstances, democratic institutions may best serve the interests of the whole, and in these situations, they ought to be employed, but not as a matter of absolute right.

This denial of the right to self-government, the most stark expression of Burke's denial of the centrality of choice in political life, was sure to set off Paine, for whom the right to rule is the essential civil right from which all others flow. Paine has no patience for Burke's complex meanderings around the basic question of self-government. He sees in Burke's reconception of rights an empty mysticism aimed at defending illegitimate rule:

> He puts the nation as fools on one side, and places his government of wisdom, all wise men of Gotham, on the other side, and he then proclaims, and says that "Men have a RIGHT that their WANTS should be provided for by this wisdom." Having thus made proclamation, he next proceeds to explain to them what their wants are, and also what their rights are. . . . [I]n order to impress them with a solemn reverence for this monopoly-government of wisdom, and of its vast capacity for all purposes, possible or impossible, right or wrong, he proceeds with astrological mysterious importance, to tell to them its powers.

This, Paine suggests, is just a way to keep Burke's readers from seeing through Burke's denial of the basic principles of liberty: "As the wondering audience, whom Mr. Burke supposes himself talking to, may not understand all this learned jargon, I will undertake to be its interpreter. The meaning, then, good people, of all this, is: That government is governed by no principle whatever; that it can make evil good, or good evil, just as it pleases. In short, that government is arbitrary power."[39]

Burke's notion of government, Paine worries, provides no protections of liberty, because it does not define in advance the precise rights of man that no government may intrude upon and because it does not lay out the limits of government. It substitutes vague and varying notions of advantages and relations for a clear idea of the protection of every individual's freedom to choose.

Without question, Burke's reimagining of the social contract deprives him of one great advantage of the Enlightenment-liberal contract theorists: a clear principle by which to limit the scope of government action to oppose coercion. Government, in Burke's view, is limited by the complex obligations, relations, and distinctions that compose every society. Paine seeks to flatten these distinctions but impose in their place explicit limits on the state in defense of individual liberty. Paine thinks the principles of liberty will better protect individual freedom than the institutions of society. Where Paine imposes on government the obligation to respect the freedom of action of each of its citizens, Burke imposes on government a much less exacting (if somewhat more demanding) obligation to meet the wants of the people and advance the interests of the complex social whole. Order and interest, more than individual liberty and choice, is the end of Burke's notion of government. And he thinks the nation's social topography will be a better guardian of the people's liberty in practice than a set of abstract rules, however exacting they might be.

But here again, Burke attempts to employ the rhetoric and vocabulary of the more radical liberals to his own rather different purposes. He will not let the Enlightenment liberals own the term *liberty*, either. "The effects of the incapacity shown by the popular leaders in all the great members of the commonwealth are to be covered with the 'all-atoning name' of liberty," he writes of events in France. "But what is liberty without wisdom, and without virtue? It is the greatest of all possible evils; for it is folly, vice, and madness, without tuition or restraint. Those who know what virtuous liberty is, cannot bear to see it disgraced by incapable heads, on account of their having high-sounding words in their mouths." [40]

And just what is this "virtuous liberty"? How does it differ from the notion that Paine or the French revolutionaries have in mind? Burke offers an answer in a 1789 letter to a young Frenchman named Charles-Jean-François Depont, who had suggested to him that the revolution then unfolding in Paris was a great example of liberty in action. The French surely deserved liberty, Burke responded, but they had mistaken the meaning of the term. True liberty "is not solitary,

unconnected, individual, selfish liberty, as if every man was to regulate the whole of his conduct by his own will. The liberty I mean
is social freedom. It is that state of things in which liberty is assured
by the equality of restraint. . . . This kind of liberty is indeed but
another name for justice; ascertained by wise laws, and secured by
well-constructed institutions."[41]

This is perhaps the boldest and most forthright of Burke's redef-
initions of liberal terminology. He suggests that radical individualism is the opposite of justice and, in that sense, also the opposite of
genuine liberty. He offers "social freedom" as a kind of counterpart
to "individual liberty," a term much favored by Paine and by many
Enlightenment liberals of the day, and suggests such freedom is the
deepest source of Britain's strength.[42]

This interplay of liberty and restraint is key to Burke's understanding of both government and the challenges of statesmanship.
"Men are qualified for civil liberty in exact proportion to their disposition to put moral chains upon their own appetites," he writes. "Society cannot exist, unless a controlling power upon will and appetite
be placed somewhere; and the less of it there is within, the more there
must be without. It is ordained in the eternal constitution of things,
that men of intemperate minds cannot be free. Their passions forge
their fetters."[43]

Thus an intemperate people, including a people pushed toward
intemperance by a radical political philosophy, will be less capable
of liberty and thus more likely to find themselves oppressed by their
regime, regardless of how noble the philosophy expounded in their
declarations of rights might be.

Finding the balance between freedom and restraint is an immensely difficult challenge, which the revolutionaries, certain of their
ability to establish a regime from scratch, are too likely to ignore.
"To make a government requires no great prudence," Burke writes
in the *Reflections*. "Settle the seat of power; teach obedience; and the
work is done. To give freedom is still more easy. It is not necessary
to guide; it only requires to let go of the rein. But to form a free
government: that is, to temper together these opposite elements of

liberty and restraint in one consistent work, requires much thought, deep reflection, a sagacious, powerful, and combining mind."[44] Liberty and restraint cannot be balanced by a stark application of Enlightenment-liberal syllogisms drawing on the natural rights of every individual, because the balance must always occur in the complicated context of social life and therefore must consider the numerous obligations, privileges, and habits that shape a society. Liberty in practice is a compromise between restraint and freedom. In a letter to some prominent constituents in Bristol, Burke lays out his case against the Enlightenment-liberal notion of freedom:

> Far from any resemblance to those propositions in geometry and metaphysics, which admit no medium, but must be true or false in all their latitude; social and civil freedom, like all other things in common life, are variously mixed and modified, enjoyed in very different degrees, and shaped into an infinite diversity of forms, according to the temper and circumstances of every community. The EXTREME of liberty (which is its abstract perfection, but its real fault) obtains nowhere, nor ought to obtain anywhere. Because extremes, as we all know, in every point which relates either to our duties or satisfactions in life, are destructive both to virtue and enjoyment.[45]

The only genuine liberty, Burke argued in 1774, "is a liberty connected with order: that not only exists along with order and virtue but which cannot exist at all without them. It inheres in good and steady government, as in its substance and vital principle."[46] This ordered liberty, Burke argues, is the essence of what a good government owes its people. It is what the social contract protects, what the rights of men properly understood involve, and what freedom really means. It is secured by prudent statesmen, alert to the non-voluntary social relations that shape society, and to the unique history, habits, and mores their people have developed to meet their obligations and pursue gradual and incremental political and social progress.

Burke and Paine therefore approach the question of social relations—of choice and obligation as ends of society—in profoundly different ways, moved by their different premises about the character of human life and especially by their deep divergence on the question of context: the importance of the given world to shaping our options and defining our duties. Their general views on this question shape many of their particular opinions and instincts on the immense array of issues both men take up in their writings. But these opinions take shape in complicated and often surprising ways.

To see these complications in more detail, we can examine the two men's views on two sets of issues in particular: patriotism (or duty to country) and social-welfare policy (or obligation to one's fellow citizens).

THE NATION AND THE POOR

Thomas Paine seeks to put universal principles into practice. In basing man's rights and liberties on nature, not on history, he understands them as equally true and applicable everywhere and therefore not rooted in any particular nation's circumstances or ideals. His writings are therefore remarkably devoid of appeals to patriotism and duty to homeland. Even in his Revolutionary War writings in America, including the *Crisis* papers, which were intended to strengthen the resolve of the populace, Paine almost always appeals to the universal cause of freedom and not to the particular love of America.

As R. R. Fennessy has put it, "Paine's only loyalty was, in fact, to his own principles. When America adopted them, he was to be an American citizen. . . . When, later, he thought that France was about to follow America's example, he was happy to accept French citizenship—and he was just as happy to relinquish it when he found that the French, after all, did not understand political principles."[47] Paine often described himself in the same terms. "My country is the world, and my religion is to do good," he wrote on several occasions.[48]

In his writings, Paine clearly asserts that his principles require him to put himself above mere national identity in this way. Contrasting the old and the new ways of thinking about government in *Rights of Man*, Paine notes that "the one encourages national prejudices; the other promotes universal society."[49] He sees social obligations as obligations to one's fellow man. They may flow through one's community or country, but they are not obligations *to* the community or country. Paine finds it difficult to justify a pure regard for one's own, and for him, love of country is not a substitute for clearheaded judgment of the legitimacy of the government.

Edmund Burke, of course, placed a far greater emphasis on the social and generational context of politics, arguing that the intermediaries between each man and mankind at large were crucial to political order and that the nation was especially crucial. The nation is the means by which order is made and kept, and by which order is made beautiful. A nation builds upon its past accomplishments through prescription by looking to its common history and finding in this history both sources of pride and principles for reform and improvement. Family affections become community affections and, finally, national ties. Every individual thus finds himself enmeshed in multiple communities—his geographic neighbors, his fellow workers or merchants or nobles—and all of these point up toward the nation, and only from the nation and through it toward mankind as a whole.[50]

This does not mean that we must simply accept everything about our country, right or wrong. But we must begin from a disposition of gratitude for what it provides us. And the statesman must sustain the attachments of the people to their country. "To make us love our country, our country ought to be lovely," Burke writes in the *Reflections*.[51] But whether it is lovely or in need of reform, our country is not simply one instance of universal principles in action. As Paine describes it, every country would be more or less the same if all were to abide by the principles of freedom and justice, but Burke thinks the historical experience of each nation defines its forward path. Each society has its own traditional institutions and trajectories and gives its people something unique of their own to love. "Our country is not a thing of mere physical locality," Burke writes. "It consists, in a great measure, in the ancient order into which we are born."[52]

But if their differences about the nature of public obligations led Burke and Paine to divergent views on patriotism, the very same differences ironically led them to quite similar views on economic relations and the then-emerging theories of capitalism. The right and left both began with high hopes for capitalism, but for very different reasons and with very different notions of what it would mean for society and its members—and especially what material obligations citizens had toward one another.

Paine several times makes it clear that he is a believer in commerce because he believes open trade and free economics will advance his radical causes by uprooting traditional social and political arrangements.[53] It would do this by focusing men on their material needs and showing them a rational means of meeting those needs. The system of the old European governments, Paine argues, was held in place by deceptions and distractions (including especially the nearly permanent specter of war) that could be, and were already beginning to be, dissipated by a rational economics. "The condition of the world being materially changed by the influence of science and commerce, it is put into a fitness not only to admit of, but to desire, an extension of civilization," Paine writes. "The principal and almost only remaining enemy it now has to encounter is prejudice."[54]

Burke's support for largely unimpeded trade and industry began from roughly the opposite corner. He argued that government manipulation of the economy could be profoundly disruptive to the social order because it involved gross manipulation of very complicated economic and social forces that are almost inevitably beyond the understanding of legislators. Even in its own material terms, he argues, the economy functions best when left to itself, referring in one essay to "the laws of commerce, which are the laws of nature, and consequently the laws of God."[55] A free economy, as Burke saw it, would help sustain the stability of society and therefore its wealth—some of which could (and should) then be used by the wealthy to help the poor.

The passion for wealth was by no means an unmitigated good, but trying to mitigate it through policy would be a mistake, Burke argued.

It would have to be counteracted by the culture, not by politics, which should just seek whatever good could be drawn from it. "The love of lucre, though sometimes carried to a ridiculous, sometimes to a vicious excess, is the grand cause of prosperity to all States. In this natural, this reasonable, this powerful, this prolific principle, it is for the satirist to expose the ridiculous; it is for the moralist to censure the vicious; it is for the sympathetic heart to reprobate the hard and cruel; it is for the Judge to animadvert on the fraud, the extortion, and the oppression: but it is for the Statesman to employ it as he finds it; with all its concomitant excellencies, with all its imperfections on its head."[56]

Legislators are always tempted to employ the weight of government to undo economic inequalities, but such attempts always produce more harm than good, in Burke's view. He recognizes that the modern economy does relegate some people to desperate poverty or to demeaning occupations, and he frets about "the innumerable servile, degrading, unseemly, unmanly, and often most unwholesome and pestiferous occupations, to which by the social economy so many wretches are inevitably doomed."[57] But the costs of remedying their situation, not only to society as a whole but even to the particular wretches involved, would be far worse than their current suffering, Burke argues, because these people are the most vulnerable to economic dislocations, which are made more likely by clumsy government manipulations of prices or wages.

In a short essay titled *Thoughts and Details on Scarcity* (much of it written in 1795, the last year of his life, to advise the prime minister against an attempt to manage the pay of farm laborers through legislation), Burke expresses a profound mistrust of government interference in the economy, especially on behalf of the poor: "My opinion is against an over-doing of any sort of administration, and more especially against this most momentous of all meddling on the part of authority; the meddling with the subsistence of the people."[58] The needs of the poor are of the utmost importance, he argues, but they should be addressed by charities, which should be amply supported by the wealthy and the noble. Government cannot take that care upon itself, as doing so would never work and, in the process, would disrupt the social order. Care of the poor is not in this sense a public obligation, but a private one.

Burke's ardent capitalism was noticed by no less an authority on the subject than his contemporary, Adam Smith, who wrote that "Mr. Burke is the only man I ever knew who thinks on economic subjects exactly as I do, without any previous communications having passed between us."[59] But ironically, Paine criticizes Burke's economic thinking precisely by citing Smith. "Had Mr. Burke possessed talents similar to the author of 'On the Wealth of Nations,' he would have comprehended all the parts which enter into, and, by assemblage, form a constitution," Paine writes in *Rights of Man*, when dismissing Burke's complaints about the revolutionaries' supposed mismanagement of the French economy.[60]

Paine was undoubtedly right about some of the social consequences of free-market economics, and Burke was surely mistaken to argue that free trade and capitalism would keep the elements of society in their place and aid stability. Few forces in the modern West have been as disruptive (for good and for bad) of established order. But the two men's deeper difference, it turns out, was not about the consequences of capitalism but about the community's obligation to the poor. While the often communitarian Burke argues that care for the needy ought to remain a private function in large part for the sake of the needy, the often libertarian Paine makes a forceful case for something like a modern welfare system. In so doing, Paine helps show how the modern left developed from Enlightenment liberalism toward embryonic forms of welfare-state liberalism as its utopian political hopes seemed dashed by the grim realities of the industrial revolution.

Paine's views in this regard offer a rare instance of his clearly changing his position in the course of his career. In his earlier writings, Paine describes a very limited scope for government: "Government is no farther necessary than to supply the few cases to which society and civilization are not conveniently competent, and instances

are not wanting to show, that every thing which government can use-
fully add thereto has been performed by the common consent of society, without government."[61] But by 1791, having witnessed in Paris
and London the early effects of the approaching industrial economy
and having thought through the implications of his views about the
origins of the social order, Paine was writing with eloquent passion
of "the moral obligation of providing for old age, helpless infancy,
and poverty."[62] Meeting this obligation, he argues in the second part
of *Rights of Man*, is a key purpose of government. "Civil government
does not exist in executions; but in making such provision for the
instruction of youth and the support of age, as to exclude, as much as
possible, profligacy from the one and despair from the other."[63] He
calls for provisions for poor parents when a child is born, for government support in paying for elementary education, for pensions to
the elderly who cannot work, and even for public help with funeral
expenses for those who cannot afford them.[64] "This support," he then
argues, "is not of the nature of a charity but of a right."[65] Public assis-
tance to the poor turns out to be a true social obligation.

In 1797, Paine devoted a short pamphlet titled *Agrarian Justice* to
laying out more fully his case for this proto–welfare state and for why
it should be viewed as a right of those in need. The case, it turns out,
draws on Paine's usual method of reasoning from human origins:

The earth, in its natural, cultivated state was, and ever would have
continued to be, *the common property of the human race*. In that state
every man would have been born to property. . . . But the earth in
its natural state, as before said, is capable of supporting but a small
number of inhabitants compared with what it is capable of doing in
a cultivated state. And as it is impossible to separate the improvement made by cultivation from the earth itself, upon which that
improvement is made, the idea of landed property arose from that
parable connection; but it is nevertheless true, that it is the value of
the improvement, only, and not the earth itself, that is individual
property. Every proprietor, therefore, of cultivated lands, owes to

the community *ground-rent* (for I know of no better term to express the idea) for the land which he holds; and it is from this ground-rent that the fund in this plan is to issue.[66]

Since the first human generation had a right to all the earth, and since subsequent ones have denied that right to most, it is only proper that compensation should be paid, drawn from a tax on property and made available to all. He is very clear on this last point: Not only the poor but all (including landowners themselves) would receive payment from this common fund. He writes, "It is proposed that the payments, as already stated, be made to every person, rich or poor. It is best to make it so, to prevent invidious distinctions. It is also right it should be so, because it is in lieu of the natural inheritance, which, as a right, belongs to every man, over and above property he may have created, or inherited from those who did. Such persons as do not choose to receive it can throw it into the common fund."[67]

Paine expressly disagrees with Burke's notion that charities can take care of the poor:

There are, in every country, some magnificent charities established by individuals. It is, however, but little that any individual can do, when the whole extent of the misery to be relieved is considered. He may satisfy his conscience, but not his heart. He may give all that he has, and that all will relieve but little. It is only by organizing civilization upon such principles as to act like a system of pulleys, that the whole weight of misery can be removed. . . . In all great cases it is necessary to have a principle more universally active than charity; and, with respect to justice, it ought not to be left to the choice of detached individuals whether they will do justice or not.[68]

Poverty, it seems, is taken by Paine to be one of those coercive realities that constrain the people's freedom, from which the state ought to protect the people, so as to allow their will and choice free rein. "The rugged face of society, checkered with the extremes of affluence and want, proves that some extraordinary violence has been committed upon it, and calls on justice for redress," Paine writes. "The great mass of the poor in countries are become an hereditary race, and it is next to impossible for them to get out of that state of themselves."[69] This persistent poverty creates a social obligation upon others—poverty is a threat to freedom that yields in a right to be liberated from poverty.

To Burke's mind, meanwhile, poverty is one of the realities that always exists and is part of the larger human condition, not a departure from it. Wealthy individuals have a moral and religious duty to help ameliorate poverty, but it could never be eradicated by the government. Poverty is surely a constraint on choice, but not a failure of government, since the protection of choice is not a fundamental purpose of government, in Burke's view.

Paine thus looks to politics to overcome impediments to our freedom to live as we choose, which leads him in time to look to the state to ameliorate severe material deprivation. He argues that such deprivation originates from the (sometimes necessary, sometimes avoidable) distortions of mankind's equal right to the fruits of the earth and is exacerbated over time by regimes that neglect or ignore the rights of their people. To correct for this error, he argues, government has a role in alleviating the misery of the most miserable and giving all something closer to an equal chance of rising by their own merits. In this way, again, Paine understands social obligations as arising primarily out of the importance of individual freedom and choice. Government exists to address violations of rights to freedom and choice, and it must occasionally do so by a modest redistribution of material resources to keep the poorest from falling beneath even the minimal standard of human dignity. Paine is thus an ardent capitalist but one alert to some of the effects of capitalism on the poor. Before the full emergence of the industrial revolution, Paine understood that economic progress would not eliminate poverty and, on the contrary, might create circumstances that could necessitate unprecedented public action.

Burke, meanwhile, believed our obligations are functions not of our right to choose but of our deeply embedded place in the social order.

Each of us lives in a particular relation to society, which carries with it both duties and privileges, and society will only function well if all its members meet their particular obligations. The care of the poor is surely among these obligations, but the duty falls to the rich, not to the state acting on behalf of all, because it is not something the state could do without causing even greater harm. Precisely because Burke draws a less stark distinction between society and government—treating both as described by the social contract, which is a partnership in all things—he also has a more limited notion of the role of the government. Paine makes a great deal of the difference between government and society, but in practice this difference often means that duties that are taken to be public obligations are all assigned to the government, while private life is kept conceptually separate from politics.

Burke's and Paine's understandings of social relations, therefore, differ dramatically, and along lines similar to (and rooted in) those of their disagreement over nature and history. Edmund Burke begins from the given world and seeks to strengthen social and political life as a means of contending with circumstances we did not choose. Thomas Paine begins from the principles of liberty, equality, and natural rights and builds political institutions on those grounds to defend the prerogatives of the individual. The two men differ sharply on just how much what has been done before matters and just how pliable human relations will be to philosophically inspired efforts at fundamental reconstruction.

In their differing views, we also find echoes of their more general approaches toward effecting political change. The thinker, who works primarily with ideas and principles, looks at circumstances not of people's choosing and considers them consequences of past applications of principle. Such a person sees in circumstances that are less than ideal the imprint of principles that are less than correct. He therefore seeks to improve on circumstances by offering a new beginning in principles that are more correct. The statesman, who works with political circumstances, begins necessarily from his (mostly given rather than chosen) affiliations with and obligations to his particular community and its various subdivisions and so starts from what exists and seeks within it ways to improve on it. In this way, the distinction between choice and obligation finds its match in the distinction between reason and prescription, as the former distinction applies to the ends of politics and the latter to its means. We therefore turn next to Burke's and Paine's profound disagreement on the relative merits of reason and prescription and, with them, of theory and practice.

FIVE

REASON AND PRESCRIPTION

I F NATURAL EQUALITY IS THE CRUCIAL PREMISE OF Enlightenment-liberal politics, and government by consent its essential form, then human reason is its great moving force. Reason cuts through the pious platitudes of the old order, demonstrates the truth and consequences of our rights, and helps us to shape a new order built to serve justice. The age of revolutions understood itself as advancing the cause of reason in political life.

In America, the revolutionary leaders assumed that "a decent respect to the opinions of mankind requires that they should declare the causes which impel" their actions for inspection under the searing light of reason. In France, the most ardent revolutionaries considered themselves a kind of "cult of reason," as the revolutionary leader Jacques Hebert put it. And for a great many Europeans who described their time as an age of enlightenment, it was human reason unleashed (especially by the new natural sciences and their methods) that shed new light on old quandaries.

Given how central the idea of a truly rational politics was to the self-understanding of the champions of Enlightenment liberalism, this ideal was, not surprisingly, a point of great contention between Burke and Paine. Paine understood his own time as "The Age of Reason" (as he dubbed it in the title of his last book). He thought that the combination of new insights into the science of politics and greater freedom for citizens to exercise their own individual reason upon public questions would free liberal societies of countless ancient prejudices and open the way to a new politics of liberty. Burke thought the governing of human communities was much too complex a task to be simplified into a series of pseudoscientific questions and resolved by logical exercises. It required, in his view, a degree of knowledge and wisdom about human affairs that could only be gathered from the experience of society itself. Their views, in other words, were direct extensions of the broader worldviews presented thus far and offer a deeper understanding of the foundational political questions of modern politics. Their dispute therefore deepens as it moves from the ends to the means of political thought.

BURKE'S PRESCRIPTION AND THE LIMITS OF REASON

Edmund Burke's belief in the complexity of human nature and the insufficiency of choice leads him to be far more skeptical than most of his peers about reason's potential for guiding political action. Burke routinely mocks the idea that the radicals' rationalism had unleashed a great enlightenment upon a hitherto dark world. Having read, as he puts it, "more than he can justify to any thing but the spirit of curiosity of the works of these illuminators of the world," Burke reports himself perplexed at their claims to a new path to wisdom. "Where the old authors whom he has read, and the old men whom he has conversed with, have left him in the dark, he is in the dark still."[1]

There is more to this than a sarcastic jab at self-appointed beacons of reason. Burke believes that Enlightenment liberals' and radicals' emphasis on human reason begins from a misunderstanding of human nature—the mistaking of a part for the whole: "Politics ought to be adjusted not to human reasonings but to human nature, of which the reason is but a part, and by no means the greatest part."[2] By ignoring the greater parts—especially the sentiments and attachments that move people in politics—one misses the most important factors behind political actions and social attachments. Many of the greatest challenges a statesman must confront arise from the less rational elements of the human character.

Governing is, of course, a rational activity, and political thought must certainly be guided by some general principles, but it's a mistake to assume that effective principles can be drawn from abstract premises rather than actual experience. The general must be derived from the particular, not the other way around. "It seems to me a preposterous way of reasoning, and a perfect confusion of ideas, to take the theories which learned and speculative men have made from [the practice of] government, and then, supposing it made on those theories which were made from it, to accuse government as not corresponding with them."[3]

This confusion of the relationship between theory and practice in politics can have dangerous consequences, Burke warns, because as political life becomes an enactment of a theory rather than a response to particular social needs and wants, it becomes unmoored both from the ends that should guide politics and from the limits that should restrain it. He believes that the importation of theory too directly into political life is among the foremost errors both of the British government in its dealings with America in the late 1770s and of the revolutionaries in France a decade later. Again and again he warns against mistaking politics for metaphysics, and he describes his concerns in terms of three distinct but closely related worries.

First, Burke believes that the attempt to apply what he calls metaphysical methods in politics confuses politicians and citizens about the purpose of politics—leading them to think that governing is about proving a point rather than advancing the interests and happiness of a nation. The trouble is not that principles do not belong in politics.

On the contrary, Burke writes, "I do not put abstract ideas wholly out of any question; because I well know that under that name I should dismiss principles, and that without the guide and light of sound well understood principles, all reasonings in politics, as in everything else, would be only a confused jumble of particular facts and details, without the means of drawing out any sort of theoretical or practical conclusion."[4] Rather, the problem is the insistence on abstract precision in political questions and thus on measuring practice by fine theoretical metrics. This insistence can confuse us about what the purpose of politics actually is. Government is "a practical thing, made for the happiness of mankind," Burke writes, not "to gratify the schemes of visionary politicians." It runs into trouble, therefore, when statesmen "split and anatomiz[e] the doctrine of free government, as if it were an abstract question concerning metaphysical liberty and necessity and not a matter of moral prudence and natural feeling."[5]

Burke's objection is in essence methodological. Politics cannot be understood by a method too exacting and abstract for the subject. Since "man acts from adequate motives relative to his interest, and not on metaphysical speculations," politics must be attuned to his motives and interests.[6] This does not mean that no distinctions can be made in politics, but it does mean that hairsplitting, speculative distinctions are often far too fine to be of service. "No lines can be laid down for civil or political wisdom. They are a matter incapable of exact definition. But, though no man can draw a stroke between the confines of day and night, yet light and darkness are upon the whole tolerably distinguishable."[7]

Practitioners of politics therefore should not expect precise knowledge and must accustom themselves to making prudential and uncertain judgments. "Every political question I have ever known has had so much of the pro and con in it that nothing but the success could decide which proposition was to have been adopted," Burke confesses to a friend.[8] In the moment, a politician cannot avail himself of scientific certitude, and in seeking it, he corrupts his practice, which must consist of informed approximations. "It is, I own, not uncommon to be wrong in theory and right in practice," Burke notes.[9]

And the success of policy must be measured in practice, not by its adherence to a speculative theory. "A statesman differs from a professor in [a] university," Burke remarked in a 1781 speech, "the latter has only the general view of society; the former, the statesman, has a number of circumstances to combine with these general ideas, and to take into his consideration."[10]

This difference points to Burke's second great concern about theory in politics, which is that theory often ignores circumstances and particulars crucial to the success of policy and the happiness of society. Theory is general and universal, but politics must always be very particular. "Circumstances (which with some gentlemen pass for nothing) give in reality to every political principle its distinguishing color and discriminating effect. The circumstances are what render every civil and political scheme beneficial or noxious to mankind."[11] In this respect politics is more, not less, precise than theory: It is concrete and particular. And Burke believes that concrete characteristics, needs, and interests are undermined when politics is turned into a kind of applied metaphysics. In a letter to constituents in Bristol, Burke assured his voters: "I never ventured to put your solid interests upon speculative grounds."[12] It is absurd to make political judgments in the abstract, he writes in another letter: "I must see the thing, I must see the men."[13] It is impossible to govern well without taking heed of these distinctions and differences. "The legislators who framed the ancient republics," Burke writes in the *Reflections*,

knew that their business was too arduous to be accomplished with no better apparatus than the metaphysics of an undergraduate, and the mathematics and arithmetic of an exciseman. They had to do with men, and they were obliged to study human nature. They had to do with citizens, and they were obliged to study the effects of those habits which are communicated by the circumstances of civil life. They were sensible that the operation of this second nature on the first produced a new combination; and thence arose many diversities amongst men, according to their birth, their education, their professions, the periods of their lives, their residence in towns or in the country, their several ways of acquiring and of fixing property, and according to the quality of the property itself, all which rendered them as it were so many different species of animals. . . . For the legislator would have been ashamed, that the coarse husbandman should well know how to assort and to use his sheep, horses, and oxen, and should have enough of common sense not to abstract and equalize them all into animals, without providing for each kind an appropriate food, care, and employment; whilst he, the oeconomist, disposer, and shepherd of his own kindred, subliming himself into an airy metaphysician, was resolved to know nothing of his flocks, but as men in general.[14]

When statesmen practice such egalitarian abstraction, they fail to know their people. And this failure translates into practice as a failure to account for crucial differences and attachments, which Burke deemed essential to political life. Rather than govern the people through their native or organically emergent categories and distinctions, Burke writes, the radicals in France seek "to confound all sorts of citizens, as well as they could, into one homogeneous mass; and then they divided this their amalgama into a number of incoherent republics."[15] He has in mind a decision of the revolutionary assembly to divide France into perfect square districts, rather than govern its traditional regions. The eradication of traditional attachments and practices that would follow such a move (and that indeed was its purpose) would not eliminate prejudices and attach the people to their national identity, as the revolutionaries hoped. Instead, Burke argues, it would crush all attachment to community and leave an unrestrained Paris government in charge of a greatly weakened nation.

In these protestations against the rational eradication of traditional distinctions, we find a hint of Burke's essential moderation, which rejected not only chaos but also an excess of order. Reductive theories of politics seemed to him an almost despotic force in society. They first undid all existing arrangements, weakening the people beyond repair, and then imposed an artificial order unconnected and ill suited to the character of those being governed. And in this radical rearrangement, he feared, were the seeds of an unrestrained political extremism, employing society as a kind of metaphysical laboratory.

That very fear points to the third concern Burke has about theory in politics. He is concerned that an overreliance on theory may unleash extremism and immoderation by unmooring politics from the polity. "Their principles always go to the extreme," Burke writes of the radicals of his day.[16] Because they pursue the vindication of a principle, they cannot stop short of total success. Even when their aims are well conceived, the radicals will not accept a good thing if it "does not come up to the full perfection of the abstract idea," and instead, they will "push for the more perfect, which cannot be attained without tearing to pieces the whole contexture of the commonwealth."[17] Burke believed that when the perfect is thus made the enemy of the good, political life can never be satisfactory, since there is no perfection in politics.

The quest for theoretical perfection is thus in practice a pursuit of extremes. And precisely because the pursuit is empowered by sophisticated theories, its extremism resists restraint. Old-fashioned grievances—moved by local or national loyalties or material necessities—have their natural bounds. Old-fashioned despotism—moved by a naked desire for power on the part of a charismatic tyrant—cannot readily mask its excesses. But a mob moved by a theory has no natural stopping point and cannot easily be assuaged, and leaders claiming to advance a truth obtained by philosophical speculation do not fit the familiar profile of the tyrant. The ancient tyrants could only wish to get away with what the modern speculative revolutionaries can achieve.[18]

In the pursuit of such extremes, moreover, the fidelity of the people to society is always in question. "Those vexatious questions, which in truth rather belong to metaphysics than politics," Burke writes, "can never be moved without shaking the foundations of the best governments that have ever been constituted by human wisdom."[19] When politics becomes a means of playing out speculative premises, every political practice, institution, and allegiance must explain itself in philosophical terms, so that no long-standing tradition, institution, or cherished habit can resist the searing light of speculative analysis. A politics built on modern reason inevitably becomes a self-fulfilling prophecy: rejecting all that cannot explain itself in terms of modern reason and therefore leaving in place only those elements of political life that meet its standards—regardless of what society may actually need or what has proven capable of serving the community in years gone by. By seeking a generalized theoretical precision in politics, ignoring circumstances and particulars, and unleashing a spirit of extremism, the speculative method of the Enlightenment radicals threatens to break the links between human nature and political life, as Burke understands them. And it does all this on the back of a notion of human reason that vastly exaggerates the capacity of the individual mind to discern political truths directly.

Beyond his concern about importing the *methods* of speculative philosophy into politics, therefore, Burke expresses profound concern about the *concept* of reason at the heart of these methods: an individual rational faculty that on its own, drawing upon evident principles derived from reflections on nature, can assess the truth or falsehood of any proposition and apply general rules to every circumstance. This modern ideal of reason, Burke fears, partakes far too much in the modern myth of individualism, suggesting that every truth must be demonstrable to the rational individual. On the contrary, Burke argues, human reason, important as it is, is far more limited than this ideal suggests, and those limits point human beings rather to their mutual dependence than to a radical individualism. The nature of reason, including its limits, is crucial to understanding the proper means of political thought and action.

From his very earliest writings, Burke was deeply impressed with the limits of human reason and its inability to resolve very basic philosophical questions. In his *Philosophical Enquiry into the Origin of Our Ideas of the Sublime and the Beautiful*, Burke notes that "on the whole one may observe that there is rather less difference upon matters of taste among mankind than upon most of those which depend upon the naked reason."[20] We are, he argues, far more likely to agree on the quality of a poetic passage in Virgil than on whether one of Aristotle's theories is true. And this implies that there are limits to what reason can fully resolve.

The persistence of these limits over centuries of disputation by brilliant philosophers suggested to Burke that some limits on our rational capacity are simply permanent—there is only so much we could know for sure. "That man thinks much too highly, and therefore he thinks weakly and delusively, of any contrivance of human wisdom, who believes that it can make any sort of approach to perfection," Burke writes.[21] And it is not our unwillingness to follow our reason that accounts for these permanent imperfections, but the limits of reason itself. "It is true indeed that enthusiasm often misleads us," Burke writes, but "so does reason too. Such is the condition of our nature; and we cannot help it."[22] This means that we must balance our reason against our passions and vice versa, but even such a balance can offer little confidence. No person has within him the capacity to overcome the radical infirmity and imperfection of man. No individual is up to it, regardless of his intelligence or his grasp of the principles of science or the facts of nature. Rather, we must learn from the combined experience of many, and particularly from the lives of those who lived before us.

"We are afraid to put men to live and trade each on his own private stock of reason, because we suspect that the stock in each man is small, and that the individuals would do better to avail themselves of the general bank and capital of nations and of ages," Burke writes in the *Reflections*.[23] Even when we as individuals cannot readily perceive the significance of the wisdom inherent in our cultural capital, the very fact of its having come down to us with the reverence and regard of previous generations should cause us to take it seriously as a standard to guide our actions and inquiries, or at least to give it a very significant benefit of the doubt. In a particularly revealing passage in the *Appeal from the New Whigs to the Old*, Burke writes: "If ever we should find ourselves disposed not to admire those writers or artists, Livy and Virgil for instance, Raphael or Michael Angelo, whom all the learned had admired, [we ought] not to follow our own fancies, but to study them until we know how and what we ought to admire; and if we cannot arrive at this combination of admiration with knowledge, rather to believe that we are dull, than that the rest of the world has been imposed on."[24]

We should in this sense be open to allowing some questions to be prejudged for us by the collective wisdom of past generations and to accept—if not quite blindly, then surely faithfully—the weight and gravity of their combined reason as greater than our own individual capacity. Those past generations were engaged in the same pursuits that we pursue—seeking fulfilling lives as individuals and societies and making the most of their imperfect human nature—and the fact that they found certain tools especially helpful should mean something to us.

Burke employs the word *prejudice*, a loaded term even in his own day, to describe such received wisdom. A prejudice, he argues, can obviously be a very bad thing when it is a mere individual bias without evidence or reason. But it can be a very good thing when it is a habit of opinion or action formed by long social usage and communicated by tradition. Since no individual can hope to reconsider every question from scratch, there must be some received opinions, but the best of these are formed by large communities over time. The revolutionaries, in seeking to uproot all the prejudices of their countrymen, in fact just work to replace the product of generations of reasoning with a set of far lesser prejudices of their own, based on ill-considered premises about human nature and politics. The friends of the English constitution, Burke contends, act differently: "Many of our men of speculation, instead of exploding general prejudices, employ their sagacity to discover the latent wisdom which prevails in them. If they find what they seek (and they seldom fail), they think it more wise to continue the prejudice, with the reason involved, than to cast away the coat of prejudice and to leave nothing but the naked reason; because prejudice, with its reason, has a motive to give action to that reason, and an affection which will give it permanence."[25]

The misguided explosion of prejudice would leave men unable to act in politics, Burke worries. Properly aged and developed prejudices, on the other hand, allow men to act on proven principles without the need to reason to them from scratch, and support the moral sentiments required for social peace.[26]

And when such age-old prejudice is not available, other means of drawing on the wisdom of many must be employed. The absence of clear guidance from the past is not a reason to rely on the unaided reason of the individual alone or to look to naked theory for standards. Instead, it is a reason to desire collective deliberation and collective action in politics. "Political arrangement, as it is a work for social ends, is to be only wrought by social means. There mind must conspire with mind," Burke writes.[27] The point of such cooperation is not to determine the will of the majority, however. Indeed, Burke argues that not will but precisely reason (in light of its limits, as he understands them) must underlie political action. His radical opponents, he argues, misguidedly employ an individualist reason to rationalize their way to the case for politics as the expression of sheer majority will. "If government were a matter of will upon any side," he tells his voters in Bristol, "yours, without question, ought to be superior. But government and legislation are matters of reason and judgment."[28] His is merely a different and less individualist notion of reason and judgment. "I have known, and, according to my measure, have co-operated with great men," Burke writes of his political career, "and I have never yet seen any plan which has not been mended by the observations of those who were much inferior in understanding to the person who took the lead in the business."[29] Politics is not a matter of individual genius, but is a matter of joint activity directed to common benefit.

This sense of the limits of individual human reason and the importance of joint deliberation and action made Burke a forthright champion of political partisanship—a most unusual view in his time, even more so than in ours. Parties have long been thought incommensurate with good government, because they represent particular interests rather than the good of the whole. The Enlightenment radicals argued that if reason were properly brought to bear on politics, individuals could—through rational thought, persuasion, and the application of the proper principles—arrive at the conclusions necessary for good government. Parties have no role in this process; they would only obscure the truth. Paine certainly held this view and suggested that party dispute was a distraction from governing: "I wish with all the devotion of a Christian that the names of Whig and Tory may never more be mentioned."[30]

Burke wholeheartedly disagrees and grounds his case precisely in the views discussed above: a sense of the limits of reason and theory, and a sense that men need to work together to be wise and effective. First, he thinks, it is a gross mistake to imagine that reason could resolve all partisan political disputes, because these disputes result precisely from the permanent imperfections of human knowledge and human reason. Participants in politics, he suggests, pursue their understanding of what is best for the whole, not just for themselves. But we are not equipped by nature to know the whole or to completely understand what is best, and the theoretical methods of the Enlightenment liberals do not in fact overcome this limitation. We can know only parts, and different people are shaped by their life experiences, moved by study, or perhaps just persuaded by arguments, to emphasize different parts. For some, the danger of disorder may be paramount; for others, the injustice of arbitrary power, respect for the will of God, the traditions of our ancestors, the promise of progress, or other priorities may be at play. Politics in a free society is a competition among the "partisans" of these different parts. Statesmen confront options for action, and what they emphasize about human nature, politics, or the circumstances of a situation—the parts of human knowledge they possess or deem most crucial—will shape the choices they make.

Partisans make their case by offering reasons for emphasizing the parts of human knowledge they deem most important, but these reasons will never be persuasive to everyone, because different people are shaped differently by their experiences and circumstances and are thus inclined to emphasize different parts. Partisanship will therefore never be argued out of existence. We can never know enough to stand above it, and no party could ever persuade everyone to stand with it. Each of the different parties has part of the truth, but none has all of it. For this reason, Burke writes, "we know that parties must ever exist in a free country."[31] Knowing this does not make the knower a nonpartisan or put him above the partisan fray. He still has his views and thinks it is his obligation to participate avidly in the great partisan debates of the day.

The opponents of party, Burke argues, too easily mistake it for faction. But large political parties in Britain are not private factions. Rather, as he uses the term, "party is a body of men united for promoting by their joint endeavor the national interest upon some principle in which they are all agreed."[32]

Politics is a negotiation of these principled differences in response to particular needs and events, and in that process, the participants benefit immensely from common action both in formulating their views and in putting them into effect—in both cases because no man's individual reason and ability are up to the task. Party politics should not be looked down upon as unseemly, Burke argues. On the contrary, it is the means by which well-intentioned politicians join together as honorable compatriots to advance what they see as the best course for their country. The effort to espouse common views and bring people who hold them into power is a noble pursuit, "easily distinguished from the mean and interested struggle for place and emolument."[33] This does not mean a blind preference for one's party. The views that drive a statesman to join with others ought to be what motivate him, and if the party ceases to advance them, he is right to abandon it. Indeed, for all his championing of partisanship, Burke himself very publicly broke with his party over the French Revolution, at great cost to both him and his party.

But as long as one's views are, in general, shared by co-partisans, and especially if opposing views are represented by parties of their own, it is incumbent upon any serious politician to hitch his wagon to a party and to work in concert with others. "No man," Burke writes, "who is not inflamed by vainglory into enthusiasm, can flatter himself that his single, unsupported, desultory, unsystematic endeavors, are of power to defeat the subtle designs and united cabals of ambitious citizens. When bad men combine, the good must associate; else they will fall, one by one, an unpitied sacrifice in a contemptible struggle. It is not enough, in a situation of trust in the commonwealth, that a man means well to his country." A statesman must find the means to turn his good intentions into effective action, and most of the time, only party politics offers that means.[34] It is not the partisan but rather the politician who claims to put himself above party who must be suspected of advancing only private interests.[35]

But partisanship is not the most significant consequence of the limits of individual reason for Burke. It offers a means of organizing political activity given those limits, but it does not itself offer an alternative guide to political judgment and action. If the premises of Enlightenment liberalism are inadequate, and if the resulting faith in modern reason is unjustified, what is the alternative organizing principle of, and the appropriate means for thinking about, political change? Burke's answer draws on all that we have seen of his critique of speculative politics, his emphasis on the given, and his understanding of human nature. It is prescription—Burke's great anti-innovationist innovation.

The term *prescription* originated in Roman property law, where it referred to ownership by virtue of long-term use, rather than by formal deed. Burke uses the term to describe the means by which practices and institutions that have long served society well are given the benefit of the doubt against innovations that might undermine them and are used as patterns and models for political life. In this way, reforms and innovations are judged by their conformity to, and continuity with, existing political forms.

Burke's case for this novel concept is firmly grounded in his sense of the limits of individual reason. Generations of statesmen have dealt with the kinds of challenges the present age must face, and "if we do not take to our aid the foregone studies of men reputed intelligent and learned, we shall be always beginners."[36] Humility before the wisdom of the past, however, does not mean just learning from the arguments that great men of prior generations made in writing and speech. Their legacy is the nation itself—its institutions, practices, and forms, all of which are "the result of the thoughts of many minds, in many ages."[37] Prescription therefore means, above all, respecting and preserving the political order as it has been handed down and even according it reverence.

Prescription thus begins in a kind of humble gratitude. Because building a working political arrangement is extremely difficult, we who inherit one such arrangement should be grateful for it even when we cannot fully understand the sources of its success. In any effort at reform, Burke writes, "I set out with a perfect distrust of my own abilities; a total renunciation of every speculation of my own; and with a profound reverence for the wisdom of our ancestors, who have left us the inheritance of so happy a constitution and so flourishing an empire."[38] To approach the constitution as the radicals do, with an eye to measuring it against a speculative theory and no inherent regard for its established forms, is to prefer one's own reason over the collective wisdom of generations of one's countrymen.[39] The French revolutionaries made precisely this mistake, Burke argues. Addressing himself to them in the *Reflections*, he writes that while the old regime had terrible flaws, it also contained the seeds of possible improvement:

> You began ill, because you began by despising everything that belonged to you. You set up your trade without a capital. If the last generations of your country appeared without much luster in your eyes, you might have passed them by, and derived your claims from a more early race of ancestors. Under a pious predilection for those ancestors, your imaginations would have realized in them a standard of virtue and wisdom, beyond the vulgar practice of the hour: and you would have risen with the example to whose imitation you aspired. Respecting your forefathers, you would have been taught to respect yourselves.[40]

Burke thus does not argue that the English constitution itself is an ideal regime for all, but rather that each society ought to draw on the best of its own tradition in addressing challenges and problems. The French should appreciate the past successes of their own fathers rather than abandon their ancestors' accomplishments in favor of a theoretical ideal.

The temptation to do otherwise is great, Burke acknowledges. It is human nature to lose sight of the value of what we possess and be taken instead with the potential of what we imagine possible. It is therefore necessary to awaken in the people an appreciation for what they have and should not take for granted, and even to build up some pride in resisting reckless innovation.[41]

Burke thus seeks to describe his fellow Britons as uniquely and admirably sensible about the dangers of abandoning the achievements of their ancestors. "Thanks to our sullen resistance to innovation, thanks to the cold sluggishness of our national character, we still bear the stamp of our forefathers," he writes.[42] "From the Magna Charta to the Declaration of Right, it has been the uniform policy of our constitution to claim and assert our liberties as an *entailed inheritance* derived to us from our forefathers, and to be transmitted to our posterity; as an estate specially belonging to the people of this kingdom, without any reference whatever to any other more general or prior right."[43] In a private letter to the poet Richard Cumberland (who had written to Burke praising the *Reflections* but wondering if their countrymen were really worthy of Burke's praise), Burke is remarkably up-front about his rhetorical purposes and methods: "Whether I have described our countrymen properly, time is to show; I hope I have, but at any rate it is perhaps the best way to persuade them to be right by supposing that they are so. Great bodies, like great men, must be instructed in the way in which they will be best pleased to receive instruction; flattery itself may be converted into a mode of counsel."[44]

Such flattery aims to suggest to the English that they already possess the materials needed to address the many challenges they confront. And this means they are able not only to stand their ground against ill-conceived innovation but also to respond effectively to changing circumstances by building on what they have.

Burke's foremost fear, particularly in the period of the French Revolution but also in the incessantly eventful preceding decade and a half, was that in crisis conditions, the English would be tempted to seek after what he derided as speculative metaphysical politics. He therefore first of all offers prescription as a means of resistance. Long before the French Revolution and speaking of the dangers of British overreaction in the American crisis in 1775, Burke offered this advice to the House of Commons:

> If you apprehend that on a concession you shall be pushed by metaphysical process to the extreme lines, and argued out of your whole authority, my advice is this; when you have recovered your old, your strong, your tenable position, then face about—stop short—do nothing more—reason not at all—oppose the ancient policy and practice of the empire as a rampart against the speculations of innovators on both sides of the question; and you will stand on great, manly, and sure ground. On this solid basis fix your machines, and they will draw worlds toward you.[45]

Long-held assumptions and time-tested prejudices, too, are useful in a crisis. "Prejudice is of ready application in the emergency; it previously engages the mind in a steady course of wisdom and virtue, and does not leave the man hesitating in the moment of decision, skeptical, puzzled, and unresolved. Prejudice renders a man's virtue his habit; and not a series of unconnected acts. Through just prejudice, his duty becomes a part of his nature."[46]

But the essence of Burke's teaching on prescription is not directed to resistance in a crisis. Rather, prescription is above all a means of controlled and gradual modification in response to felt public needs—not to oppose all change, but rather to pursue change carefully, preferring changes to substance over changes to form where possible, and incremental over radical reform where necessary.[47] Burke was by no means a radical traditionalist opposed to all reform. Far from it; he was a leading (in some respects *the* leading) reformer in Parliament in his time (see Chapter 6). But he believed that successful reform must begin from existing circumstances, not from theoretical speculations. The maxim of the English, Burke writes, is "never entirely nor at once to depart from antiquity."[48] That does not mean no departure may be attempted, but rather means that departures must be partial and incremental—aimed at improving or correcting, not beginning anew.

Indeed, Burke argues that change, understood in this way as "a principle of growth," is not only permissible but essential, and essential precisely to the task of preserving the existing order.[49] "A state without the means of some change is without the means of its conservation," he writes.[50] Such a principle of growth or means of change is intended to be a permanent feature of the regime, not just a path to an ultimate and correct arrangement that would not change further.

In this sense, Burke's approach is actually more open to change than that of many of his radical opponents, including Paine. They were looking to establish the right permanent principles to guide the work of government. Burke argues that change is itself a permanent principle, and that while the ends of government do not change, the means to those ends must be altered as needed, and these sometimes must include even the details of the form of the government.

The preservation of the overall political order, which is among Burke's chief concerns, requires and must be suited to accommodate constant change and must ensure that any change is continuous and gradual rather than disruptive and sudden.[51] This precisely is what prescription aims to do: to ground the new in the old, to make change into extension, and so to provide for continuity and stability so that problems are addressed while the overall order is not unduly disturbed. Burke wants political judgments even in extreme situations to be guided by the pattern of the normal and the usual, not the other way around. He argues that such an approach, drawing as we have seen on the model of inheritance, "furnishes a sure principle of conservation and a sure principle of transmission; without at all excluding a principle of improvement. . . . [I]t leaves acquisition free; but it secures what it acquires. Whatever advantages are obtained by a state proceeding on these maxims, are locked fast as in a sort of family settlement."[52]

Burke's model for such careful gradualism is the legal profession, which he deeply admires. Lawyers, he says, always seek for precedents and always present innovations as modest enlargements of precedent. He acknowledges that these efforts sometimes strain credulity and misrepresent the nature of the precedent to obscure the degree of genuine innovation in question, but he actually praises this practice as an indication of the lawyers' desire to minimize social disruption— suggesting perhaps that his own efforts include such obscuring of real disruption.[53] Lawyers understand that the authority of the law depends on its stability and that people build their lives around certain assumptions that should not be disrupted needlessly. This is all the more true when the disruption in question is more profound than in most legal cases—when the form or function of the regime itself is in question. Gradual change that carefully builds on existing materials allows society to adjust and to employ its strengths to address its weaknesses.

This reliance on precedent does not mean that Burke believed that all circumstances had analogies in prior historical events. There were surely unprecedented political challenges. When confronting the government's failure to contain the colonial revolt in America, Burke told his parliamentary colleagues that Britain's long history offered nothing like it to consider.[54] Of the European war he saw emerging in the wake of the French Revolution in the last years of his life he said, "I cannot persuade myself that this war bears any the least resemblance (other than that it is a war) to any that has ever existed in the world—I cannot persuade myself that any examples or any reasonings drawn from other wars and other politics are at all applicable to it—and I truly and sincerely think that all other wars and all other politics have been the games of children."[55] But precisely in the face of such unprecedented difficulties and crises that called for new thinking, Burke believed the nation had to call on the strength and stability of its ancient constitution, adapted as it had been over centuries to address a broad variety of challenges. It was valuable not because it had dealt with crises just like those of his day, but because it had dealt effectively with a bewildering array of different and novel kinds of problems.

The constitution is valued, after all, not because it is old but because it has been developing and evolving for a long time and so is well suited to the nation, its character, and its needs. The constitution is in this sense very up to date and is adapted and adaptable to real-world circumstances. It is therefore likely to be far better than any theory at contending with novel circumstances since theory has high expectations and is very rigid while a long-standing regime is accustomed to adjusting itself as things change.

The changes and reforms the constitution undergoes, moreover, do not all point in any one direction, but are responses to events that seek to bring the system into equilibrium. Sometimes, the appropriate response is to enlarge the scope of representative institutions, as the theories of the Enlightenment liberals would suggest should always happen, but at other times, the appropriate response is to enlarge the prerogative of the monarch or the aristocracy.

As we have seen in Chapter 3, Burke believed that the structure of the constitution and the regular practices of preceding generations offered the only available means of reaching for standards of measure beyond utility, and he does argue that politics should answer to, and be shaped in accord with, these standards. But these standards are discovered through gradual improvements tried by the test of time. History, Burke suggests, is not an unfolding, but rather a process of clarification through experience, and political change is among its constant features. No particular change sets a single direction for future development. All are prudential modifications in response to unique circumstances and demands. "These exceptions and modifications are made not by the process of logic, but by the rules of prudence," Burke writes. "Prudence is not only first in rank of the virtues, political and moral, but she is the director, the regulator, the standard of them all."[56] The rules of prudence are applied, and therefore developed, in response to events, not in advance of them, and their validity is measured by their practical success or failure in keeping the people safe, happy, and free.

Institutions that have grown in this organic way may not be tidy, but they are strong and functional, and the attempt to force them into accord with a theory foreign to their development will not end well. "The old building stands well enough, though part gothic, part Grecian, and part Chinese, until an attempt is made to square it into uniformity. Then it may come down upon our heads altogether, in much uniformity of ruin."[57] Rather than pursue such uniformity, Burke argues, we ought to see how well the evolved institutions serve the public's needs and desires.

This organic approach establishes for Burke a different and more practical standard not only for policy but also for political principles. "The practical consequences of any political tenet go a great way in deciding upon its value," he writes. "Political problems do not primarily concern truth or falsehood. They relate to good or evil. What in the result is likely to produce evil, is politically false: that which is productive of good, politically is true."[58] Thus within the bounds of the constitution, politics is not a branch of philosophy, in an express search for truth or its application, but is rather in the business of producing good practical outcomes, which help point to higher truth but not directly. Burke makes this point exceptionally explicit several times in his career, perhaps most notably in reference to the American crisis: "I will not enter into the question of how much truth is preferable to peace. Perhaps truth may be far better. But as we have scarcely ever the same certainty in the one that we have in the other, I would, unless the truth were evident indeed, hold fast to peace."[59]

Thus Burke returns to the limits of reason. Our ability to know the practical consequences of a particular policy far exceeds our ability to ascertain the truth of a philosophical claim. In politics, therefore, we almost always ought to judge by effects and not by speculation.

Burke understands that because his alternative to modern reason begins from a rejection of modern reason, his approach would prove to be exceedingly vulnerable to attempted applications of such reason. For prescription to serve its purpose, it must be accepted implicitly, not argued for or about.[60] He hopes that its practical success will protect its roots from undue curiosity. "The bulk of mankind on their part are not excessively curious concerning any theories whilst they are really happy," he writes, "and one sure symptom of an ill-conducted state is the propensity of the people to resort to them."[61] But Burke also sees that the Enlightenment radicals want to investigate the regime in their theoretical terms regardless of its practical success, and he understands the danger this scrutiny can pose to a prescriptive regime. "It has been the misfortune, not as these gentlemen think it, the glory, of this age, that every thing is to be discussed," he writes, "as if the constitution of our country were to be always a subject rather of altercation than enjoyment."[62] Once the foundation of the regime becomes a subject of argument, the implicit fidelity of the people may well be lost forever.

It is not that no argument could be made in defense of the English constitution. Far from it, Burke believes. But no argument could achieve the force of attachment that prescription creates by habit, enjoyment, and untroubled loyalty. Through legalistic arguments, a statesman can show that his regime is legitimate, but he cannot make his fellow citizens love the country through such arguments, or make sacrifices for it in a crisis, and indeed he could easily undermine such patriotism by making the country a subject of such impudent investigation.[63] A working regime, with roots deep in the past and a history of incremental development that has suited it well to the needs of its people, should have the benefit of the doubt, in Burke's view, and should not be subjected to the searing light of the Enlightenment philosopher's misguided investigation, driven as it is by an exaggerated notion of the power of reason. The radicals and their schemes must bear the burden of proof, and their ideas should be subjected to extreme scrutiny. "The arrogance of their pretensions in a manner provokes and challenges us to an enquiry into their foundation," Burke writes.[64] This is why Burke goes to such lengths to examine the revolutionary regime and its claims, methods, actions, and results in the *Reflections*. While prescriptive regimes should enjoy some immunity from such prosecution on the basis of their proven success, novel revolutionary regimes should expect to be scrutinized.

Burke's case regarding the limits of human reason in politics can easily be taken as an anti-intellectual case against the use of reason in politics, or the use of reason at all, and it very often has been. But it is better understood as an argument about the particular character of the political sphere. Burke clearly does not deny the value of the contemplative life in its own terms, and indeed at times he argues that the contemplative virtues are superior to the active ones. In June 1777, Burke received a letter from William Richardson, a Scottish professor of the humanities, together with a copy of a book Richardson had written analyzing the philosophical underpinnings of some of Shakespeare's plays. In his letter (which does not survive), Richardson apparently praised with great humility Burke's political vocation as superior to his own more speculative life. Burke in his response vehemently disagreed with the characterization: "How could you think I could be indifferent to the opinions of a gentleman in your honorable and happy situation, secluded though you conceive it to be from the importance of political occupation? . . . The contemplative virtue is in the order of things above the active; . . . the other, at best, is but a very gross and concrete body, constantly dependent, frequently defeated, always obstructed."[65]

And yet, the superiority of the contemplative virtue does not entitle it to supplant the active virtue in its proper sphere. Political life, Burke suggests, is the realm of the active virtue, since politics governs human action and not human thought. To pretend otherwise and import a speculative theorizing frame of mind into politics is both to distort the character and purpose of politics and to exaggerate the nature and the power of reason. Enlightenment liberalism does so as a result of the premises from which it begins regarding human nature, individualism, choice, reason, and the given world. Burke's sullen resistance to these premises shapes his vehement rejection of the rationalist politics of the radicals of his day and shapes his innovative alternative: prescription as a mode of change and preservation.

Burke thus offers his case for prescription as a response to the elevation of reason at the heart of both Enlightenment thought and Thomas Paine's political philosophy. But Paine, almost alone among the Enlightenment liberals and radicals of his day, not only advances the vision of reason that Burke opposes, but also responds directly to Burke's alternative and reaffirms a faith in reason.

Paine's Rationalism and the Age of Reason

Thomas Paine viewed reason as a profoundly liberating force that can help man learn his rights and establish governments equipped to guard and champion those rights. "There is a morning of reason rising upon man on the subject of government, that has not appeared before," Paine writes. "As the barbarism of the present old governments expires, the moral conditions of nations with respect to each other will be changed."[66] Paine's self-declared purpose is to advance the cause of this rational politics. "It is time that nations should be rational, and not be governed like animals, for the pleasure of their riders."[67] Making nations rational was in one way or another his goal in every political exertion.

Paine argues plainly that political principles must precede political institutions, rather than, as Burke would have it, be derived from them. In *Rights of Man*, he asserts that his aim is "to establish a system of principles as a basis on which governments ought to be erected."[68] And this was his goal not only in his time in France. In an 1806 letter to John Inskeep, the mayor of Philadelphia, Paine reflects on his eventful career: "My motive and object in all my political works, beginning with *Common Sense*, the first work I ever published, have been to rescue man from tyranny and false systems and false principles of government, and enable him to be free and establish government for himself."[69] These false systems and unreasonable principles are central to all of Paine's descriptions of the world, especially as the chief causes of war and despotism. "Man is not the enemy of man, but through the medium of a false system of Government," he writes.[70] If only regimes were established on the proper principles, in line with reason, mankind would flourish as never before.

Building on the Enlightenment-liberal view of human nature and the polity, Paine argues that the crucial premise of Enlightenment thought—the natural equality of man—inescapably leads to a politics of individualism and individual reason. If men are equal, then none can simply command the assent of another and none will accept on faith the superior wisdom of others. The equality of man dictates that in a legitimate government, everything must be open for discussion and analysis by all. And this is a great virtue, not, as Burke had argued, a vice of modern politics. "In the representative system," Paine writes, "the reason for everything must publicly appear. Every man is a proprietor in government, and considers it a necessary part of his business to understand. It concerns his interest, because it affects his property. He examines the cost, and compares it with the advantages; and above all, he does not adopt the slavish custom of following what in other governments are called leaders."[71] Burke's insistence that the core of the regime must not be questioned or open to inspection seems to Paine like a self-interested reaction of those who "are called leaders" against this new rational politics. They defend their prerogatives by clothing them in fancy names, and they assert the danger of unaided reason in politics because "they tremble at the approach of principles, and dread the precedent that threatens their overthrow."[72]

To avert that overthrow, Paine writes, they make government seem far too subtle and fragile for citizens to approach, "blinding the understanding of man and making him believe that government is some wonderful mysterious thing."[73] But understood in the proper, rational terms, government is not a mystery at all.[74] The science of government ought therefore to be a science of principles, not of single instances, and these principles are accessible to the reason of every rational individual. The French Revolution, Paine argues, should be understood in this context. What matters most about it is not that it is a sharp break from the patterns of the past, but that it is a replacement of wrong with right principles.

Burke, in Paine's view, seeks to obscure the question of principle by focusing instead on historical particularities: on persons and the details of institutions. It is difficult to discern anything clearly "when circumstances are put for arguments, which is frequently the case with Mr. Burke," he writes.[75] Burke's case that abstract principle is foreign to political life therefore strikes Paine as simply an excuse to avoid the question of the principles of his beloved English constitution, which causes Burke in turn to excuse appalling injustice in France on similar grounds. In *Rights of Man* Paine writes:

> Mr. Burke appears to have no idea of principles, when he is contemplating government. "Ten years ago," says he, "I could have felicitated France on her having a government without enquiring what the nature of that government was, or how it was administered." Is this the language of a rational man? Is it the language of a heart feeling as it ought to feel for the rights and happiness of the human race? On this ground, Mr. Burke must compliment every government in the world, while the victims who suffer under them, whether sold into slavery, or tortured out of existence, are wholly forgotten. It is power, and not principles, that Mr. Burke venerates; and under this abominable depravity, he is disqualified to judge between them.[76]

Precisely this kind of confusion of persons for principles and power for reason is behind the defense of hereditary government, Paine argues. "Mr. Burke does not attend to the distinction between men and principles."[77] Hereditary rule is "a mere animal system," with no rational component attached. Its advocates could never persuade the people to establish such a system were it not already in place (having gotten there illegitimately long ago).[78]

And the fact that the system has been there for ages is hardly a case for its persistence. To argue that long usage transforms an unjust practice into a just one is absurd, Paine writes, "for either it is putting time in the place of principle, or making it superior to principle; whereas time has no more connection with, or influence upon principle than principle has upon time."[79] An institution or practice must prove itself before the bar of reason. Laws cannot derive authority from age, but only from "the justness of their principles."[80]

Throughout his writing Paine rejects appeals to authority and demands instead appeals to reason as a standard of judgment. He even prides himself in his own work on avoiding making points by quotation of familiar and learned authorities—a practice Burke engages in frequently. "I scarcely ever quote; the reason is, I always think," Paine writes.[81] Even when others pointed to places in which his work clearly drew on noted authorities, Paine staunchly resisted the implication. There is certainly something odd in an obviously learned man's insisting he is not conversant with the great writers of his age and of the Western canon, but for Paine the substantive point is worth more than the biographical one: Direct reference to original principles is more important than a demonstrated grasp of precedents. The emphasis on individual and unaided reason is crucial for the case he seeks to make. He argues that every individual is capable of employing his own reason to discern the truth or falsehood of a political question, so that no reliance on the past or on collective reasoning is required. In this way, again, Paine believes that every individual has the capacity to begin from scratch, rather than beginning where others have left off.

On the question of reason, as on others we have seen, this assertion of self-sufficiency starkly divides Burke and Paine. Paine seeks to demonstrate the capacity of the individual for self-rule by holding every individual separate from a larger whole—both social and temporal. In order to follow the dictates of reason, we must put aside all the context and authority of the given world and pursue the abstract and universal truth directly. And the reason unleashed by the Enlightenment allows us (and indeed requires us) to do just that. This unaided modern reason is our means of knowing the truth, and we need not take any claims to truth on the authority of others.

Reason can take the place of authority even in the realm of religion—indeed perhaps especially in that realm, which for so long had been the domain of authority and faith. Paine's most express and outright claims for the power of unaided reason appear in his writings on religion and especially his two-volume case for Enlightenment Deism, titled (not coincidentally) *The Age of Reason*.

The Age of Reason is in some respects an astonishingly intemperate book and may therefore unduly distract its readers from Paine's case for reason. He launches blistering attacks on all forms of organized Christianity and works his way through the Bible pointing out inconsistencies and implausibilities. "The most detestable wickedness, the most horrible cruelties, and the greatest miseries that have afflicted the human race have had their origin in this thing called revelation, or revealed religion," Paine writes.[82] It is absurd and insulting to God himself, he contends regarding the origins of Jesus, "to believe that the Almighty committed debauchery with a woman engaged to be married."[83]

But beyond his attacks on the particular dogmas and consequences of organized religion, Paine's final book contains his most extensive and assertive case for the centrality of individual human reason. His rejection of organized religion is an elevation of individual reason: "I do not believe in the creed professed by the Jewish Church, by the Roman Church, by the Greek Church, by the Turkish Church, by the Protestant Church, nor by any church that I know of. My own mind is my own church."[84] He rejects any religious authority's claims that cannot be independently verified by every rational person. "A thing which everybody is required to believe requires that proof and evidence of it should be equal to all, and universal."[85] We simply cannot be expected to take on authority what we have not seen ourselves, even in the case of revelation. "When it is revealed to me, I will believe it to be a revelation," Paine writes, "but it is not, and cannot be incumbent upon me to believe it to be revelation before."[86] Rather than in books claiming the authority of revelation, human beings ought to search for God in his creation, which is available to all through their unaided senses and reasoning faculty:

> The creation is the Bible of the deist. He there reads, in the handwriting of the creator himself, the certainty of His existence and the immutability of His power, and all other Bibles and testaments are to him forgeries. . . .

. . . We can know God only through His works. We cannot have a conception of any one attribute but by following some principle that leads to it. We have only a confused idea of His power, if we have not the means of comprehending something of its immensity. We can have no idea of His wisdom but by knowing the order and manner in which it acts. The principles of science lead to this knowledge; for the Creator of man is the Creator of science, and it is through that medium that man can see God, as it were, face to face.[87]

Thus modern science, employing modern reason, offers us the path to authoritative and verifiable truth, even about God. "That which is now called natural philosophy, embracing the whole circle of science, of which astronomy occupies the chief place, is the study of the works of God, and of the power and wisdom of God in His works, and is the true theology."[88]

Paine thus argues that the unleashing of reason through science and its further refinement and employment in the political revolutions of the day would inevitably unleash new modes of knowing God and his works, too, and so would inspire a revolution in religion. "Soon after I published the pamphlet *Common Sense* in America," Paine writes, "I saw the exceeding probability that a revolution in the system of government would be followed by a revolution in the system of religion."[89] Reason, conceived in Enlightenment terms as an individual analytical faculty, is the means to knowing the truth. No claim of authority or seniority has standing to assert itself over reason. If this is true of people's knowledge of God and so of morality, it is surely all the more true of their knowledge of political things. Politics, no less than theology and morals, must be an application of unaided reason and must be designed and managed to facilitate its operation.

And indeed, politics as Paine describes it is an exceptionally intellectual undertaking—almost purely an exercise in reason. Again and again, he distinguishes a properly functioning regime (by which he means something like a representative republic) from the despotism of the aristocracy on the grounds of their differing relations to the exercise of reason:

> Those two distinct and opposite forms erect themselves on the two distinct and opposite bases of Reason and Ignorance. As the exercise of Government requires talents and abilities, and as talents and abilities cannot have hereditary descent, it is evident that hereditary succession requires a belief from man to which his reason cannot subscribe, and which can only be established upon his ignorance; and the more ignorant any country is, the better it is fitted for this species of Government. On the contrary, Government, in a well-constituted republic, requires no belief from man beyond what his reason can give. He sees the rationale of the whole system, its origin and its operation; and as it is best supported when best understood, the human faculties act with boldness, and acquire, under this form of government, a gigantic manliness.[90]

Paine actually raises Burke's own words in defense of this position, particularly Burke's assertion in the *Reflections on the Revolution in France*: "Government is a contrivance of human wisdom" (see Chapter 4).[91] In that passage, Burke is arguing that political institutions are not works of nature but creations of man (though he downplays the difference between the two). But Paine rather deftly employs the reference to suggest that governing is an act of raw intellect. In *Rights of Man*, Paine argues: "Admitting that government is a contrivance of human wisdom, it must necessarily follow, that hereditary succession, and hereditary rights (as they are called), can make no part of it, because it is impossible to make wisdom hereditary."[92]

This is a crucial part of Paine's case against monarchy—that since governing is intellectual work, there is no reason to expect that the ability to govern well will be hereditary, and in any case no one could possibly be wise enough to be given as much power and privilege as a king is granted. "For a man to merit a million sterling a year from a nation, he ought to have a mind capable of comprehending from an atom to a universe, which, if he had, he would be above receiving the pay," Paine writes.[93] For this reason, the very fact of monarchy demonstrates, in Paine's view, an intentional rejection of a politics of reason. "Hereditary succession is a burlesque upon monarchy. It puts it in the most ridiculous light, by presenting it as an office which any child or idiot may fill. . . . This sort of superstition may last a few years more, but it cannot long resist the awakened reason and interest of man."[94] In a society that properly understands the fully rational character of politics, no such practice could make sense.

Such a politics of rational assessment, of course, relies on the premise that if reason is allowed free rein, the right choices will be made. Paine's republicanism rests on the view that reason is well (though not equally) distributed across society, and if left to its own devices, it will move the majority to both elect to power those with the greatest mental gifts and make the correct kinds of choices directly. "It is always the interest of a far greater number of people in a nation to have things right, than to let them remain wrong; and when public matters are open to debate, and the public judgment free, it will not decide wrong, unless it decides too hastily."[95]

Paine therefore flatly disagrees with Burke's view that political judgment requires more wisdom than the unaided reason can muster and that therefore long-standing and successful prejudices should be given some weight: "No man is prejudiced in favor of a thing, knowing it to be wrong. He is attached to it on the belief of its being right; and when he sees it is not so, the prejudice will be gone."[96]

Long-standing use provides no exemption. "The question is not whether those principles are new or old, but whether they are right or wrong."[97] And a refusal to directly confront that question leads society to accept many wrongs and persist in much injustice—and especially in needless wars. In the emerging age of reason, "the objects for war are exceedingly diminished, and there is now left scarcely anything to quarrel about, but what arises from that demon of society, prejudice, and the consequent sullenness and untractableness of the temper," Paine writes in 1782.[98]

One crucial reason why society cannot easily overcome that demon of prejudice, Paine argues, is precisely the reliance on precedent that Burke values so highly. "Government by precedent, without any regard to the principle of the precedent, is one of the vilest systems that can be set up," Paine writes.

> By associating those precedents with a superstitious reverence for ancient things, as monks show relics and call them holy, the generality of mankind are deceived into the design. Governments now act as if they were afraid to awaken a single reflection in man. They are softly leading him to the sepulcher of precedents, to deaden his faculties and call attention from the scene of revolutions. They feel that he is arriving at knowledge faster than they wish, and their policy of precedents is the barometer of their fears.[99]

Moreover, because the oldest precedents are valued most highly, the doctrine of precedents suggests that human history is a decline, "that wisdom degenerates in governments as governments increase in age, and can only hobble along by the stilts and crutches of precedents."[100] Paine thus rejects the view at the core of Burke's doctrine of prescription: that practices that have passed the test of time deserve respect and have gradually evolved to best meet the needs of the present. In fact, he argues, the practices of the past were not built upon reasoned knowledge and so do not provide a model of politics. Paine even objects to the employment of precedent not only in political life but also in the law courts.[101]

And for the same reasons, he thinks the wisdom of many has no special standing over that of one—all must pass the same test of reason, as employed by every individual. Paine thus flatly rejects the idea that party politics allows for many minds to work together and that the limits of reason mean that parties are inevitable in a free society, as different people emphasize different parts of the truth in different ways. For Paine, the truth is knowable by reason and should be persuasive to all, and therefore parties in politics can only be factions in search of private ends over the public good. His ideal of a republican legislature "was always founded on a hope that whatever personal parties there might be in the state, they would all unite and agree in the general principles of good government—that these party differences would be dropped at the threshold of the statehouse, and that the public good, or the good of the whole, would be the governing principle of the legislature within it."[102] A politics freed from prejudice and enlightened by reason need not be a politics of partisanship. Just as Burke's case for party emerges from his understanding of human nature and the limits of reason, so Paine's case against it is grounded in his own understanding of human nature and of the power of reason.

Similarly, Paine dismisses the notion that each nation should follow the patterns of its own history and that no universal principles of political form or function can speak to all. Such a view, he argues, begins by assuming that politics has nothing to do with reason and knowledge and so does not answer to principles of any kind but only to contingent experience. If there is a case for monarchy, for instance, surely one group of Englishmen in Britain should be able to explain it to another in America, even if they live in different circumstances. "If there is anything in monarchy which we people of America do not understand, I wish Mr. Burke would be so kind as to inform us," Paine writes.[103] But in fact the opposite is the case:

> I see in America a government extending over a country ten times as large as England, and conducted with regularity, for a fortieth part of the expense which Government costs in England. If I ask a man in America if he wants a King, he retorts, and asks me if I take him for an idiot? How is it that this difference happens? Are we more or less wise than others? I see in America the generality of people living in a style of plenty unknown in monarchical countries; and I see that the principle of its government, which is that of the equal Rights of Man, is making a rapid progress in the world.[104]

Surely if it is good for America, it will be good for others, too, because it is verifiably grounded in accessible arguments.

For all these reasons, Paine believes that Burke's concerns about the danger of uprooting long-standing prejudices and practices are misplaced and that his politics (based as it is on the limits of reason) is misguided. It is not at all a misfortune that everything is to be discussed, Paine argues. Discussing everything openly is the means of rationalizing politics and, by so doing, the way to properly define, guide, and implement political change. Once basic principles like the equality of man and the necessity of consent are laid out, the kinds of gross injustice evident in so many of the regimes of the world become untenable. "It is impossible that such governments as have hitherto existed in the world, could have commenced by any other means than a total violation of every principle sacred and moral," Paine writes.[105] He argues against Burke's assertion that these governments do most things well and we should therefore not focus on the few things they fail to do. The truth is the opposite, Paine says: These governments' most basic forms are wrong, and the few things that do work are merely exceptions that prove the rule.[106]

A legitimate and working government, therefore, will combine the proper principles with their attendant forms. In this sense, politics really does answer to abstract principles for Paine, but it does so out of the conviction that the right principles are inescapable prerequisites for the right practices, and that once reason and proper principles are unleashed in political life, a course is irrevocably set that will lead to a fairer and more effective government. The revolution Paine has in mind is thus primarily one of knowledge, enabled by reason, and those who oppose it are essentially agents of willful ignorance. Paine writes: "The Revolutions of America and France have thrown a beam of light over the world, which reaches into man. The enormous expense of governments has provoked people to think, by making them feel; and when once the veil begins to rend, it admits not of repair. Ignorance is of a peculiar nature: once dispelled, it is impossible to re-establish it. . . . Mr. Burke is laboring in vain to stop the progress of knowledge."[107]

A government founded on such advances in knowledge therefore argues for itself in rational terms in its very forms and functions. It makes its case explicitly so that every citizen can consider the case, and it wears its principles on its sleeve. This means, for one thing, that the government must explicitly present its principles and forms to the world through a written constitution. Such a document, Paine argues, must give expression to the proper origin of government in a contract among the people and is in effect the actual legal form of that contract. Such a constitution thus embodies what is known by reason about the origins of government and the nature of man, and it speaks in plain terms to the reason of every reasonable person, so that no one can question its legitimacy. What Burke calls the English constitution—which is not a document but the actual forms and structures of the English government—is to Paine not a constitution at all, but just the accumulated practices of an essentially unjust regime.

Their definitions of a constitution embody Burke's and Paine's views on reason and political change. For Burke the constitution is the product of prescription, and its defense is the aim of prescription. Paine believes that the constitution is the product of explicit reasoning on abstract principles and is defended by reasoned argument. Burke's constitution is a regime, if not a nation. Paine's constitution is a legal document. A constitution, Paine writes, "is not a thing in name only, but in fact. It has not an ideal, but a real existence; and wherever it cannot be produced in a visible form, there is none. Can, then, Mr. Burke produce the English Constitution? If he cannot, we may fairly conclude that though it has been so much talked about, no such thing as a constitution exists, or ever did exist, and consequently that the people have yet a constitution to form."[108]

Such a straightforward constitution, which in plain black-and-white describes the government in rational terms and in its entirety, also greatly simplifies the function of government and avoids the enormous and needless complexity and inefficiency of the English system, with its countless vestigial limbs retained out of pure inertia and unwillingness to change. This complexity is itself a mark of the unreasonable character of the British regime. Rationalization translates to simplification. "I draw my idea of the form of government from a principle in nature, which no art can overturn, viz. that the more simple any thing is, the less liable it is to be disordered; and the easier repaired when disordered," Paine writes in *Common Sense.*[109]

This point again stands in for Paine's larger disagreement with Burke about the relation of political life to reason and science, as understood by the Enlightenment philosophers. Burke explicitly rejects the notion that simplicity in government is a virtue. Complicated institutions built up over time are far more likely to work well because they have developed to balance competing pressures and ambitions against one another. Human beings are not simple, and their governments cannot be, either. "When I hear the simplicity of contrivance aimed at and boasted of in any new political constitutions, I am at no loss to decide that the artificers are grossly ignorant of their trade, or totally negligent of their duty. The simple governments are fundamentally defective, to say no worse of them," Burke writes.[110]

But to practice politics by balancing countervailing excesses, Paine says, "amounts to an accusation upon Providence, as if she had left to man no other choice with respect to government than between two evils."[111] Since he does not believe that is the case, he rejects the kind of checks-and-balances approach to institutional design that characterizes even most liberal political philosophers and argues that mixed government is unacceptable. Paine is in this respect a true Enlightenment radical, more like the French Revolutionaries than the American.

Burke's various defenses of the aristocracy and the prerogatives of the king always defend the whole mixed regime—the king, the nobles, and the common people balancing each other's interests to achieve a stable political life. "I hold [the Lords] to be of absolute necessity in the constitution, but I think they are only good when kept within their proper bounds," Burke writes.[112] This, as he explains it, is why he defended Parliament against royal power grabs in the 1760s but then become a staunch defender of the royal prerogative against the advocates of republicanism in the 1780s.[113]

But Paine believes that such instability and irregularity result from a failure to apply the proper principles to government. A mixed regime is a jumbled mess and falls short of legitimacy to the extent it falls short of true republicanism.[114]

For similar reasons, Paine does not generally advocate checks and balances *within* a republican regime. He does not argue that a very specific arrangement of the representative system is a necessary function of republican principles; it is a matter of preference as long as the representative principle is adhered to.[115] But Paine's own preference is for simplicity and minimalism in institutional design.

In *Common Sense*, he offers an idea of what he believes should be the shape of American self-government after the British are expelled. He calls for annually elected unicameral state assemblies with no state executives (or governors). The assemblies are to be empowered over all domestic questions but subject to the authority of the Continental Congress in foreign affairs. At the federal level, he wants the different states divided into equal districts that would each send a large number (perhaps thirty each) of representatives to the national congress, which would also be a unicameral body. All votes in the congress should require a three-fifths majority; the congress would choose its president by drawing the states by lot, and each state in turn would have its chance to preside. Little to no discord could arise in such a structure, Paine suggests, as it would best represent the true will of the people while allowing for the rational assessment of political problems.[116] The structure is aimed at facilitating rational decision making and ignores almost entirely the role of ambition, interest, and passion in human affairs—all of which Paine takes to be avoidable by a proper attention to the correct principles of government.

Paine's rejection of bicameralism (which he modified a little in the 1790s but never rejected during his career) is particularly telling in this regard. In *Rights of Man*, he argues that "two houses arbitrarily checking or controlling each other is inconsistent; because it cannot be proved on the principles of just representation, that either should be wiser or better than the other."[117] These words were published in 1792 and probably written in late 1791, well after the adoption of the U.S. Constitution, which, of course, involved a very different institutional structure. Though Paine never says so explicitly, his constitutional writings of the 1790s strongly suggest he had serious principled objections to the design of the American constitutional system, with its complicated efforts to corral ambition and channel envy and the hunger for power through counteracting institutions.

For Paine, simplicity in government is the appropriate expression of the simple and accessible truths that underlie it. Thus, he not only opposes intricate designs in the constitution but also rejects the kind of pomp and circumstance that often attaches to the power of the state. While Burke argues that elevating the institutions and great persons of the state "with majesty and sober pomp" helps form the crucial sentimental attachments and ennoble the whole enterprise of politics, Paine calls it all a means to disguise the fundamental injustice and unreasonableness of the regime. He seeks to desentimentalize politics. The haughty pretensions of the aristocracy are ridiculous, he says. "Titles are but nicknames, and every nickname is a title."[118] And the self-importance of the monarchy is ludicrous: "I compare it to something kept behind a curtain, about which there is a great deal of bustle and fuss, and a wonderful air of seeming solemnity; but when, by any accident, the curtain happens to be open and the company see what it is, they burst into laughter."[119]

Burke does not disagree with the notion that exposing the monarchy to ridicule would weaken it, but for him this is precisely the reason for treating it solemnly—the seeming solemnity is truer and more valuable to human nature than the laughter. But Paine rejects this as an insult to human nature. "As to Mr. Burke," he writes, "he is a stickler for monarchy. . . . He has taken up a contemptible opinion of mankind, who, in their turn, are taking up the same of him. He considers them as a herd of beings that must be governed by fraud, effigy, and show; and an idol would be as good a figure of monarchy with him, as a man."[120] The revolutionaries express their higher views of man by putting aside these demeaning displays. "The patriots of France have discovered in good time that rank and dignity in society must take a new ground. The old one has fallen through. It must now take the substantial ground of character, instead of the chimerical ground of titles; and they have brought their titles to the altar, and made of them a burnt-offering to Reason," Paine writes.[121]

If all the pretensions and chimeras of the aristocracy were dropped, and if the political principles laid bare by reason were allowed to govern, Paine believed that the concerns to which Burke's correctives were directed would prove unfounded. A politics of reason, Paine argues, will largely resolve what may appear to be inherent tensions in human nature. Mistaken principles of government and the regimes built on them were the essential causes of human problems like poverty and war. If reason were unleashed, it would first demonstrate to the people that the principles are false and so the systems are illegitimate. "I do not believe that monarchy and aristocracy will continue seven years longer in any of the enlightened countries in Europe," Paine wrote in 1792. "If better reasons can be shown for them than against them, they will stand; if the contrary, they will not." [122] And once the reasons have been arrayed and the old governments brought down, new regimes better founded in reason will resolve what have always seemed intractable problems. The existence of desperate poverty in many countries, Paine writes, "lies not in any natural defect in the principles of civilization, but in preventing those principles having a universal operation; the consequence of which is, a perpetual system of war and expense, that drains the country, and defeats the general felicity of which civilization is capable." [123] He later argues:

If men will permit themselves to think as rational beings ought to think, nothing can appear more ridiculous and absurd, exclusive of all moral reflections, than to be at the expense of building navies, filling them with men, and then hauling them into the ocean, to try which can sink each other fastest. Peace, which costs nothing, is attended with infinitely more advantage, than any victory with all its expense. But this, though it best answers the purpose of nations, does not that of court governments, whose habited policy is pretence for taxation, places, and offices. . . . When all the governments of Europe shall be established on the representative system, nations will become acquainted, and the animosities and prejudices fomented by the intrigue and artifice of courts, will cease. The oppressed soldier will become a freeman; and the tortured sailor, no longer dragged through the streets like a felon, will pursue his mercantile voyage in safety.[124]

Paine believed fervently that war was grounded in the consequences of error and of intentional denial of the truth. In an age of reason, war will become a thing of the past. Once the proper political principles are put into effect, there will remain only questions of opinion and preference. These questions will range from the more minor details of the institutions of the regime (the more major ones being in fact questions of principle) to other, less significant momentary questions of policy and will. They may not be answered by direct recourse to abstract principle, but in a system designed in line with such principles, these questions of opinion will be resolved very efficiently by rational democratic deliberation and swift trial and error. No error will continue long, Paine writes.[125]

"It will sometimes happen that the minority are right and the majority are wrong," Paine writes, "but as soon as experience proves this to be the case, the minority will increase to a majority, and the error will reform itself by the tranquil operation of freedom of opinion and equality of rights."[126] As long as the broad structure and principle of the regime is properly established and reason is free to reign, the people will choose well.

Paine realizes, of course, that no system will be perfect. He acknowledges, too, that changing circumstances will require changes in the law, even when the government is founded on the right principles. He approves of the provisions in the U.S. and French constitutions allowing for amendment on these grounds. Though he believes that reasoned principles should shape the regime, the subject to which that reason is applied changes with time, so the laws must too. "It is perhaps impossible to establish anything that combines principles with opinions and practice, which the progress of circumstances, through a length of years, will not in some measure derange, or render inconsistent," Paine writes.[127] But these deficiencies will be modest and will be quickly noticed and corrected, provided that the overall system of government is established on the principles of equality and representation and that the people are left free to employ their reason to political problems without deception or oppression. When prejudice and habit are replaced with rational examination and the application of principle in politics, the age of reason, though not a perfectly untroubled paradise, will enjoy peace, prosperity, and progress.

Indeed, the progressive character of the transformation Paine envisions is crucial to his larger case. He believes that the Enlightenment project will unleash human reason long kept in chains. It will unseat the institutions and practices that have caused the most profound human problems and replace them with institutions and practices that will further empower reason over human affairs. Moreover, Paine believes that once empowered, human reason will allow for a continuing series of good judgments and choices. These positive developments, Paine believes, represent the outset of a great forward motion in history—a future that will get better and better as improvements build on one another.

This view informs Paine's openness to the possibility of improvement in political institutions, even over those he himself proposes. "The best constitution that could now be devised, consistent with the condition of the present moment, may be far short of that excellence which a few years may afford," he writes. The age of reason is only dawning.[128] And because knowledge once learned cannot be unlearned, this type of political transformation will not be reversed, but will advance with time. Guided by reason, the new free republican institutions will champion the cause of rights, justice, commerce, science, and knowledge, and these will each build upon the others. It is truly an unprecedented time. Rather than look back for guidance, Paine argues we must look to reason and, with its help, move forward.

Paine rejects Burke's charge that because he, Paine, always looks forward, his cause will always lack for concrete proof of its effectiveness. Paine, too, wants to prove his political philosophy by its effects, not just by speculation: "When it shall be said in any country in the world, my poor are happy; neither ignorance nor distress is to be found among them; my jails are empty of prisoners, my streets of beggars; the aged are not in want, the taxes are not oppressive; the rational world is my friend, because I am the friend of its happiness: when these things can be said, then may that country boast its constitution and its government."[129] His claim to be able to bring about such effects must be largely prospective, since he champions an untried innovation, while Burke speaks for a long-established constitution. Paine therefore seeks to prove by reason that what he advocates will bring about a progressive transformation of social life. But in the debate over the French Revolution, when Paine's heralding of reason was at its height, he did also point to a crucial and prominent practical success of his principles: He pointed to America.

Both during and after the American Revolution, Paine understood and explained the revolution in terms of universal principles and the march of reason and rights. It therefore served for him as the first example of an enactment of his kind of Enlightenment vision of politics and as the model for what he hoped might happen in France and beyond. And yet for Burke, the same American crisis offered a case study in a nearly opposite view of human reason and its place in public affairs.

THE MEANING OF AMERICA

Burke and Paine were in effect on the same side of the American question, the side (eventually) of independence for the colonies. But, as becomes most clear in light of their differences about reason in politics, they were moved by starkly opposed analyses of the events in question and their significance.

"The independence of America, considered merely as a separation from England, would have been a matter of but little importance, had it not been accompanied by a revolution in the principles and practice of governments," Paine asserted a decade after the American Revolution in *Rights of Man*. "She made a stand, not for herself only, but for the world, and looked beyond the advantages herself could receive."[130] For Paine, from his very earliest public writings about America until the very end of his life, the American story was a story of the vindication of Enlightenment reason and the principles it helps to uncover. As we have seen, he began his call for American independence in *Common Sense* with a case for Enlightenment-liberal equality and liberty, and Paine was always keen to make clear that the essence of the cause was a matter of principle, not mere practical exigency. "The cause of America is, in the greatest measure, the cause of all mankind," he declares.[131]

When in 1782 the Abbé Raynal, a French priest and scholar, wrote a short book on the (still ongoing) American Revolutionary War, accusing the Americans of revolting over nothing greater than a petty tax complaint, Paine responded with a heated public letter to the abbot, asserting the essentially principled character of the struggle. The American Revolution, he argued, was an utterly novel political act, unlike any seen before in history: "Here the value and quality of liberty, the nature of government, and the dignity of man were known and understood, and the attachment of the Americans to these principles produced the Revolution as a natural and unavoidable consequence. They had no particular family to set up or pull down. Nothing of personality was incorporated with their cause." At issue instead was the vindication of reason and principle.[132] "The true idea of a great nation is that which extends and promotes the principles of universal society," Paine writes.

What the Americans had begun, far from a mere petty squabble among Englishmen, would "be distinguished by opening a new system of extended civilization."[133] By their claim to authority over the colonies without the extension of voting rights and other protections, the English had opened the question of rational liberty, and the people of America were uniquely well suited to understand the question and its proper answer and to act on that understanding. Once independent, they would establish a model of republicanism that undoubtedly would attract the attention and the emulation of others and would demonstrate that the principles of enlightenment rationalism could offer solid foundations for a thriving political community.

Over the subsequent two decades, as (albeit not without obstacles and hiccups) the American experiment did indeed appear to have been well launched, Paine resorted constantly to the model of America as an example of the potential of his revolutionary principles. The Americans succeeded not for reasons specific or local to them—on the contrary, circumstances were much arrayed against them. They succeeded because they had employed the proper principles for founding a new regime. In 1792 Paine put it this way:

> If there is a country in the world where concord, according to common calculation, would be least expected, it is America. Made up as it is of people from different nations, accustomed to different forms and habits of government, speaking different languages, and more different in their modes of worship, it would appear that the union of such a people was impracticable; but by the simple operation of constructing government on the principles of society and the rights of man, every difficulty retires, and all the parts are brought into cordial unison. There the poor are not oppressed, the rich are not privileged. Industry is not mortified by the splendid extravagance of a court rioting at its expense. Their taxes are few, because their government is just: and as there is nothing to render them wretched, there is nothing to engender riots and tumults.[134]

America is the very thing that Burke insists is lacking in Paine's argument: concrete proof in the life of a real community that Paine's principles of government can work in practice. This evidence allows him to turn the tables and accuse Burke of ignoring actual circumstances in favor of abstract worries. With characteristic flourish, Paine argues in *Rights of Man* that "a metaphysical man, like Mr. Burke, would have tortured his invention to discover how [the Americans] could be governed. He would have supposed that some must be managed by fraud, others by force, and all by some contrivance; that genius must be hired to impose upon ignorance, and show and parade to fascinate the vulgar."[135] Instead of all this sound and fury, Paine argues, the Americans chose the simplicity of reason and Enlightenment liberal principles and have shown by their success that nothing more is needed and that other regimes, founded on other principles, are needlessly oppressive and unjust. "One of the great advantages of the American Revolution has been that it led to a discovery of the principles, and laid open the imposition, of governments. All the revolutions till then had been worked within the atmosphere of a court, and never on the great floor of a nation." The American Revolution was a practical experiment in the new science of government and one that proved the efficacy of its principles and its understanding of human reason in politics.[136]

But Edmund Burke drew more or less the opposite lesson from the story of American independence. He was deeply involved in the British debate over America and was quite possibly the most prominent and vocal of the friends of America in Parliament. But Burke never attributes a philosophical character to the views and actions of the Americans. Not once in his public or known private writings on the subject does he refer to the events in America as a revolution, referring always to the American crisis, the American war, or even describing the events as a civil war. In his view, it was the English, not the Americans, who had broken with prescription in the name of merely speculative theoretical claims about government by imposing an unprecedented regime of taxation and limits on commerce in America on the premise that Parliament had an unlimited authority to govern colonial affairs directly.

The Americans, in his view, merely sought to continue and preserve the traditions of the English constitution and the privileges they had always enjoyed. Burke does worry that the example of the Americans so ably pursuing their independence and seemingly suffering so little for it might move others around the world to attempt it, but he does not attribute the appeal of their example to any philosophical underpinnings of their cause, and he blames only the British for provoking it.[137] The Americans were defending their long-standing implicit rights and the nature of their past relationship with London—they wanted continuity, and Parliament would not allow it. Burke in effect reads the second half of the Declaration of Independence (a document he surely knew but scrupulously avoids mentioning) and not the first, while Paine does the opposite.

In fact, Burke's case against the actions of the British government involved some of his clearest and most adamant defenses of prescription against abstract reason, all directed against the English, not the Americans. The move to tax the colonies for revenue rather than merely to control Britain's international trade (that is, the move from customs and tariffs to internal taxation of consumption) was utterly unprecedented, and it was this novelty, not the cost of the tax, that alarmed the Americans and moved them to resist, he argued. "Whatever the right might have been, this mode of using it was absolutely new in policy and practice."[138]

The move was defended by Lord North's administration on the grounds that Parliament has every right to tax the colonies in any way it wished. The principles of sovereignty and the charters of the colonies permitted it. Burke never denied this point; he only argued that politics must take account of more than abstract principles. "The question with me is not whether you have a right to render your people miserable," Burke told the Parliament, "but whether it is not in your interest to make them happy. It is not what a lawyer tells me I may do; but what humanity, reason, and justice tell me I ought to do."[139] The Americans had lived for many years essentially as Englishmen, with the apparatus of self-rule and a developed sense of independence. When Parliament decided, without involving them in consultation, to alter the scheme of their taxation, it rudely reminded them of the limits of their independence, in what amounted to a needless provocation. "People must be governed in a manner agreeable to their temper and disposition," Burke writes, "and men of free character and spirit must be ruled with at least some condescension to this spirit and this character."[140] Rather than break so harshly with the grain of American sentiments, Parliament could instead have increased the levies on trade and thereby improved its revenue without disturbing the Americans. Burke insisted they would have stood for it, because they were used to it. "Men do bear the inevitable constitution of their original nature with all its infirmities," he argued. "The act of navigation [of 1660] attended the colonies from their infancy, grew with their growth, and strengthened with their strength. They were confirmed in obedience to it even more by usage than by law."[141]

Being right in principle was no excuse for being wrong in practice, and Burke warned Parliament that forgetting this truth would carry heavy costs, because it would move the Americans to question their entire relationship with London. Precisely because he did not believe the Americans were making a case against prescription or raising genuine threats to the regime (as he believed did occur in France in the following decade), Burke thought it terribly unwise for the English to break with the patterns of their past practices.[142]

Again and again in 1775 and early 1776, Burke implored the Commons to pay attention to "the true nature and the peculiar circumstances" of the conflict, because, he argued, "whether we will or not, we must govern America according to that nature, and to those circumstances; and not according to our own imaginations; not according to abstract ideas of right; by no means according to mere general theories of government, the resort to which appears to me, in our present situation, no better than arrant trifling."[143] In time, this line of argument caused Burke to conclude that the Americans should be allowed to go their separate way, as Parliament had pushed too hard against the grain of the American character and the English constitution, and left no hope of reconciliation. Human affections, he argued on this front as on others, were the key to any functional society, and once disaffection takes hold, social and political bonds have little hope of surviving.

Burke said and wrote remarkably little about America after the end of the war in 1783. Unlike Paine, he did not resort to the American crisis for an example in later political struggles. His only extended reference to it was in a passage of the *Appeal from the New to the Old Whigs* in 1791. In this discussion, he essentially restates his case against the government's policy in the American crisis and his belief (affirmed, he says, by conversations with Benjamin Franklin in London) that the Americans did not want independence or pursue affirmation of philosophical principles, but rather reacted understandably to an unwise provocation. The Americans stood at that time "in the same relation to England as England did to King James the Second in 1688," Burke writes.[144]

For both Burke and Paine, the American crisis served as proof of their very different understandings of reason and political change. Paine's case for American independence is a case for a politics of

Enlightenment reason and rational principle. Burke's case for American independence is a case for prudence and prescription. In championing opposing sides of the question of the French Revolution a decade later, each man made almost exactly the same case he had argued about America. Their agreement over America reflected quite different understandings of events there, while their disagreement over France reflected a general agreement over what the French revolutionaries were up to. In both cases, Burke and Paine disagreed profoundly about human nature, political change, and the proper relation of reason and politics.

DEBATING REASON

Throughout his public and private writings on a range of political subjects over several decades, Thomas Paine offers an extensive and determined case for the supremacy of unaided, individual human reason as understood by Enlightenment liberalism over habit and tradition. With this assertion comes the need to subject every political institution, practice, question, and ideal to the rational inspection of every individual. Because society and politics answer to rational and universal principles, they must be answerable to the reason of one and all, he argues.

Throughout his own many political writings, speeches, and letters in the same period, Edmund Burke offers vigorous objections to this mode of thinking about politics. These objections are grounded in his very different view of human nature, political life, and the limits of reason. Burke offers a case for political action guided by prescription and aimed at gradual change in response to particular felt needs. This approach to politics makes up for limited knowledge and the permanent limits of reason through a reliance on past precedents and an aggregation of individual views in (inevitably partisan) politics.

This dispute between universal principles and historical precedents—between a politics of explicit knowledge and a politics of implicit knowledge—cuts to the core of the debate that still defines our politics.

To this day, progressive voices argue that our political system must empower expertise to directly address social and political problems with technical prowess. And today's conservatives argue that we must empower institutions (like families, churches, and markets) that channel the implicit knowledge of many individuals and generations and that have passed some test of time and contain in their very forms more wisdom than any person could possess. This dispute, which Burke and Paine made so explicit, is another version of the disagreement about whether political thought must consider abstract, solitary, rational individuals or must take up particular human societies in their social and historical settings. The question forms a unifying thread throughout the Burke-Paine debate. As they argue about reason, Burke and Paine disagree about the given past and its relation to the present—about whether the circumstances that greet us when we enter the world can legitimately make demands on the way we think about politics.

These disagreements combine into a deep difference over the nature of political change and improvement. Their differing assessments of the nature of events in America masks this dispute somewhat, but as the age of revolutions approached its climax in France, Burke's and Paine's differences rose swiftly to the surface and shaped a heated public debate between them. The disagreement over reason and prescription is at its core an argument about the theoretical or conceptual foundations of politics. But Burke's and Paine's two positions have very practical consequences when applied to political change. From reason and prescription, and from the views of human nature and society on which they draw, Paine and Burke arrive at the arguments for which they are best known: the arguments for revolution and reform.

SIX

REVOLUTION AND REFORM

URKE AND PAINE WERE KEENLY AWARE THAT POLITICAL ideas pointed to political action. Both men were writers and thinkers, but both were also deeply involved in political affairs at a time when the links between ideas and action were unusually clear. Their political ideas therefore point toward two views of political action and change—with Burke drawing on his vision of prescription to make the case for slow, incremental reform and Paine building on his case for a rational politics to argue that only a wholly new beginning from first principles can redeem an illegitimate government.

These views were evident in Burke's and Paine's writings from their earliest political engagements and follow plainly, as we have seen, from their reflections on society and man. But they came to the fore most forcefully in the period of the French Revolution, when the question of just how the means and the ends of political change were related became suddenly urgent and prominent. Burke and Paine were better prepared than most of their contemporaries to take up these questions, and the passion and intensity with which they did so have ever since defined their legacies.

Paine's Revolution for Justice

Thomas Paine was a self-declared and unabashed revolutionary. "To have a share in two revolutions is living to some purpose," he proudly wrote to George Washington.[1] That purpose, from Paine's earliest political exploits to the end of his life, was the cause of justice, pursued by an application of reason and principle to government. And as we have seen, Paine believed that such an application must begin from the beginning, so that a profoundly corrupt or broken regime needs to be replaced rather than mended.

Again and again, he expresses disgust with the excuses illegitimate governments make for their mistreatment of their people in an effort to hold on to power. "As time obliterated the history of their beginning," he writes of the despots who founded every old nation, "their successors assumed new appearances, to cut off the entail of their disgrace, but their principles and objects remained the same."[2] It is simply not possible to fix discrete problems in regimes of this sort, because the principle of despotism has soaked through into every corner and crevice. "When despotism has established itself for ages in a country, as in France," Paine writes, "the original hereditary despotism resident in the person of the king divides and sub-divides itself into a thousand shapes and forms, till at last the whole of it is acted by deputation."[3]

Nothing short of a total remedy can address such a profound corruption of government. To speak of revolution, therefore, is for Paine to speak of overthrow, of the lifting up of the burden of generations of misrule and iniquity, leaving only the society itself, essentially in its natural state.

Paine was under no illusion that such a general revolution would be easy; nor did he take lightly the risks and problems it entailed. "Mischief is more easily begun than ended," he writes, and revolutions will always carry behind them a train of mischief.[4] He insists therefore that he is not enamored of revolutions for their own sake. As a general matter, he writes, "it is better to obey a bad law, making use at the same time of every argument to show its errors and procure its repeal, than forcibly to violate it."[5] Only when the regime is so fundamentally corrupt as to make the very idea of a good law impossible is more extreme action required. Paine is careful to emphasize this caveat because he wants to be perfectly clear that a government established on the proper principles, not the revolution required to get to such a government, is the goal of his efforts: "It is in the first place necessary that we distinguish between the means made use of to overthrow despotism in order to prepare the way for the establishment of liberty and the means to be used after the despotism is overthrown."[6]

The aim of the revolution is to establish a new order, not a permanent revolutionary state, and only the promise of that new order, together with the abuses of the old one, justifies the revolution. It is an insurrection that aims at the establishment of some stable political arrangement. "The authority of the present Assembly is different from what the authority of future Assemblies will be," Paine writes of the French parliament in the early stages of the revolution. "The authority of the present one is to form a constitution; the authority of future assemblies will be to legislate according to the principles and forms prescribed in that constitution; and if experience should hereafter show that alterations, amendments, or additions are necessary, the constitution will point out the mode by which such things shall be done, and not leave it to the discretionary power of the future government."[7]

But for all these caveats, the mandate Paine describes for revolution is exceptionally broad because he faults the very idea of "monarchical and hereditary government," and not just the particular abuses of particular regimes, for leaving man in a wretched condition.[8] In some writings (particularly in the first part of *Rights of Man*, written while some of the French revolutionaries, including Paine's friend the Marquis de Lafayette, were still trying to retain some symbolic role for the king in the new regime, and therefore written with some caution) Paine reluctantly acknowledges the right of the people to choose a monarch. But by the height of the French Revolution, and very clearly by the second part of *Rights of Man*, which was written a little over a year after the first, he declares himself an uncompromising republican. "All hereditary government is in its nature tyranny," Paine writes, and passionately attacks the very notion of monarchy and hereditary aristocracy.[9]

When legitimate governments are established around the world, revolutions should be scarce and citizens should seek to redress grievances by persuasion and legislation. But as long as that is not the case (which it was not in his time in any country except America and revolutionary France, Paine believed), the only remedy at hand was to begin again. The old European regimes were simply no longer adequate in the era of modern knowledge about politics. "Whether the forms and maxims of Governments which are still in practice were adapted to the condition of the world at the period they were established is not in this case the question," Paine writes. "The older they are, the less correspondence can they have with the present state of things. Time, and change of circumstances and opinions, have the same progressive effect in rendering modes of Government obsolete as they have upon customs and manners."[10] The advance of knowledge and civilization, themselves aided by the advance of modern reason and science, make the inadequacy and illegitimacy of old regimes increasingly acute, and the illegitimacy itself can only be addressed by total revolution.

In practice, therefore, Paine argues that the moment requires a complete and utterly new political beginning. People in every nation must throw off the old governments that burden them and must begin again from their social foundations, this time constructing political institutions in accord with the principles of equality, choice, and representation made evident by reason. Paine's idea of revolution is thus less a remedy to a particular set of social and political grievances and more a response to the absence of proper political foundations. He wants to see a return to the natural society that he believes precedes the formation of government and, from that point, the construction of entirely new institutions and practices, unconnected to any that have existed in the old regime. This requires the design and implementation of thoroughly novel social and political forms. Continuity with the old regimes would itself be proof of the inadequacy of reform. A constitution, in order to work well, "must be a novelty, and that which is not a novelty must be defective," Paine writes.[11] Nothing of the prior regime should be retained, and it makes very little sense to look at even more ancient models, like those of Greece and Rome, in establishing a new regime. "Mankind have lived to very little purpose if, at this period of the world, they must go two or three thousand years back for lessons and examples."[12] Instead, we must look not to history but to our new understanding of nature and of the principles of justice and society and begin nothing less than a rebirth.

Clearly, given both his enthusiasm for revolution and his caveats regarding the limited circumstances under which it could be called for, Paine believed that what matters most is what the revolution builds, not what it tears down, and he was careful to make this point explicit too. "In contemplating revolutions," he notes in *Rights of Man*, "it is easy to perceive that they may arise from two distinct causes; the one, to avoid or get rid of some great calamity; the other, to obtain some great and positive good." He continues:

> In those which proceed from the former cause, the temper becomes incensed and soured; and the redress, obtained by danger, is too often sullied by revenge. But in those which proceed from the latter, the heart, rather animated than agitated, enters serenely upon the subject. Reason and discussion, persuasion and conviction, become the weapons in the contest, and it is only when those are attempted to be suppressed that recourse is had to violence. When men unite in agreeing that a thing is good could it be obtained, such for instance as relief from a burden of taxes and the extinction of corruption, the object is more than half accomplished. What they approve as the end, they will promote in the means.[13]

Yet even in this very passage, Paine betrays the difficulty of distinguishing destruction and construction in his view of the world. The positive goods he calls upon as examples are "relief" from burdensome taxes and "the extinction" of corruption—both of which are in fact negative goods. Because he believes a legitimate government can fall into line with the rational and natural order of things, he considers injustice a kind of imposition. Therefore, the enactment of justice is the removal of a burden; the good is the elimination of the bad. For this reason, Paine's revolutionary writing is in fact almost entirely devoted to the enterprise of bringing down despots and tyrants. Revolution is the elimination of impositions and burdens, which in practice requires the total elimination of the governments responsible for them.

Paine believes that since governing is essentially intellectual work, people have the ability to build a proper government from scratch provided they respect the principles of individual equality and liberty. But the necessary prior task of dismantling a despotic regime is a much more difficult challenge that requires immense political exertion, courage, and commitment. He sees himself above all called to contribute to meeting this challenge, an effort that requires the best and the brightest in an oppressed society—"all that extent of capacity which never fails to appear in revolutions"—to help the people see their way to understanding the failings of their government and to argue for a return to beginnings for the construction of an alternative.[14]

Paine believed his particular talent for political argument was especially well suited to the nature of the challenge, which required a kind of awakening. The forms and habits of the old regime can easily disguise its fundamental injustice from the people, since people after all tend to love their country and its symbols and forms and so will bear a lot of pain out of habit. But, Paine writes, "it is, however, curious to observe how soon this spell can be dissolved. A single expression, boldly conceived and uttered, will sometimes put a whole company into their proper feelings: and whole nations are acted on in the same manner."[15]

Properly disillusioned and then instructed in the proper principles of government, every nation has the capacity to liberate itself through revolution and replace a decrepit despotism with a free regime. It is in this sense that Paine famously assures his fellow Americans in 1776 that they can choose to effectively to begin the world anew.[16] We have it in our power to shake loose of old presumptions, begin from the correct first principles, and so construct a proper government.

Put this way, Paine's revolutionary ethic turns out to be (in its means, as well as its ends) an applied form of his theory of political life. He seeks to institute change by starting over from scratch, just as he seeks to assess political arrangements by looking back to first origins. He wants to take the method of reasoning about politics employed by Enlightenment liberalism and turn it into a method of acting on politics.

Because his idea of revolution is grounded in principle in this way and involves a kind of liberation of man's nature from the oppression of false ideas and tyrannical government, Paine believes that its progress will be essentially unstoppable once the obstacles of the old regimes are properly removed. "Government founded on a moral theory, on a system of universal peace, on the indefeasible hereditary Rights of Man, is now revolving from west to east by a stronger impulse than the government of the sword revolved from east to west," he writes. "It interests not particular individuals, but nations in its progress, and promises a new era to the human race."[17] This is a revolution concerned not with the replacement of one leader with another. It is moved not by hatred of one king or preference for another, but by the desire for justice enabled by a search for the truth.

Even as things turned sour in France and Paine found himself imprisoned for nearly a year by the revolutionary regime for associating with insufficiently radical factions, he continued to argue that the proper principles were there to be applied, and that any failures of the revolution were merely failures to apply them fully and properly. "All the disorders that have arisen in France during the progress of the revolution have had their origin not in the principle of equal rights, but in the violation of that principle," he wrote in 1795.[18] Nine years later, having seen the collapse of his great dream and the rise of Napoleon, Paine told a group of French-speaking inhabitants of Louisiana: "You see what mischief ensued in France by the possession of power before they understood principles. They earned liberty in words, but not in fact. The writer of this was in France through the whole of the Revolution, and knows the truth of what he speaks; for after endeavoring to give it principle, he had nearly fallen victim to its rage."[19] To the extent the revolution did not fully succeed, Paine concludes, it was because it was incomplete, not, as Burke might suggest, because it sought a complete enactment of an inadequate and excessively speculative vision.

This view makes Paine a thoroughgoing revolutionary, well before the idea of the revolutionary as a political character or type had come into vogue. Believing that political change must be total and uncompromising, he is excited by the prospect of overthrowing the existing order so that a new and more rational one may sprout in its place. Paine was exceptionally frank about his advocacy for total revolution, especially once he was ensconced in France. He saw all resistance to a complete new beginning as an expression of corruption or of some invidious private motive and believed that during the exceptional period of the revolution, resistance and opposition must be squashed for the good of the cause.

It is important to understand how far beyond the liberalism of most English Whigs Paine went by espousing these views. By rejecting monarchy in principle, he allied himself with the fringe of the English radicals of the day, but even most of those radicals never went as far as to suggest the abolition of the monarchy in Britain itself. For Paine, despotism was the result of a failure to fully apply the principles of liberty in practice, and so the liberal principles that had emerged from the Whig worldview necessitated an unbending republicanism. It was in this context that in his final letter to Burke, on January 17, 1790, Paine wrote of the zeal of the revolutionaries and their determination to destroy themselves or their country rather than abandon their revolutionary plan.[20]

It is easy to see why Paine was excited. The events he described, in the opening months of the French Revolution, perfectly embodied his view of how meaningful political change must occur and how a regime properly grounded in Enlightenment rationalism ought to replace an ancient monarchy. The very same events, however, also gave perfect expression to his correspondent's worst fears and deepest worries. Burke's and Paine's sharp differences were never clearer than at the outset of the revolution in France.

BURKE'S COUNTERREVOLUTIONARY REFORM

"There was a time when it was impossible to make Mr. Burke believe there would be any revolution in France," Paine explains in *Rights of Man*. He was referring to his discussions with Burke just a year before the revolution broke out.[21] Total revolution in the very heart of Europe seemed to Burke too radical a prospect to believe. And for that very reason, when the revolution did come, Burke could hardly contain his worry about its consequences. The revolution embodied every concern Burke had spent his political life trying to address. It was an outbreak of philosophically inspired radicalism driven by the very theories of human nature and politics Burke had criticized for decades, it sought to cut off a society's links to its past, and it proceeded by acts of mob violence and extremism.

Not surprisingly, therefore, Burke's response, from the moment he became aware of the scale of the violence in Paris until the end of his life about seven years later, was an intense and fiery opposition to developments in France. He had an unswerving dedication to opening the eyes of his countrymen to what he took to be a profound and unprecedented peril. The French regime, Burke writes, "is not a new power of an old kind. It is a new power of a new species."[22] Nothing like it had been seen before on the European scene, but it expressed in real-world form the dangers that had for some time been building in the intellectual world. "Never before this time was a set of literary men converted into a gang of robbers and assassins; never before did a den of bravoes and banditti assume the garb and tone of an academy of philosophers," Burke writes in one characteristic flourish of disconcertion.[23]

In the American crisis, which he never called a revolution, Burke believed the colonies rebelled against British misrule. But the French were rebelling, he thought, out of zeal for a new theory of man and society and in the process were overturning far more than political structures. In this sense, it was precisely because the revolution was about pursuing a new order, rather than just rejecting a particular policy or ruler, that Burke thought it went too far. Paine's justification was identical to Burke's indictment. "It is not a revolution in government," Burke writes. "It is not the victory of party over party. It is a destruction and decomposition of the whole society; which never can be made of right by any faction, however powerful, nor without terrible consequences to all about it, both in the act and in the example." [24]

France after its revolution, according to Burke, was not so much a nation with a different government as a party in an intellectual dispute that spanned borders and had ambitions to reach into every European state. "My ideas and my principles led me in this contest to encounter France not as a state but as a faction," Burke writes in the *Letters on a Regicide Peace*.[25] "It is a war between the partisans of the ancient, civil, moral, and political order of Europe against a sect of fanatical and ambitious atheists which means to change them all. It is not France extending a foreign empire over other nations: it is a sect aiming at universal empire, and beginning with the conquest of France." [26]

And Burke's vehement opposition was clearly motivated by the concern that the revolutionary sect's next conquest would be Britain and indeed that England's own political radicals were avidly working to set the scene for a new English revolution to follow the French. He was worried that the agitations of such radicals in Britain would give the people, as well as foreigners, the impression that the nation as a whole was about to rebel. And in the *Reflections*, he worked to dispel this notion while reminding his countrymen of the principles of their regime and making the case against revolution as a mode of political change.[27]

Burke did not deny that the need for serious political change sometimes arose; nor did he deny that the old regime in France had serious faults (though he surely did play these down at times).[28] "I am no stranger to the faults and defects of the subverted government of France," he writes, "and I think I am not inclined by nature or policy to make a panegyric upon anything which is a just and natural object of censure. But the question is not now of the vices of that monarchy, but of its existence. Is it then true, that the French government was such as to be incapable or undeserving of reform; so that it was of absolute necessity that the whole fabric should be at once pulled down, and the area cleared for the erection of a theoretic, experimental edifice in its place?"[29] Burke did not object to the desire for political change, but objected to throwing out the entire regime, and with it, he believed, the political tradition of France, to realize such change.

Some of the particular policies of the new regime could well improve the lot of the people in the short run, he notes, as "they who destroy every thing certainly will remove some grievance" and "they who make every thing new, have a chance that they may establish something beneficial." But to excuse the violence and radicalism of the revolution by pointing to some particular benefit of it, a person would have to prove that the benefit could not have been achieved through less radical reform, and this, Burke argued, was simply false. And more important, the harm done by the means and ends of the revolution was far greater than these modest benefits. "The improvements of the national assembly are superficial; their errors, fundamental."[30] The old regime may have been barbaric, Burke writes, but the violent revolution has merely unleashed on the world another no less barbaric regime.[31]

Surely these are not the only options. "Have these gentlemen never heard, in the whole circle of the worlds of theory and practice, of anything between the despotism of the monarch and the despotism of the multitude?" he asks.[32] "It is with them a war or a revolution, or it is nothing."[33] Burke argues that the failure to see or pursue a middle ground is not an oversight but a prominent feature of the radical worldview of the revolutionaries: "Their despair of curing common distempers by regular methods, arises not only from defect of comprehension, but, I fear, from some malignity of disposition."[34]

The overthrow of a government is of course not unprecedented, even in the history of Britain. But for the British as for most civilized nations, Burke claims, revolution has been considered justifiable only as a matter of absolutely unavoidable necessity. "Revolution will be the very last resource of the thinking and the good."[35] The French, however, have made it a rule. "Their idea of their powers is always taken at the utmost stretch of legislative competency, and their examples for common cases from the exceptions of the most urgent necessity."[36] This kind of extremism is very poorly suited to political life. "He that sets his house on fire because his fingers are frostbitten can never be a fit instructor in the method of providing our habitations with a cheerful and salutary warmth," Burke writes.[37]

Moreover, necessary revolutions in Britain have generally been undertaken to return the constitution to some balance. They have not sought to completely replace the system of government. Such total revolution, Burke argues, cannot be justified even by necessity, because its consequences are so dire and grave that there must always be a better option. By cutting off political life from all prescription and instituting Enlightenment radicalism as a kind of state religion, the revolution goes beyond the bounds of any necessity and puts in place an incorrigible system—a government so riddled with fundamental problems it can never be made good.[38]

Why should the revolutionary regime be so thoroughly (and permanently) unsalvageable? Burke sees the regime as the instantiation of the radical views of nature, choice, and Enlightenment reason described thus far, and he believes that when all these are combined and put into action, the result is an unmitigated political disaster, and one that closes off the path to its own improvement.

To begin with, the revolution undoes checks and incentives for moderation and sets wild spirits loose. Its leaders treat France like a conquered country, erasing all vestiges of prior identity and strength.[39] They turn the people against one another to weaken every part of society except the new government and seek in particular "to subvert the whole frame and order of the best constructed states by corrupting the common people with the spoil of the superior classes."[40] They turn the talents of the nation's best and brightest against the wealth of its great families.[41] All of this creates new habits of action and thought that powerfully undermine all political order. These habits began before the revolution itself and were essential to it. "A silent revolution in the moral world preceded the political, and prepared it."[42] And once connected with the spectacles of an actual revolution, these habits create a hunger for radical political action—a hunger that leaves people dissatisfied with normal life and thus disinclined to seek stability. "A cheap, bloodless reformation, a guiltless liberty, appear flat and vapid to their taste. There must be a great change of scene; there must be a magnificent stage effect; there must be a grand spectacle to rouse the imagination."[43]

Once roused, Burke argues, the imagination will remain so and will seek a target for further spectacles and stage effects. Burke fears the unleashing of political zealotry and fanaticism. A regime built on such theories with a public moved to fanaticism, he writes, will quickly become a "tyranny of a licentious, ferocious, and savage multitude, without laws, manners, or morals, and which so far from respecting the general sense of mankind, insolently endeavors to alter all the principles and opinions which have hitherto guided and contained the world, and to force them into a conformity to their views and actions."[44]

Setting loose these forces, Burke argues, not only undermines social stability, but also sets the people and the state on a collision course, because the public will soon enough grow tired of its new regime and its unavoidable restrictions on individual liberty just as it was taught to grow tired of the old regime. And the state is certain to overwhelm the populace in such a clash. A revolution driven by a faith in choice and individualism will in time therefore yield a regime that crushes choice and individualism. The political ideas behind the revolution encourage disloyalty to one's country in favor of Enlightenment principles. But when that disloyalty extends to the new regime itself, the regime will have far fewer resources than its predecessor to call upon in exerting its authority, since it will have crushed the people's natural calm. Having leveled society, the regime will have only force at its disposal and will find itself compelled to crush dissent. "Kings will be tyrants from policy when subjects are rebels from principle," Burke writes.[45] And in that crisis, Burke predicts, the only recourse will be to a military regime and, with it, the end of all the lovely talk about the rights of man. In the *Reflections*, Burke predicts the rise of a charismatic general to power in such a crisis—a prediction that eerily prefigures the coming of Napoleon.[46]

Indeed, it is precisely because the new regime is built upon a rational plan that it has the potential to wield immense and previously inconceivable power and overrun the individual. "France differs essentially from all those Governments which are formed without system, which exist by habit, and which are confused with the multitude, and with the complexity of their pursuits," Burke writes.

> It is systematic; it is simple in its principle; it has unity and consistency in perfection. In that country entirely to cut off a branch of commerce, to extinguish a manufacture, to destroy the circulation of money, to violate credit, to suspend the course of agriculture, even to burn a city, or to lay waste a province of their own, does not cost them a moment's anxiety. To them, the will, the wish, the want, the liberty, the toil, the blood of individuals is as nothing. Individuality is left out of their scheme of Government. The state is all in all.[47]

Ironically, the regime built explicitly upon the rights of man stands to trample those rights more effectively than any ancient despotism, Burke believes. The revolutionaries have mistaken the external signs of despotism (like nobles and priests) for the causes of it and so, as often happens in history, have fought the wrong enemy and may turn out to embody the very evil they seek to combat. "It is thus with all those, who, attending only to the shell and husk of history, think they are waging war with intolerance, pride, and cruelty, whilst, under color of abhorring the ill principles of antiquated parties, they are authorizing and feeding the same odious vices in different factions, and perhaps in worse."[48]

Here again, Burke argues that the effort to rationalize politics, to eliminate those sentimental attachments and seemingly vestigial organs, will end up liberating not reason and justice but the passion for power. His difference with Paine regarding human nature leads to very different expectations of the age of revolutions. Political ideas have consequences, Burke writes, and these should be understood in light of both the permanent limitations of human nature and the successes and the failures of the past. Revolution, he argues, is an inappropriate means of political change because it is not well suited for capitalizing on the implicit lessons of the past or for leaving room for the permanent imperfection of all human undertakings. The challenges of governing are simply too subtle and complex to allow for such blunt force.

The French revolutionaries, as he understood them, simply ignored this complexity. "An ignorant man, who is not fool enough to meddle with his clock, is however sufficiently confident to think he can safely take to pieces, and put together at his pleasure, a moral machine of another guise, importance and complexity, composed of far other wheels, and springs, and balances, and counteracting and co-operating powers," Burke writes. "Men little think how immorally they act in rashly meddling with what they do not understand. Their delusive good intention is no sort of excuse for their presumption."[49]

The pleasure that the revolutionaries seemed to take in such destruction of long-standing arrangements only further confirms Burke in his worries. "It is a sour, malignant, envious disposition, without taste for the reality, or for any image or representation of virtue, that sees with joy the unmerited fall of what had long flourished in splendor and in honor," he writes. "I do not like to see any thing destroyed; any void produced in society; any ruin on the face of the land."[50] He believes that this hunger for ruin is a function of a lack of appreciation for the given world. "Ingratitude is indeed their four cardinal virtues compacted and amalgamated into one," he writes in the *Letter to a Noble Lord*.[51]

Thus again, Burke's deepest objections to the revolutionaries and their approach to political change have to do with their attitudes about the past and their relation to it—their assertion that political change must overcome the past, rather than build on it. Burke argues that this view, together with the closely related assumptions of the revolutionaries regarding nature, choice, and reason, leads to a profoundly misguided approach to political action and political change. What's more, the resulting revolutionary regime not only stands to do terrible damage to society, but would also close off the paths to correcting its own mistakes.

For all these reasons, Burke considers it absolutely crucial to resist the revolution, both by opposing its extension and growth in France and, more importantly, by preventing its importation into Britain. If it is not firmly resisted at the outset and is allowed to seep into the political bloodstream of the British, its effects could be irreversible, he worries. In a famous passage at the conclusion of the *Thoughts on French Affairs*, Burke highlights the difficulty and the danger that counterrevolutionaries since his day have always faced: "If a great change is to be made in human affairs, the minds of men will be fitted to it, the general opinions and feelings will draw that way. Every fear, every hope, will forward it; and then they, who persist in opposing the mighty current of human affairs, will appear rather to resist the decrees of Providence itself, than the mere designs of men. They will not be resolute and firm, but perverse and obstinate."[52] Burke clearly worries that the intellectual and almost spiritual appeal of the revolution's call for justice will overwhelm its great practical deficiencies in the minds of the people and that once the revolution has taken firm root, it will be essentially impossible to undo its effects or to remind the people of what it has cost.

He is alert, as well, to the danger of appearing to be merely opposed to change—of seeming to defend the status quo for no other reason than that it is the way things are. On the contrary, Burke argues, he is not defending the status quo but is rather defending an effective means of reform against an ineffective one that threatens to cut society off from the possibility of real improvement.

In light of his vehement opposition to the French Revolution, we are today too easily inclined to dismiss this assertion and to see Burke as merely a defender of the established order. But the facts of his career and the nature of his case against the revolution plainly argue otherwise. Burke was a leader in almost every reform effort undertaken in Parliament during his three decades in elected office. He sought (often but not always successfully) to reform the nation's finances, trade, and restrictions on Catholics and dissenters. He sought to moderate the excesses (especially the excessive punishments) of the criminal law, to rein in the East India Company, and to bring the gradual end of the slave trade. And he effectively backed the American Revolution. But he always approached the reform of existing institutions from a regard for their pedigree and their worth, seeking to build on what worked to correct what did not, rather than to overturn the foundations of the regime and begin again.

In this sense, Burke's opposition to the French Revolution, especially as laid out in the *Reflections*, involves a contrast between two modes of political change, rather than between two types of regime or views of politics. The contrast Burke draws in the *Reflections* between France and Britain is really a contrast between revolution and reform. The French, he argues, have cut themselves off from their glorious traditions and so, in an effort to correct the faults of their former regime, have introduced worse faults than anyone could have imagined. Their parliament is filled with inexperienced miscreants, their economy in shambles, their population declining, their bureaucracy inept, their laws ill-formed, their credit gone, their money worthless, their coffers empty, their king a slave, their judges fools, and their army falling apart. Meanwhile, England in his telling is basking in the glorious warmth of its old and revered constitution—safe, sound, free, orderly, wealthy, and comfortably munching on crumpets.

There is no question, as Thomas Paine frequently seeks to show, that Burke is exaggerating in both accounts. The details of his descriptions of the revolutionary regime and the events surrounding its emergence are often inaccurate, and his description of the prior two centuries of English history (when his countrymen had, after all, beheaded one king and deposed another) is, to put it mildly, sanitized to make a point.

The point is not that whatever exists must be good, but that reform must proceed gradually for practical, political, social, and moral reasons. In one especially striking passage of the *Reflections*, Burke works through a long discussion of the achievements and glories of the French throughout the centuries of the Bourbon monarchy. He wonders how the beneficiaries of it all, even in light of the many abuses and other faults of the later years of the regime, could have determined that nothing but total revolution could improve it: "I do not recognize, in this view of things, the despotism of Turkey. Nor do I discern the character of a government, that has been, on the whole, so oppressive, or so corrupt, or so negligent, as to be utterly unfit *for all reformation.* I must think such a government well deserved to have its excellencies heightened; its faults corrected; and its capacities improved into a British constitution."[53]

When he speaks of the British constitution in this context, Burke means the model of slowly enlarged precedent, not the model of the Lords and the Commons in particular. Reformers should build on their national traditions.

The fundamental insight of his positive case for reform is that a statesman ought to begin from gratitude for what works in his society, rather than from outrage at what does not work. He must begin from a sense of what he has and what is worth preserving and from there build toward what he wants and what is worth achieving. But without question, change is not only inevitable but desirable. And without developing an effective means of change, a nation "might even risk the loss of that part of the constitution which it wished the most religiously to preserve."[54]

This difficult task of preservative improvement is, to Burke's mind, the most demanding and most important of the challenges of political life:

> When the useful parts of an old establishment are kept, and what is superadded is to be fitted to what is retained, a vigorous mind, steady persevering attention, various powers of comparison and combination, and the resources of an understanding fruitful in expedients are to be exercised; they are to be exercised in a continued conflict with the combined force of opposite vices; with the obsti-

nacy that rejects all improvement, and the levity that is fatigued and disgusted with every thing of which it is in possession.[55]

Thus, as he famously put it, "a disposition to preserve, and an ability to improve, taken together, would be my standard of a statesman."[56] And a key to that disposition is that what Burke considers reform must be addressed to specific, discrete problems. "The change is to be confined to the peccant part only; to the part which produced the necessary deviation."[57] Rather than see the whole state as a problem, he seeks to discern the good from the bad in it. This inclination speaks to his understanding of the character of regimes in general. As we have seen, Burke believes governments exist for very broad reasons, not to advance one particular set of views or rights, but to account for the general welfare of the people and to serve the needs of a complicated society. Rather than see the whole of the system as one success or one failure, he thus sees it as a patchwork of accumulated institutions that may require reform now and then as difficulties present themselves, but that for the most part ought to be left to function.

Unlike the planned regime of the revolutionaries, "the States of the Christian World have grown up to their present magnitude in a great length of time, and by a great variety of accidents. They have been improved to what we see them with greater or less degrees of felicity and skill. Not one of them has been formed upon a regular plan or with any unity of design," Burke writes in the *Letters on a Regicide Peace*.[58] When something goes awry in this kind of complex organism, the treatment required is more like medicine than engineering: a process of healing that seeks to preserve by correcting.

There is a real art to knowing just how to pull off such a balancing act. And when it is done well, a timely and gradual reform can avert public disaffection and thus avert more disruptive or wholesale changes. "Early reformations are amicable arrangements with a friend in power; late reformations are made under a state of inflammation. In that state of things the people behold in government nothing that is respectable. They see the abuse and they will see nothing else. They fall into the temper of a furious populace provoked at the disorder of a house of ill-fame; they never attempt to correct or regulate; they go to work by the shortest way: to abate the nuisance, they pull down the house." [59]

A decade before the French Revolution, Burke led an effort at just such an artful and preventive reform, intended to curb waste and abuse in the appropriation of public money, especially money spent on the lavish upkeep of the royal family and assorted official jobs in the royal residences. These plum jobs often involved no real work and simply rewarded the friends and relatives of the politically well-connected. Seeing the potential for public disaffection with the larger system of government over such waste and abuse, Burke led a successful initiative to clean up public expenditures by painstakingly reviewing every expense on the royal households. Toward the end of his life, he reflected back upon this reform effort, employing terms drawn from medicine to describe the statesman's task: "I found a great distemper in the commonwealth; and, according to the nature of evil and of the object, I treated it. The malady was deep; it was complicated, in the causes and in the symptoms. Throughout it was full of contra-indicants." And his mode of treatment was motivated by an understanding of the difference between fixing and replacing an established system that works but that has some problems:

> I knew that there is a manifest marked distinction, which ill men, with ill designs, or weak men incapable of any design, will constantly be confounding, that is, a marked distinction between Change and Reformation. The former alters the substance of the objects themselves; and gets rid of all their essential good, as well as of all the accidental evil annexed to them. Change is novelty; and whether it is to operate any one of the effects of reformation at all, or whether it may not contradict the very principle upon which reformation is desired, cannot be certainly known beforehand. Reform is, not a change in the substance, or in the primary modification of the object, but a direct application of a remedy to the grievance complained of. So far as that is removed, all is sure. It stops there; and

if it fails, the substance which underwent the operation, at the very worst, is but where it was.[60]

The challenge, of course, is to tell the difference between what must be preserved and what must be reformed, and Burke acknowledged to the Commons that he could not be entirely certain he had done so correctly in his economic proposals. He could state with confidence only that he had based his proposals on the specifics of the situation rather than a speculative theory of how the royal households should work.[61] And above all, he pursued his reform with a sense of the risks of altering the institutions of the state.[62] But it was necessary, he says, to avoid public disaffection and to rescue the good name and opinion of Parliament and the monarchy, and so he set out not to innovate but quite literally to re-form, to bring the regime back to health by addressing its particular ailment.

Wholesale innovation, Burke argues, is not a means of progress but rather undercuts the prerequisites for progress by breaking with the past and thus regressing to beginnings. It disrupts a long-standing political order and therefore makes improvements vastly more difficult, as "good order is the foundation of all good things."[63] Instead, statesmen must begin from what they have.

The British have long understood this crucial point, Burke argues. True English principles—true Whig principles—militate against reckless innovation and argue instead for the importance of continuity and stability. Even when they were forced to resort to a kind of revolution themselves, the old Whigs who are his models did so with an eye to preservation. Burke describes how they accomplished this:

The two principles of conservation and correction operated strongly at the two critical periods of the Restoration and Revolution, when England found itself without a king. At both those periods the nation had lost the bond of union in their ancient edifice; they did not, however, dissolve the whole fabric. On the contrary, in both cases they regenerated the deficient part of the old constitution through the parts which were not impaired. They kept these old parts exactly as they were, that the part recovered might be suited to them.[64]

The failure of the French to do the same meant that their revolution would tear down the old but not build up the new.

THE EMERGENCE OF RIGHT AND LEFT

Because he understood the old Whigs in these terms, Burke reacted with particular resistance and alarm to the attempt by some radicals to portray the Glorious Revolution of 1688 as a kind of preface to the French Revolution. The idea that the Whigs of 1688 had turned their ancient monarchy into merely an elected kingship was central to the case made by the British defenders of the French Revolution, and his alarm at such an argument drove Burke to compose the *Reflections*.

He thus devotes the opening of the *Reflections* and the great bulk of the *Appeal from the New to the Old Whigs* to answering this argument. In these tellings, the Whigs of 1688, as defenders of the ancient English order, sought to address a severe crisis of legitimacy by finding a means of preserving the structure of the regime and the line of succession despite gross misbehavior by the monarch, rather than starting anew on novel principles. The revolution of 1688, Burke argues, was a necessary exception, but the Whigs of the day made sure it did not become the rule. It was decidedly "not a nursery of future revolutions."[65] Indeed, he argues in the *Appeal*, 1688 was "a revolution not made but prevented."[66]

The debates of his own time, Burke thought, bore no real resemblance to those of 1688, and the simplistic notion that Whigs should be in favor of revolution and that to be against the French radicals made one a Tory mistook the meaning of the crisis. In the early years of the French Revolution, a great many of Burke's Whig co-partisans disagreed and charged him with betraying the principles of the party. Burke at first brushed off such charges, but as the French Revolution wore on, he came to think that his own differences with his fellow Whigs contained an important lesson about what the French Revolution meant to the politics of Britain. The British debate about the French Revolution, he concluded, was in a certain sense a debate among Whigs. Or at least it was detached from the debate between parliamentary and royal power—a debate long understood as the distinction between Whigs and Tories. The revolution had wrought a profound transformation of the political landscape and created two new parties divided along a new question.

In the *Letters on a Regicide Peace*, Burke argues that it simply no longer made sense to speak of Whigs and Tories as those terms had once been used. "These parties, which by their dissensions have so often distracted the Kingdom, which by their union have once saved it, and which by their collision and mutual resistance, have preserved the variety of this Constitution in its unity, be (as I believe they are) nearly extinct by the growth of new ones, which have their roots in the present circumstances of the times." And what are these new parties? One party, Burke says, is filled with men who "consider the conservation in England of the ancient order of things, as necessary to preserve order every where else, and who regard the general conservation of order in other countries, as reciprocally necessary to preserve the same state of things in these Islands." And opposing this party of conservation is "the other party which demands great changes here, and is so pleased to see them every where else, which party I call Jacobin."[67]

In the wake of the French Revolution, Burke suggests, the Whigs and Tories have been replaced by a party of conservation and a Jacobin party. The question between them is no longer about the prerogatives of the king versus those of Parliament, but is rather about the prerogatives of the existing given regime versus a revolutionary republicanism that would wash it away. In other words, the question that now defined British politics was the question of revolution and reform.

On this point, Burke and Paine largely agreed. Although Burke cites Paine at length as the chief example of the republican arguments he attributes to the radical Whigs, Paine in fact never claims the mantle of the Whigs. Far from attempting to appropriate the authority of 1688, as many English radicals did, Paine disparages the Glorious

Revolution, which he says had been "exalted beyond its value." He even openly mocks the old Whigs who undertook it. "Mankind will then scarcely believe that a country calling itself free would send to Holland for a man, and clothe him with power on purpose to put themselves in fear of him, and give him almost a million sterling a year for leave to submit themselves and their posterity, like bondmen and bondwomen, for ever." [68] The influence and appeal of the Glorious Revolution, he argues, "is already on the wane, eclipsed by the enlarging orb of reason, and the luminous revolutions of America and France. In less than another century it will go, as well as Mr. Burke's labors, 'to the family vault of all the Capulets.'" [69] Of William and Mary themselves, long venerated by Whig champions of the rights of 1688, Paine says they "have always appeared to me detestable; the one seeking to destroy his uncle, and the other her father, to get possession of power themselves." [70]

Paine effectively makes Burke's point that the French Revolution, properly understood, does not seek to advance the Whig principles of 1688, but rather sees them as sorely inadequate to the task of correcting unjust regimes. To alter a fundamentally unjust regime in order to preserve it strikes Paine as both illegitimate and pointless. No government has "a right to alter itself, either in whole or in part," he writes, so that reform without recourse to an original condition or a national convention can only be either inadequate or illicit. [71] In fact, a partial reform strikes him as no better than no improvement at all. "It will always happen when a thing is originally wrong that amendments do not make it right, and it often happens that they do as much mischief one way as good the other." [72] In an ill-founded society, the principles of injustice become "too deeply rooted to be removed, and the Augean stables of parasites and plunderers too abominably filthy to be cleansed by anything short of a complete and universal Revolution." [73] Such universal revolution is in fact the only effective means of reform, Paine argues, and he utterly dismisses the distinction Burke insists upon between revolution and reform: "Reforms, or revolutions, call them which you please." [74]

For his own reasons, therefore, Paine concludes just as Burke does that the familiar political divide in Britain has lost its salience and been replaced by a new question. "It is not whether this or that party shall be in or not, or Whig or Tory, high or low shall prevail; but whether man shall inherit his rights, and universal civilization take place. Whether the fruits of his labors shall be enjoyed by himself or consumed by the profligacy of governments. Whether robbery shall be banished from courts, and wretchedness from countries."[75]

This new question now pressed upon Europe with great urgency and made for a moment of political transformation. In Paine's view, the advancement of reason and science made his own time a moment of profound change unlike any prior era and set the tone for a far brighter future: an age of reform, by which he means an age of revolutions, as he puts it in the final words of the first volume of *Rights of Man*:

> From what we now see, nothing of reform in the political world ought to be held improbable. It is an age of Revolutions, in which everything may be looked for. The intrigue of Courts, by which the system of war is kept up, may provoke a confederation of Nations to abolish it: and an European Congress to patronize the progress of free Government, and promote the civilization of Nations with each other, is an event nearer in probability, than once were the revolutions and alliance of France and America.[76]

"The iron is becoming hot all over Europe," Paine then writes in the second volume. "The insulted German and the enslaved Spaniard, the Russ and the Pole, are beginning to think. The present age will hereafter merit to be called the Age of Reason, and the present generation will appear to the future as the Adam of a new world."[77] This period will be remembered as the moment of transformation, he argues: "The farce of monarchy and aristocracy, in all countries, is following that of chivalry, and Mr. Burke is dressing for the funeral. Let it then pass quietly to the tomb of all other follies, and the mourners be comforted."[78]

But in Burke's view, his time differed from the past not because some new truth had been learned or great advance achieved, but simply because the excesses and corruptions of the revolution itself had distorted and transformed English politics: "The present time differs from any other only by the circumstances of what is doing in France."[79] The basic realities of human nature and of politics have not changed at all, except inasmuch as they must now confront a political force that seeks to ignore or undermine them. And politics seeks in particular to ignore the obligations of the present to the past, and therefore to the future, as Burke sees it.

In this sense, Burke's and Paine's disparate ideas about revolution and reform—a difference that both men suggested was quickly becoming their era's defining disagreement in European politics—can be understood as a disagreement about the relation of the present to the past and about the obligation of every generation to sustain and improve what it was given and to pass it along to those who follow. The dispute over political change concerns the relations of generations in politics. Burke's objection to total revolution draws on his horror at the prospect of abandoning all that has been arduously gained over centuries of slow, incremental reform and improvement. He sees it as a betrayal of the trust of past generations and of the obligation to future ones. Paine's objection to such plodding reform, meanwhile, is that it gives credence to despotism and is moved more by the desire to sustain iniquity than by the desire to address injustice.

Burke believes that human nature and the rest of nature make themselves known in politics through long experience, that human beings are born into a web of obligations, and that the social problems we confront do not lend themselves to detached scientific analysis. For all these reasons, he believes that improvements in politics must be achieved by cumulative reform—by building on success to address failure and by containing the effects of innovation within a broader context of continuity.

Paine, on the other hand, believes that nature reveals itself in the form of abstract principles discovered by rational analysis, that human beings are entitled to choose their government freely, that government in turn exists to protect their other choices, and that reason can help people see beyond the superstitions that have long sustained unjust regimes. For all these reasons, he believes that improvements in politics must be achieved by thoroughgoing revolution—by throwing off the accumulated burdens of the past and starting fresh and properly.

Their assorted disagreements therefore repeatedly point to a confrontation over the authority of the past and the prerogatives of the present in political life. That profound and unusual terrain of dispute is where we now turn.

SEVEN

GENERATIONS AND THE LIVING

W HAT IS THE PROPER RELATION BETWEEN GENERA-
tions in a society? Just because our parents' generation
did something a certain way, should we do the same, or
can we put aside their practices and blaze our own path? Do we owe
it to our children to preserve the social and political institutions that
we ourselves inherited so our descendants can live as we did, or do we
owe them the freedom to find their own way? Is it even possible to
understand our civic life in terms of consent and freedom of choice
if it involves a political order we inherited at birth and so had no real
part in choosing? Do both the society we happened to inherit and our
place in that society have any legitimate authority over how we ought
to live our lives?

As we have already begun to see, the Burke-Paine debate has
a great deal to tell us about both why and how we ought to think
about these vexing questions. The dilemma of the generations in a
liberal society looms exceptionally large in their political thought
and is present just below the surface of many of the disputes that

divide them. Paine and Burke bring up the subject frequently and in a wide variety of contexts, so that more than just another theme of their dispute, it forms a kind of unifying thread among the themes we have discussed.

Paine seeks to understand man apart from his social setting, while Burke thinks man is incomprehensible apart from the circumstances into which he is born—circumstances largely the making of prior generations. Burke describes a densely layered social whole that defines the place of each of its members, while Paine thinks each person is born with an equal right to shape his destiny. Paine's case for a politics of reason argues for direct recourse to principle in the face of long-established but unreasonable practices. Burke's case for prescription is based on generational continuity. This argument leads Burke to prefer gradual reforms that preserve what has come down from the past, while Paine pursues a revolutionary break as the only way to escape the heavy burden of long-standing injustice.

The question of the generations recurs so frequently in their discussions because the Burke-Paine debate is about Enlightenment liberalism, whose underlying worldview unavoidably raises the problem of the generations. Enlightenment liberalism emphasizes government by consent, individualism, and social equality, all of which are in tension with some rather glaring facts of the human condition: that we are born into a society that already exists, that we enter this society without consenting to it, that we enter it with social connections and not as isolated individuals, and that these connections help define our place in society and therefore often raise barriers to equality.

These facts suggest either that Enlightenment liberalism is in some important ways unworkable in practice given the relations between generations or that those relations must be transformed to make such liberalism possible. Because they took up the question of Enlightenment liberalism at the moment when it was becoming a question of practice, Burke and Paine were unusually attentive to these problems and approached the matter of generational relations as a genuinely practical and open question.

PAINE'S ETERNAL NOW

Thomas Paine's view of political life points toward a politics of timelessness. An individual's rights and place in society should have nothing to do with what preceded his birth. Every human individual in every generation has the same relation to society as every other person in every other generation, so that the political actions, decisions, rules, and achievements of past generations do not constrain the present or define it. The present is defined instead in direct relation to original principles, which are just as plain and true today as they were at the beginning of human history. They are equally true for different generations just as for different individuals. Therefore, Paine insists, "every generation is equal in rights to generations which preceded it, by the same rule that every individual is born equal in rights with his contemporary."[1]

This equality among the generations does not mean, however, that past and present generations have an equal claim on present political judgments. The past had its chance, and now the present generation is entitled to its own, as future generations someday will be. "Every age and generation must be as free to act for itself in all cases as the ages and generations which preceded it."[2] The movement of generations is in this sense less cumulative than repetitive. "All men are born equal, and with equal natural right, in the same manner as if posterity had been continued by creation instead of generation," Paine argues, "the latter being only the mode by which the former is carried forward; and consequently every child born into the world must be considered as deriving its existence from God. The world is as new to him as it was to the first man that existed, and his natural right in it is of the same kind."[3]

This desire for a direct connection to original principles can make it difficult to contend with the consequences of the passing of generations—indeed with the very fact that people are born at all. Consent requires that every generation see the world as fully open before it, rather than taking as given what existed when it arrived. Free men must be able to live freely in the present, and they cannot do so if they are obliged to obey the edicts of their predecessors. Paine makes this point remarkably explicit in essentially all of his political writings—before, during, and after the French Revolution. It is perhaps put most starkly in his 1795 *Dissertation on First Principles of Government*: "Time with respect to principles is an eternal NOW: it has no operation upon them; it changes nothing of their nature and qualities. But what have we to do with a thousand years? Our lifetime is but a short portion of time, and if we find the wrong in existence as soon as we begin to live, that is the point of time at which it begins to us; and our right to resist it is the same as if it never existed before."[4]

This extraordinary notion of the eternal now powerfully clarifies Paine's understanding of time in political life. His is a politics of the present. As he puts it in *Rights of Man*, "it is the living, and not the dead, that are to be accommodated" in political life.[5] Paine does not deny the fact of generations of course, but rather the authority of the accumulated practices of the past. Indeed, he takes the constant movement of nations through generations to be itself an argument for the eternal now in politics:

A nation, though continually existing, is continually in a state of renewal and succession. It is never stationary. Every day produces new births, carries minors forward to maturity, and old persons from the stage. In this ever running flood of generations there is no part superior in authority to another. Could we conceive an idea of superiority in any, at what point in time, or in what century of the world, are we to fix it? To what cause are we to ascribe it? By what evidence are we to prove it? By what criterion are we to know it?[6]

Precisely because life itself is not timeless, Paine insists that politics must be timeless—for why would the past be inherently better or worse than the present or the future? And precisely because Paine does believe in progress, in a movement of political life toward a better understanding of the timeless principles of justice, he argues that this progress points toward a politics of permanent principle in which truth rather than habit reigns supreme. He thus understands hereditary monarchy and aristocracy not only as unjust impositions on the liberty of the individual but as unjust impositions by the past upon the present.

Paine particularly presses this point in his response to Burke's assertion of the permanent allegiance of the British people to the monarchy. In the *Reflections on the Revolution in France*, in an effort to refute the claim of Richard Price that the Glorious Revolution had created a right to choose the monarch, Burke notes that the Parliament of 1688 pledges to William and Mary that "we do most humbly and faithfully submit ourselves, our heirs and posterities, for ever." Paine quotes this passage in the opening of *Rights of Man* and accuses Burke of arguing that this submission by one particular generation of legislators is inexorably binding on all future Englishmen.[7] "The English Parliament of 1688 did a certain thing, which, for themselves and their constituents, they had a right to do," but which they had no right to do for subsequent generations.[8]

> There never did, there never will, and there never can, exist a Parliament, or any description of men, or any generation of men, in any country, possessed of the right or the power of binding and controlling posterity to the "end of time," or of commanding for ever how the world shall be governed, or who shall govern it. The vanity and presumption of governing beyond the grave is the most ridiculous and insolent of all tyrannies. Man has no property in man; neither has any generation a property in the generations which are to follow. . . . Every generation is, and must be, competent to all the purposes which its occasions require.[9]

The deep connection between Paine's individualism and his rejection of the authority of the past is powerfully evident in this passage. Paine thinks of different generations as essentially distinct and unconnected—not as extensions of one another. In effect, he suggests that we who are alive today, the people who once inhabited our country, and the people who will inhabit it in the future are simply not one people in any meaningful political sense. "That every nation, *for the time being*, has a right to govern itself as it pleases must always be admitted; but government by hereditary succession is government for another race of people, and not for itself."[10]

Hereditary government is always imposed and never chosen, Paine explains, because it is not hereditary government until the second generation of its rule, and that generation of the ruled could not have chosen its rulers. If human beings lived forever, there might be such a thing as a legitimate monarchy, but since they do not live forever, every hereditary regime becomes tyrannical by definition after one generation.[11] This next generation is forced to be governed by the descendant of the person chosen to govern in the prior generation. Force thus replaces choice, and the regime ceases to be legitimate. "The Parliament of 1688 might as well have passed an act to have authorized themselves to live for ever, as to make their authority live for ever."[12]

The right to rule is a matter of consent, which ideally is earned by a display of virtue or merit. "Whenever we are planning for posterity," Paine writes in *Common Sense*, "we ought to remember that virtue is not hereditary."[13] And as virtue is not hereditary, neither can political power be hereditary. For this reason, no man can claim the authority to govern by virtue of his link to those who have governed in the past.

Indeed, Paine's individualism, and his resulting egalitarianism, drives him to suggest that essentially nothing of any relevance is hereditary, and he minimizes the importance of the links between generations in society more generally. Human beings should be governed by their own choices and actions, rather than those of others, and the social relations one happens to have inherited upon arriving in this world ought not to be the decisive factor in the trajectory of one's life.

For much the same reason, the political arrangements and practices of the past do not possess any inherent authority over the present or the future simply for having been in effect for a time. Writing of the English constitution, Paine remarks:

In speaking on this subject (or on any other) on the pure ground of principle, antiquity and precedent cease to be authority, and hoary-headed error loses its effect. The reasonableness and propriety of things must be examined abstractedly from custom and usage; and, in this point of view, the right which grows into practice today is as much a right, and as old in principle and theory, as if it had the customary sanction of a thousand ages. Principles have no connection with time, nor characters with names.[14]

The just and right paths do not need the blessing of long custom to be adopted—in a politics attuned to proper principles and guided by reason, they will be adopted on their own merits: "That which is worth following will be followed for the sake of its worth; and it is in this that its security lies, and not in any conditions with which it may be encumbered."[15]

In a regime premised on inheritance, there is no guarantee that what is worth following will be followed, not only because custom can be blind, but because nature can be quite haphazard in its distribution of gifts, and the child of an able monarch may easily be a fool. The flood of generations disburses natural gifts, and the march of time means that even the ablest leader must eventually depart the stage. A successful political system must be able to contend with both problems, even as it holds to timeless ideals and treats every individual and every generation equally. For Paine, the key to such a system is a republican character, the essence of which is that an able person from any part of society may rise to elected power by proving his worth. Only a republic can keep the generations from trampling on one another and keep the loss of an able leader from ruining the state. "As the republic of letters brings forward the best literary productions, by giving to genius a fair and universal chance; so the representative system of government is calculated to produce the wisest laws, by collecting wisdom from where it can be found," Paine writes.[16]

The republic is a kind of solution to the cycle of generations in politics. By putting into practice liberal premises, it creates a state in which the assumptions of Enlightenment liberalism apply, and by reshaping the traditional relationship of the generations, it ensures that everyone has rights of consent and equality, despite everyone's being born into a preexisting society. It also offers a practical solution to the serious practical deficiencies of an inherited order. A monarchy not only is an unjust imposition by the past, but is also constantly interrupted by the facts of birth and death and the deficiencies of both youth and old age. "To render monarchy consistent with government, the next in succession should not be born a child, but a man at once, and that man a Solomon. It is ridiculous that nations are to wait and government be interrupted till boys grow to be men," Paine writes.[17] A republic avoids that problem. "It places government in a state of constant maturity. It is, as has already been observed, never young, never old. It is subject neither to nonage, nor dotage. It is never in the cradle, nor on crutches."[18]

A crucial part of Paine's enthusiasm for republicanism has to do with this character of the republic as he sees it: its ability to offer an escape from the ravages of time, a permanence denied to any institution that follows the life cycle, yet at the same time a legitimacy denied to any institution that denies the equality of all generations. "It is the nature of man to die, and he will continue to die as long as he continues to be born," Paine writes, but politics need not be shaped or debilitated by this fact about mankind.[19] The problematic political consequences of human mortality are overcome by a regime of choice and consent.

In this sense, modern liberal politics as Paine sees it is part and parcel of a larger project to overcome the limitations placed on mankind by his natural condition, especially his birth and death. Enlightenment liberalism both requires and (through republicanism) makes possible a state of constant maturity—an eternal now. It averts the effects, and thereby denies the importance, of the passing of generations and of the links between them. As noted earlier, Paine expressly denies that these links exercise any authority, even when laws extend across generations: "A law not repealed continues in force, not because it cannot be repealed, but because it is not repealed; and the non-repealing passes for consent."[20]

Nothing of consequence passes between the generations, Paine insists. In *Agrarian Justice*, he argues that an inheritance tax is the most just means by which to draw government revenue for the welfare system he envisions, because at the moment of inheritance—the nexus of generations—no transaction worth protecting occurs.[21] The links between generations therefore cannot serve as the foundation for political institutions or even for property. Rather, politics must focus on the present, not on the dead or those yet to be born. "Those who have quitted the world, and those who have not yet arrived in it, are as remote from each other as the utmost stretch of moral imagination can conceive. What possible obligation, then, can exist between them?"[22] Because it is impossible to legislate on behalf of those who can no longer or not yet exercise consent, legislators must focus on those who can.

Paine is not ignoring the needs of future generations, but he argues that their greatest need will be like that of the present generation: the need for freedom in accord with their natural rights. Paine rarely speaks of inheritance in a positive sense, but speaks of it only in a negative sense—that is, as an obligation not to impose on our descendants. The present should live in such a way that it does not bind the future.

Political institutions last beyond one generation, of course, but they must be designed to require continuing consent. And legislation passed by one generation should not overly burden the next—each age should legislate only for itself when possible. "As the generations of the world are every day both commencing and expiring," Paine writes, "therefore when any public act of this sort is done, it naturally supposes the age of that generation to be then beginning, and the time contained between coming of age and the natural end of life is the extent of time it has the right to go to, which may be about thirty years; for though many may die before, others will live beyond; and the mean time is equally fair for all generations."[23] Beyond that roughly thirty-year span, a law is no longer in effect primarily upon those who enacted it, and so it should be cleared away, Paine argues.[24]

Requiring all laws to expire after a generation would also help avoid the suffocating clutter of the British constitution. "The British, from the want of some general regulation of this kind, have a great number of obsolete laws; which, though out of use and forgotten are not out of force, and are occasionally brought up for particular purposes."[25] By establishing time limits on legislation, wise lawmakers would enable every age to govern itself and so would actually reinforce the laws that deserve to endure (by having them reaffirmed), while systematically filtering out those that do not. There is no sense in legislating as if legislators' reason will discern the desires and needs of all future generations forever. "The term 'forever' is an absurdity that would have no effect," Paine writes. "The next age will think for itself, by the same rule of right that we have done, and not admit any assumed authority of ours to encroach upon the system of their day. Our forever ends where their forever begins."[26]

Essentially nothing, therefore, legitimately spans generations. Because Paine believes that the rights and freedoms of the individual are at the core of political life, he argues that positive inheritance is almost entirely burdensome. What we owe the future is freedom, which is also what we must demand from the past. Politics in this sense exists for the sake of the present. It allows present citizens to legislate for themselves, free of impositions from their ancestors, and it will allow future citizens to do the same. This temporal individualism is at the heart of Paine's liberalism.

BURKE'S ETERNAL ORDER

Beginning from a very different premise, Edmund Burke comes to an entirely different view of the appropriate relations between the generations. His own understanding of politics puts not abstract natural freedom but concrete inheritance at the very core and emphasizes obligation over choice. Burke believes that what we owe the future above all is not freedom but rather the accumulated wisdom and work of the past: The task of any generation is to preserve and, where necessary and possible, improve what that generation has been given by its predecessors, with the aim of passing the benefit along to its successors. Each generation must live with a sense of its own time as transitory—more or less the opposite of an eternal now.

As noted, Burke sees society as a relationship not just between the living, but also between the living, the dead, and the people of the future.[27] Society exists not to facilitate individual choice but to meet the needs of the people, and to do so, it must draw on the wisdom of the past and be guided by the imperative to make that wisdom available to future generations as well, supplemented by lessons learned by the current generation along the way. "I attest the retiring, I attest the advancing generations, between which, as a link in the great chain of eternal order, we stand," Burke told the House of Lords in the course of the impeachment trial of Hastings.[28]

A great deal of Burke's work is built on this sense that the present is fleeting and best understood as a link in a chain, and his focus on this question grows especially pronounced in the years of the French Revolution. Burke believes that the present generation has profound obligations both to the past and to the future and that these obligations offer an important benefit to the present generation, by imposing crucial constraints upon its ambitions and its reach. Society can thrive only within such constraints and therefore with a sense of itself as linked to the past and the future. Without these constraints, all the lessons of history would be denied to the present and the future, and "personal self-sufficiency and arrogance, the certain attendants upon all those who have never experienced a wisdom greater than their own, would usurp the tribunal."[29]

Burke expressly denies that we can look out for the needs of the future even as we reject the lessons and achievements of the past. Access to those lessons and achievements is one of the most crucial needs of the future, as he sees it, so the present-centered vision of the revolutionaries must involve betraying the future as much as the past: "People will not look forward to posterity, who never look backward to their ancestors."[30] A free and ordered society will look to both, Burke argues:

One of the first and most leading principles on which the commonwealth and the laws are consecrated, is lest the temporary possessors and life renters in it, unmindful of what they have received from their ancestors, or of what is due to their posterity, should act as if they were the entire masters; that they should not think it amongst their rights to cut off the entail or commit waste on the inheritance, by destroying at their pleasure the whole original fabric of their society; hazarding to leave to those who come after them a ruin instead of a habitation, and teaching these successors as little respect to their contrivances as they had themselves respected the institutions of their forefathers.[31]

In order to build anything lasting, Burke suggests, we must respect what has been built in the past and how it has come down to us.

The idea of inheritance for Burke explains not only the descent of property and title, but also the descent of rights and obligations, which Paine takes to derive directly from the individual but which Burke believes are a function of one's relation to the past. Burke stresses that because men are born into civil society without their own consent, their rights in that society are a function not of their agreeing to certain arrangements but of their inheritance from their forefathers, who had worked to defend those rights just as members of this new generation should for themselves and their posterity. In defending the accumulated achievements of the past, however, Burke defends not only social relations and ordered freedom but also precisely the kind of inherited property and privileges that Paine so opposes. Burke argues that the noble families of Britain are essential to the nation's stability and success and provide a source of strength that a fully democratic republic could never attain. In an extraordinary letter to the Duke of Richmond in 1772, Burke writes:

You people of great families and hereditary trusts and fortunes are not like such as I am, who, whatever may be the rapidity of our growth, and even by the fruit we bear, and flatter ourselves a little that, while we creep on the ground, we belly into melons that are exquisite for size and flavor, yet still we are but annual plants that perish with our season, and leave no sort of traces behind us. You, if you are what you ought to be, are in my eye the great oaks that shade a country, and perpetuate your benefits from generation to generation.[32]

Though not blind to the dark side of the aristocracy, Burke rejects Paine's assertion that nothing of much consequence transpires at the junction of the generations. He argues that the strength and stability made possible by the aristocracy are worth the cost—and that in any case, no plausible alternative exists as a means of perpetuation.

Burke also expressly disagrees with Paine's assertion that a republic allows for institutions that reach beyond the lifespans of individuals. Republican institutions are never secure, Burke argues, because they accept no authority but the present. "They conceive, very systematically, that all things which give perpetuity are mischievous, and therefore they are at inexpiable war with all establishments," Burke writes of the revolutionaries.[33] No one can ever plan ahead securely in a republic, Burke argues, because the rules could change at any point on the momentary whim of today's majority. Only cross-generational institutions and the great aristocratic families offer a real solution to the challenge of establishing arrangements that will outlive their founders. "This nobility forms the chain that connects the ages of a nation which otherwise (with Mr. Paine) would soon be taught that no one generation can bind another," Burke argues.[34] Whereas individuals come and go, the commonwealth is more permanent. Precisely because of this difference, laws and practices that span generations are essential, so that society as a whole may persist as a body which, "in juridical construction, never dies; and in fact never loses its members at once by death."[35] Or as Burke puts it in the *Reflections*:

Our political system is placed in a just correspondence and symmetry with the order of the world, and with the mode of existence decreed to a permanent body composed of transitory parts; wherein, by the disposition of a stupendous wisdom, moulding together the great mysterious incorporation of the human race, the whole at one time is never old, or middle-aged, or young, but in a condition of unchangeable constancy, moves on through the varied tenor of perpetual decay, fall, renovation, and progression.[36]

Burke and Paine thus employ very similar language—the language of a regime always in its prime—to argue for thoroughly opposite notions of the relations between the generations in the design of political institutions. For Burke it is not by separating the generations but by joining them that we ensure that society is not debilitated by human mortality. Society flourishes not by freeing every generation from those that precede and succeed it so that it might have direct recourse to permanent principles, but by linking the generations tightly together so that they might form a permanent body. If "the whole chain and continuity of the commonwealth would be broken and no one generation could link with the other," Burke worries, then "men would become little better than the flies of a summer."[37]

The commonwealth, as a work of many generations intended to last for many more, requires an explicitly intergenerational character. It exists not in an eternal now but rather as the product of a lengthy and still ongoing process—one in which time is of very great significance and therefore in which the generations must take part together. "Where the great interests of mankind are concerned through a long succession of generations," Burke writes, "that succession ought to be admitted into some share in the councils which are so deeply to affect them. If justice requires this, the work itself requires the aid of more minds than one age can furnish."[38]

Thomas Paine, as we have seen, believes that this view subordinates the interests of the present and the future to those of the past, as it would deny every generation but the first a full share in self-government. But Burke argues that far from sacrificing the present and the future, he is defending both from being robbed of their inheritance. It is the revolutionaries who would sacrifice the interests of the present (by subjecting the present generation to the instability and danger of the revolution itself) and risk the inheritance of the future on a gamble. "In political arrangements, men have no right to put the well-being of the present generation wholly out of the question," he writes. "Perhaps the only moral trust with any certainty in our hands is the care of our own time. With regard to futurity, we are to treat it like a ward. We are not so to attempt an improvement of his fortune, as to put the capital of his estate to any hazard."[39]

That capital, to which the present and the future are entitled, is the accumulated knowledge and practice of their forefathers. The radicals, Burke argues, seek "to deprive men of the benefit of the collected wisdom of mankind, and to make them blind disciples of their own particular presumption."[40] He therefore sees himself as a defender of the present, not the past, and sees the revolutionaries as a threat to present happiness as well as to future order. "Our first trust is the happiness of our own time."[41]

Even if their plans had some chance of succeeding, Burke suggests, the revolutionaries' treatment of the present generation is therefore a dereliction of the statesman's foremost duty. And of course, for the very same reason, he also thinks their plans will fail: Because the revolutionaries do not grasp the actual character of human society, they direct themselves to the wrong ends altogether. In rejecting the accumulated achievements of the past, they reject an entire approach to political life and an entire view of the nature of man and society. Their other errors—as Burke sees it, errors about human nature and justice, human obligations and freedom, human reason and knowledge, and political change and reform—result from (and also describe) the same underlying view.

The Politics of the Given World

Anyone exploring the views of Burke and Paine will repeatedly encounter, as we have, the question of context—both social and generational. Again and again, Paine defends the prerogatives of the individual and derides all that presses upon his freedom of action. Again and again, Burke insists that no man is an island and no individual exists apart from society.

Two sets of concerns—those regarding the individual and the community, and those regarding the present and the past—are therefore constant themes of both Burke's and Paine's political thought. Paine believes that human beings are best understood apart from the community and the past, as complete and sufficient individuals endowed with natural rights whose interactions are functions of their individual choices and actions. Both tradition and society should be put aside when contemplating questions of political principle and action, because both are consequences of politics, not sources of it. Burke believes that human beings are best understood in their social and historical settings, as members of their communities with obligations to each other and as the recipients of a valuable inheritance from the past—an inheritance that they are charged to improve and pass along.

But as we review the particulars of the Burke-Paine debate laid out in the previous chapters, these two sets of concerns—about tradition and community—appear to collapse into one. The argument over tradition and the past encompasses the dispute over community for both Burke and Paine. It is the given world—those conditions we are born into without choice—that to Burke's eyes make the theory of individualism inadequate. Because human generations are not independent of one another, human individuals are not independent of one another, either. The facts of human birth and death and the social institutions built around them link individuals, families, and communities inexorably, and to pretend otherwise (let alone to sever their links) would be disastrous for political life.

For Paine, meanwhile, the theory of individualism relies on an explanatory device (the "state of nature") that takes the first human generation as its model—a generation for whom there was no given past. To apply a theory based on that premise is to deny the authority and significance of human generations and thus of tradition—and Paine is not shy about making that clear. The independence of individuals from their neighbors is a function of the independence of generations from their predecessors; this independence in the first generation is the essence of the theory of Enlightenment liberalism, which applies its timeless principles to all subsequent generations as well.

Thus, a crucial common thread in the large and varied debates between Burke and Paine is apparently a dispute about the status of the past in political life. And both Burke and Paine are exceptionally explicit about its significance and take up the question of the meaning of the past in an uncommonly overt way. Paine's abhorrence of inherited government is the core of his political philosophy, for he sees inherited government as essentially opposed to nature, choice, reason, and justice. He wants to look past history and tradition to nature, and therefore to look past given obligations to created choices, beyond received wisdom to pure reason, and beyond mere cumulative reforms to total revolution. Burke, meanwhile, says the model of inheritance is the model of nature, the appropriate means of understanding and meeting our obligations, the core of prescription, and the key to reform.

Both men are students of political change, and in a certain respect all of the themes taken up in this book are aspects of a dispute about change: its purpose, its character, its means, and its ends. But Burke's and Paine's views of the matter always clearly draw on this deep disagreement about the nature and meaning of the relations between generations. For Paine, the disjunction between the permanent principles of politics and the inherited realities of social and political life demands a revolutionary transformation—a break with the past to bring the real into alignment with the ideal made known by reason. For Burke, the evolved forms of political life, which are a valued inheritance, offer both the means and the ends of political change. When problems arise, society can employ its political institutions to address them, as those institutions have developed slowly over time to serve that purpose. But when a problem is too large for those institutions to contend with and thereby threatens their survival, statesmen must reform the institutions in an effort to strengthen and preserve them, so that these institutions might be passed down to future generations who will use them in the same way. This arrangement calls for gradual change in response to discrete needs and problems, informed by a profound respect for the given order—because for Burke the real is the only reliable means of grasping the ideal.

HERE WE FIND THE TRUE BOTTOM of the Burke-Paine debate, and from here we can begin to appreciate how their differences have helped to shape our own. They disagreed about whether some basic aspects of the human condition, especially the facts that we are all born and that we all die, should decisively shape human societies. Paine's assertive, confident, rationalist, technocratic, and progressive outlook held that through the right kinds of political arrangements, man could overcome the limits that these facts might impose and he could therefore reshape his world to his preferences and even end the long-standing scourges of injustice, war, and suffering. Burke's grateful, protective, cautious, pious, gradualist, and reformist outlook held that man could only hope to improve his circumstances if he understood his own limits, built on the achievements of those who came before him to repair their errors, and realized that some profound human miseries and vices are permanent functions of our nature—and that pretending otherwise would only make them worse.

Both are modern attitudes, and both are liberal too, but they disagree about just what modernity and liberalism mean. Indeed, that very disagreement has ultimately come to define modern liberalism.

CONCLUSION

EDMUND BURKE AND THOMAS PAINE KNEW THAT THE heated controversies that had shaped their public lives would not end with their deaths. In fact, both of them worried that they might not be allowed to rest in peace, quite literally.

As he lay ill in 1797, Burke expressed his dread that should the French radicals and their allies in Britain succeed in spreading their revolution across the channel, they would exhume his body from its resting place to make an example of their staunch opponent. He gave instructions that he should be buried in an unmarked grave kept apart from that of his son and from the plot reserved for his wife, so that his fate need not be theirs. In the end, Burke's family and friends decided to follow the guidance of his written will instead of this fevered deathbed plea, and he was buried alongside his son in a grave bearing the family name in a Beaconsfield churchyard, where his wife joined them some fifteen years later.[1]

Paine, too, found himself uneasy about the fate of his earthly remains and reasoned that his enemies (whom he assumed would be motivated by his writings against biblical religion) would be deterred only by the sanctity of a Christian cemetery. The adamant Deist (if not atheist) therefore ironically sought ultimate protection under the religion of his fathers, leaving this request in his will: "I know not if the Society of people called Quakers admit a person to be buried in their burying ground who does not belong to their Society, but if they do, or will admit me, I would prefer being buried there; my father belonged to that profession, and I was partly brought up in it. But if it is not consistent with their rules to do this, I desire to be buried on my own farm at New Rochelle."[2]

The Quakers in the end did not allow it, and Paine was indeed buried on his farm. His fears, moreover, turned out to be better founded than Burke's, if not quite for the reasons he expected. Ten years after his death, Paine's remains were surreptitiously removed from his New Rochelle grave by William Cobbett, an English radical who sought to take the body to Britain and erect a glorious memorial to his hero. But Paine's antimonarchical views had not been forgotten in Britain, and the government refused to permit a monument. Cobbett's gambit turned into a fiasco and made him a national laughingstock. Worse yet, Paine's remains were eventually lost. Their final disposition remains unknown to this day.

Burke's and Paine's exceptional concerns about their legacies should not surprise us. They were right to assume that their names and their words, if not their mortal remains, would not be left to rest but would continue to play key roles in the great debate they had helped launch. Throughout the nineteenth and twentieth centuries and into the twenty-first, both have been frequently appealed to by various political movements. Assorted radical leaders the world over—from the American abolitionist firebrand John Brown to Uruguayan liberator José Gervasio Artigas and countless others in between—laid claim to the legacy of Thomas Paine, as did the mainstream labor and progressive movements in the Anglo-American world. Conservative cultural and political movements—from Romantic poets to reforming Tories to the conservative movement that emerged in America in the middle of the last century—have laid claim to Edmund Burke's name and ideas.

Ironically, our understanding of the Burke-Paine debate has actually suffered some from such persistent political attention to both men. The revolutionaries who adopted Paine as their own would too often infuse his historical memory with socialist sensibilities that would have been largely foreign to Paine himself. And a great deal of the commentary (and even the scholarship) regarding Burke, particularly over the past century, has seemed to want to make him (even) more temperamentally conservative than he was, in the process overlooking important strains in his thinking.

There has been some modest tempering of these tendencies in both cases, if sometimes through equal and opposite distortions: Paine's role in the American Revolution, for instance, has caused some American conservatives to give him a serious look and to emphasize elements of his worldview they find agreeable. No less an icon of the American right than Ronald Reagan accepted the Republican Party's nomination for president in 1980 by reminding his supporters of Paine's call for transforming failed governing institutions. Burke's emphasis on gradualism, meanwhile, has appealed to some contemporary liberals eager to resist dramatic transformations of the welfare state. No less an icon of the American left than Barack Obama has reportedly described himself as a Burkean eager to avoid sudden change.[3]

But it is not in these uses and abuses of Burke's and Paine's own names and reputations that we can find the lasting legacy of their debate. By considering the arguments as each man first made them, and not as assorted partisans across two centuries have sought to use them, we can see how the worldviews Burke and Paine laid out still describe two broad and fundamental dispositions toward political life and political change in our liberal age.

The tension between those two dispositions comes down to some very basic questions: Should our society be made to answer to the demands of stark and abstract commitments to ideals like social equality or to the patterns of its own concrete political traditions and foundations? Should the citizen's relationship to his society be defined above all by the individual right of free choice or by a web of obligations and conventions not entirely of our own choosing? Are great public problems best addressed through institutions designed to apply the explicit technical knowledge of experts or by those designed to channel the implicit social knowledge of the community? Should we see each of our society's failings as one large problem to be solved by comprehensive transformation or as a set of discrete imperfections to be addressed by building on what works tolerably well to address what does not? What authority should the character of the given world exercise over our sense of what we would like it to be?

These questions build on one another, and step by subtle step, they add up to quite distinct ways of thinking about politics. Every person looks upon his country and sees a mix of good things and bad. But which strike us more powerfully? In confronting the society around us, are we first grateful for what works well about it and moved to reinforce and build on that, or are we first outraged by what works poorly and moved to uproot and transform it?

Our answers will tend to shape how we think about particular political questions. Do we want to fix our health-care system by empowering expert panels armed with the latest effectiveness data to manage the system from the center or by arranging economic incentives to channel consumer knowledge and preferences and address some of the system's discrete problems? Do we want to alleviate poverty through large national programs that use public dollars to supplement the incomes of the poor or through efforts to build on the social infrastructure of local civil-society institutions to help the poor build the skills and habits to rise? Do we want problems addressed through the most comprehensive and broadest possible means or through the most minimal and targeted ones? People's answers to such questions likely fall into a pattern. And the answers depend not only on our opinion of the state of our particular society at this moment but also on our assumptions about how much knowledge and power social reformers can really expect to have, and of what sort.

Ultimately, the answers depend as well on people's implicit notion of what our political order—what modern liberalism—really is, exactly. Is it a set of principles that were discovered by Enlightenment philosophers and that should be put more and more completely into practice so that our society can increasingly resemble those philosophers' ideal mix of egalitarianism and liberty? Or is it a living culture built up over countless generations of social trial and error so that by the time of the Enlightenment, especially in Britain, society had taken a form that allowed for an exceptional mix of egalitarianism and liberty? Is liberalism, in other words, a theoretical discovery to be put into effect or a practical achievement to be reinforced and perfected? These two possibilities suggest two rather different sorts of liberal politics: a politics of vigorous progress toward an ideal goal or a politics of preservation and perfection of a precious inheritance. They suggest, in other words, a progressive liberalism and a conservative liberalism.

THE TWO PARTIES TO our political debates still very often answer to these general descriptions. But of course, they do not answer to them perfectly or quite consistently. Burke and Paine offer us a window into the birth of the right and the left, but to see the birth of an idea is not to see its developed state. How both the right and the left have changed from the views laid out by Burke and Paine is at least as interesting as how their views have persisted. This book can, of course, barely scratch the surface of that complex evolution, but even the very broadest outlines can help us see how Burke and Paine remain deeply relevant both as instructive points of origin and as useful correctives for today's right and left.

The fundamental utopian goal at the core of Paine's thinking—the goal of liberating the individual from the constraints of the obligations imposed upon him by his time, his place, and his relations to others—remains essential to the left in America. But the failure of Enlightenment-liberal principles and the institutions built upon them to deliver on that bold ambition and therefore on Paine's hopes of eradicating prejudice, poverty, and war seemed to force the left into a choice between the natural-rights theories that Paine thought would offer means of attaining his goal and the goal itself. In time, the utopian goal was given preference, and a vision of the state as a direct provider of basic necessities and largely unencumbered by the restraints of Paine's Enlightenment liberalism arose to advance it.

We can begin to discern the earliest roots of this way of thinking in Paine's own later revolutionary writings, when he proposes a primordial welfare state. But it advanced a fair bit from Paine's views as over time, some American progressives, influenced by European social-democratic thinking, came to believe in an assertive national government. They thought such a government could both provide some material benefits and clear away some of the social and civic institutions that stood between the individual and the state (institutions that they considered, as Paine did, carriers of backwardness and prejudice). In this way, the government could free people simultaneously from material want and from direct moral obligations to those immediately around them. Such a government would make people more equal to one another and freer of one another, and thus better able to exercise their individual choices.

Today's left plainly exhibits this combination of material collectivism and moral individualism. The role it affords to the government and its links to European social thought might at first suggest that this attitude leans toward communitarianism. But its American form is actually a radical form of individualism, moved by much the same passion for justice that Paine had and by much the same desire to free people of the fetters of tradition, religion, and the moral or social expectations of those around them.

The deep commitment to generational continuity and to the institutions of implicit social knowledge that we have found at the core of Burke's thought remains essential to today's American right, meanwhile. But as Burke himself noted, different societies form such institutions differently, and Americans in particular have always been "men of free character and spirit" to an exceptional degree. [4] This, and the simple fact that American conservatives are conserving a political tradition begun in a revolution (even if it was not as radical a revolution as Paine insists), has long made the American right more inclined both to resort to theory and to appeal to individualism than Burke was. And the two tendencies are connected: The theory of American political thought most often and most readily at hand for today's conservatives is an adaptation of the very same natural-rights theories that Paine, Jefferson, and other Enlightenment-liberal founders of America had championed, but which the left eventually abandoned. The tradition of conservative liberalism—the gradual accumulation of practices and institutions of freedom and order that Burke celebrated as the English constitution and that in many important respects the American revolution sought to preserve (not to reject) on this side of the Atlantic—has only rarely been articulated in American terms. For this reason, it is not often heard on the lips of today's conservatives.

And yet, this very same conservative liberalism is very frequently the vision they pursue in practice. It is the vision conservatives advance when they defend traditional social institutions and the family, seek to make our culture more hospitable to children, and rail against attempts at technocratic expert government. It is the vision they uphold when they insist on an allegiance to our forefathers' constitutional forms, warn of the dangers of burdening our children with debt to fund our own consumption, or insist that the sheer scope and ambition of our government makes it untenable.

Today's left, therefore, shares a great portion of Paine's basic disposition, but seeks to liberate the individual in a rather less quixotic and more technocratic way than Paine did, if also in a way that lacks his grounding in principle and natural right. Thus today's liberals are left philosophically adrift and far too open to the cold logic of utilitarianism—they could learn from Paine's insistence on limits to the use of power and the role of government. Today's right, meanwhile, shares a great deal of Burke's basic disposition, but seeks to protect our cultural inheritance in a less aristocratic and (naturally, for Americans) more populist way than he did, if also in a way that lacks his emphasis on community and on the sentiments. Today's conservatives are thus too rhetorically strident and far too open to the siren song of hyperindividualism, and they generally lack a nonradical theory of the liberal society. They could benefit by adopting Burke's focus on the social character of man, from Burke's thoroughgoing gradualism, and from his innovative liberal alternative to Enlightenment radicalism.

Both sides of our politics therefore exhibit in practice deep continuities to their intellectual forerunners, despite being barely aware of these connections, and would be well served by better understanding them. Each group might find some of its worst excesses alleviated a bit by carefully considering the Burke-Paine debate.

One peculiar feature of some prominent contemporary policy debates can make this historical continuity of the left-right divide particularly difficult to see and so is worth a further word. As the great economic debate of the last century has loosened its grip on our politics with the fall of communism and the waning of socialist ideas, American political life has come to be defined by the social-democratic welfare state and its mounting difficulties. Today's progressives are thus often engaged in a struggle to preserve a set of public entitlement programs that their predecessors built over the past century (often employing arguments that, in the cause of preservation, sound downright Burkean). Meanwhile, today's conservatives seek to transform some key governing institutions (often resorting to arguments from classical-liberal principles that ring of Paine). The rhetoric of some key domestic debates therefore sometimes seems almost like a mirror image of the original left-right debate.

But this is a kind of second-order argument about political change—a debate about reforming a set of welfare-state institutions that are themselves intended to advance a certain vision of change. The vision is a progressive archetype that Paine would certainly have recognized: an egalitarian ideal of justice advanced through the application of technical expertise regarding society within a liberal framework. Opposing it is a more conservative ideal that Burke would have found familiar: a case for addressing social problems through evolved institutions (like the family, civil society, religious groups, and markets) that tacitly contain and convey implicit knowledge within a liberal framework. It is very much another instance of the general pattern of ideological division that we have traced back to Burke and Paine's era.

For all that they have certainly evolved over two centuries, the two sides of our politics still often express the basic underlying dispositions—toward progress and tradition, choice and obligation, technocratic prowess and a worldly skepticism—evident in Paine and Burke. When it is most itself, each of our parties rather plainly fits the profile that emerges from our study of the great debate of the age of revolutions.

I⊤ MAY BE STRANGE TO THINK that just a few layers beneath our bubbling and contentious political debates there still lurk such profound questions of political philosophy. But as both the lives and the arguments of Burke and Paine help show us, political events are always tied up with political ideas, and seeing those ties can shed a bright light on both the events and the ideas. Philosophy moves history, especially in times of profound social change. And ours, like Burke and Paine's, is surely such a time.

Burke and Paine agreed that politics is always in flux and that the challenge of the statesman is to govern change for the benefit of society. The practical questions that divided them and shaped their assorted theoretical explorations and arguments began from this basic reality. But to what ends, and by what means, should people alter their political and cultural arrangements? Burke and Paine's debate may not provide an ultimate answer, but it offers an unusually deep and serious engagement with a question we must still confront.

In our day-to-day political arguments, we hear echoes of a deeper debate that we easily mistake for remnants of an argument between capitalism and socialism, or for faint precursors of a long-predicted ultimate clash between religious traditionalism and secular cosmopolitanism. But more likely, these echoes are in fact reminders of the defining disagreement of the political order of modern liberalism. That disagreement was given early and unusually clear voice by Edmund Burke and Thomas Paine, and becomes far easier to comprehend when we pay careful attention to what they have to teach us.

ACKNOWLEDGMENTS

THIS BOOK HAS BEEN LONG IN COMING, AND SO HAS left me with enormous debts to many people whose support, guidance, good will, and (in no small measure) patience have made it possible.

It began in the Committee on Social Thought at the University of Chicago, where I found to my amazement teachers and students engaged in a genuine search for understanding and committed to a kind of scholarship that, had I not witnessed it myself, I might have easily imagined was entirely a thing of the past. I owe special thanks to Ralph Lerner, whose generous spirit, enthusiasm, astonishing breadth of knowledge, and abiding good humor helped make this work a joy. Nathan Tarcov, too, offered a model of deep and devoted engagement with texts. And Leon Kass, who was the first reader of this book, has been far more than a teacher but a mentor and model—both professional and personal. My debt to him is greater than I could hope to repay.

Although my research began in Chicago, this book was written almost entirely in Washington, where I have built up debts to many other scholars and friends. Alan Levine of American University and

Patrick Deneen (then of Georgetown University and now of the University of Notre Dame) were particularly helpful. And Adam Keiper, in this as in so much else, has been beyond invaluable—for among his countless talents he is a superb editor. More important, he is a treasured friend.

Since 2007, I have been privileged to hang my hat at the Ethics and Public Policy Center in Washington, and much of my work on this book was done there. It is an island of collegiality and intellectual engagement in a city where both are too often lacking, and for that I am grateful to its president, Ed Whelan, and to my colleagues. Since 2009, I have also been lucky enough to serve as editor of *National Affairs* magazine, and my wonderful team of colleagues there has made it a joy—my thanks to them all. Neither this book nor my other work in recent years could have been possible without the generous support, encouragement, and guidance of Roger Hertog, for which I am deeply grateful.

I am grateful, also, to a variety of colleagues, advisors, and friends who read parts or all of this manuscript and offered their wisdom and guidance. They include especially Adam White, George Weigel, Hillel Ofek, Michael Aronson, Scott Galupo, Peter Wehner, my brother Yariv Levin, and (the late) Daniel Bell. I was also privileged to have a series of conversations about Thomas Paine with the late Christopher Hitchens in what turned out to be the last year of his life, which deeply shaped my thinking about Paine and his ambitions.

In any project like this, one inevitably also accumulates debts to librarians, who have only become more important in the age of the internet. For me, this was especially the case with Thomas Paine's writings, which still cry out for an authoritative scholarly collection. The librarians of the Regenstein Library at the University of Chicago, the manuscripts collection of the Library of Congress, the British Library, and the library of the American Philosophical Society in Philadelphia offered invaluable help, in some cases remotely under circumstances that could not have been convenient for them. And I am of course much indebted to the many scholars cited in the bibliography and throughout the text, for their work and in some cases for personal conversations and guidance beyond.

At Basic Books, I have been very fortunate to work with Tim Bartlett—a learned and gifted editor who understood precisely what my manuscript was, what this book should be, and how to turn the former into the latter. Kaitlyn Zafonte managed to keep both Tim and me (and always a great deal more, it seemed) on track; Collin Tracy and Patty Boyd showed the kind of meticulous care every writer hopes for in a production and editing team; and Nicole Caputo made the final product look its best. I am very grateful to them all.

My greatest debt, however, is as always to my family. I am grateful to my parents for more than I could ever say. I am grateful to my children, Maya and Sam, for the profound joy they bring to our lives.

But above all, I am grateful to, and grateful for, my wonderful wife, Cecelia, who is the embodiment of that "unbought grace of life" that we are privileged to enjoy though we could never truly deserve. Aside from an inexplicable failure of judgment in her selection of a spouse, she has always seemed to me just perfect. I dedicate this book to her with love, because it is from her that I have learned what love and dedication really mean.

NOTES

INTRODUCTION

1. Copeland, *Our Eminent Friend Edmund Burke*, 148.

2. As we will see, because the term *liberal* is itself a matter of significant contention between Burke and Paine, the term will usually be modified when it appears in this book. *Enlightenment liberalism* will refer to
the political ideas (drawn especially from John Locke but refined and at
times also altered by some of his intellectual successors) at the heart of
the thinking of many English Whigs. With some important differences,
the term also refers to the ideals of many revolutionaries in America and
France—especially government by the consent of the governed, and natural rights underlying political association. *Radical liberalism* will describe
more extreme variants of the same approach to politics—variants that insisted on a thoroughly republican form of government and entertained
the notion of overthrowing the monarchy. *Classical-liberal*, used just once
in the book, describes a more moderate (and later) variant of liberalism
greatly influenced by the British reaction against the French Revolution,
and by Edmund Burke. In the conclusion, I will also use *conservative liberalism* to describe an element of the political thought of Edmund Burke—
which viewed liberalism as a practical achievement of the English legal and
political tradition, rather than as a discovery of principles against which
that tradition (and others) should be measured. These definitions will be
further refined in later chapters, but the terms are, of course, necessarily

shorthand and therefore somewhat anachronistic (indeed, while the word liberal was commonly used in Burke's and Paine's time, the word *liberalism* did not emerge until the second decade of the nineteenth century). Nevertheless, the terms are used here with the same meanings they are widely given in modern scholarship regarding the period.

3. Edmund Burke, *The Writings and Speeches of Edmund Burke*, ed. Paul Langford (Oxford: Oxford University Press, 1981–) (hereinafter cited as Burke, *Writings*), 8: 293. This collection, once completed, will include all of Burke's available speeches and writings with the exception of personal correspondence. Two crucial volumes in the collection still remain to be published, so that a significant number of Burke's writings, especially of the early 1790s, will be cited from other collections and noted as such.

4. Burke, *On Empire, Liberty, and Reform: Speeches and Letters of Edmund Burke*, 11.

5. Edmund Burke, *The Correspondence of Edmund Burke*, ed. Thomas Copeland (Chicago: University of Chicago Press, 1967) (hereinafter cited as Burke, *Correspondence*), 6: 303. This collection includes all of Burke's available personal correspondence.

6. Thomas Paine, *Life and Writings of Thomas Paine*, ed. Daniel Wheeler (New York: Vincent Parke & Company, 1915) (hereinafter cited as Paine, *Writings*), 5: 18n. This ten-volume collection includes all of Paine's publications and the bulk of his personal correspondence. Unless otherwise noted, all references to Paine's writings are drawn from this collection. In a few instances, cited personal letters that are available only in other, and otherwise less complete, collections will be noted individually.

7. Jefferson, *The Political Writings of Thomas Jefferson*, 207.

8. This letter to John Inskeep, mayor of Philadelphia, is included in Paine, *The Complete Writings of Thomas Paine*, 2: 1480, but not in Paine, *Life and Writings of Thomas Paine*, which is used for most other Paine citations.

9. Burke, *Writings*, 9: 31.

Chapter 1: Two Lives in the Arena

1. Burke, *Correspondence*, 5: 412.

2. Paine, *Writings*, 4: xv.

3. Some recent historical detective work by historian F. P. Lock suggests Burke might have actually been born in January 1730 (Lock, *Edmund Burke*, 1: 16–17). In fact, the date (and especially the year) of his birth has been a subject of a long-standing scholarly dispute dating back at least to Dixon Wecter's 1937 essay "Burke's Birthday" (though, with lesser scholarly probity, really

all the way back to his earliest biographers), with plausible claims placing it anywhere from 1728 to 1730. Lock's 1998 analysis of the evidence is compelling but hardly conclusive, especially because the case for 1729 is buttressed by contemporary accounts. Having no new evidence in this controversy, I have simply followed the substantial majority of modern Burke scholars who place his birth in January 1729.

4. Morley, *Burke*, 24–25.

5. Burke, *Writings*, 1: 221.

6. Walpole, *Horace Walpole's Correspondence*, 9: 380.

7. Burke, *Writings*, 8: 206.

8. Burke, *Writings*, 3: 483.

9. Burke, *Writings*, 3: 64–70.

10. Burke, *Writings*, 2: 196.

11. Ibid., 252.

12. Ibid., 458. As we will see in some detail in Chapter 2, however, this does not mean that Burke rejected all applications of theory to politics.

13. Paine, *Writings*, 5: 32–33.

14. Robbins, "The Lifelong Education of Thomas Paine," 135–142.

15. Cited in Nelson, *Thomas Paine*, 44.

16. Franklin, *The Works of Benjamin Franklin*, 361.

17. Paine, *Writings*, 2: 113–118.

18. Ibid., 196.

19. Paine frequently uses the term *republican*, which he defines rather carefully in the second part of his *Rights of Man*, as discussed in a later chapter. My use of it throughout follows his definition (which also mirrors Burke's understanding of the term). Thus, *republican* refers not to a specific system of government but to an approach to government. This approach begins from a thoroughgoing rejection of hereditary monarchy and then seeks to establish on rational principles of utility a system of government that is maximally answerable to the people.

20. Paine, *Writings*, 2: 75.

21. Exact sales and readership figures for this period are of course unobtainable. Kaye, *Thomas Paine*, 56–57, notes that about 150,000 copies of the pamphlet were apparently distributed by printers and publishers—an immense number for the time. Conway, *Life of Thomas Paine*, 25, reports a similar number from several contemporary sources. Paine himself, with his customary modesty, states in *Rights of Man* that *Common Sense* was an utterly unprecedented literary event and "the success it met with was beyond anything since the invention of printing" (Paine, *Writings*, 5: 18n). This, of course, is a rather less reliable report.

22. Washington, *The Writings of George Washington*, 3: 347.

23. Paine, *Writings*, 3: 1.

24. Paine, *Writings*, 4: 220.

25. Burke, *Writings*, 3: 305–306.

26. Burke's earliest biographer, Robert Bisset, plainly asserts such a meeting occurred, but Thomas Copeland, after poring over the evidence, argues that it appears unlikely to have happened and that the two men met for the first time only in 1788. (Copeland, *Our Eminent Friend Edmund Burke*, 155–156.) Subsequent biographers have concurred with Copeland's view, while acknowledging that it cannot be proven conclusively.

27. Burke, *Correspondence*, 5: 415.

28. Quoted in Copeland, *Our Eminent Friend Edmund Burke*, 160.

29. Edmund Burke, "An Appeal from the New to the Old Whigs," in *Further Reflections on the Revolution in France*, ed. Daniel Ritchie (Indianapolis: Liberty Fund, 1992) (hereinafter cited as Burke, *Appeal*), 136n. I have used this Ritchie collection for the *Appeal* throughout this book, as the volume of the Oxford collection of Burke's writings that will include that essay has yet to be published.

30. Paine, *Writings*, 5: 106–107.

31. Burke, *Correspondence*, 6: 1.

32. Fox made the remark in a letter on July 30, 1789. It is quoted and discussed in Evans, *Debating the Revolution*, 12.

33. Burke, *Correspondence*, 6: 10.

34. Ibid., 30.

35. Burke, *Correspondence*, 6: 70.

36. Ibid.

37. MacCoby, ed., *The English Radical Tradition*, 54.

38. Price, *The Correspondence of Richard Price*, 260.

39. Burke, *Writings*, 8: 59.

40. Edmund Burke, *The Writings and Speeches of Edmund Burke* (Boston: Little, Brown & Co., 1901) (hereinafter cited as Burke, *Writings and Speeches*), 3: 221. (A partial text of this speech, which Burke did not set down himself but which was published in the parliamentary record, is made available in this older edition of Burke's writings and speeches, but not in the contemporary academic edition otherwise used for most references.)

41. Burke, *Correspondence*, 6: 46.

42. Burke, *Writings*, 8: 116.

43. Ibid., 108.

44. Ibid., 136.

45. Ibid., 293.

46. Fennessy, *Burke, Paine, and the Rights of Man*, 1.

47. For details of its circulation, see W. B. Todd's meticulously researched study "The Bibliographical History of Burke's *Reflections on the Revolution in France*," 100–108.

48. Paine, *Writings*, 4: 69.

49. Ibid., 104.

50. Ibid., 143.

51. Paine, *Writings*, 2: 90.

52. Paine, *Writings*, 4: 200.

53. Ibid., 201.

54. Paine himself, in a letter to John Hall, claimed the book sold more than fifty-six thousand copies, but he offers no evidence and scholars generally express serious doubts about that figure (Paine, *The Complete Writings of Thomas Paine*, 2: 1,321–1,322). In any case, Paine's book clearly sold far more copies than Burke's. (Conway, *The Life of Thomas Paine*, 343).

55. Jefferson, *The Papers of Thomas Jefferson*, 20: 304.

56. Ibid., 17: 671.

57. David Bromwich, "Burke and the Argument from Human Nature," in Crowe, ed., *An Imaginative Whig*, 54–55.

58. Paine, *Writings*, 5: 97.

59. The episode is ably discussed in Nelson, *Thomas Paine*, 228.

60. Burke, *Writings*, 9: 326–327.

61. Paine, *Writings*, 6: 3.

62. Ibid., 275.

CHAPTER 2: NATURE AND HISTORY

1. Paine, *Writings*, 2: 1.

2. Paine, *Writings*, 4: 52.

3. As it was the common practice in Burke and Paine's time and would be difficult to avoid in discussing their thinking, I will use the singular male "man" to refer to human beings in general throughout this book.

4. Paine, *Writings*, 4: 53.

5. Ibid., 266.

6. Ibid., 54.

7. Paine, *Writings*, 8: 294–295.

8. Paine, *Writings*, 4: 227.

9. Claeys, *Thomas Paine*, 94, argues that this emphasis on the distinction between society and government and the antistatist implications of

this distinction are among Paine's most significant original contributions to political thought.

10. Paine, *Writings*, 4: 226.

11. Ibid., 221.

12. Paine, *Writings*, 2: 90.

13. Paine, *Writings*, 4: 255–256.

14. Ibid., 197.

15. Ibid., 240.

16. Ibid., 291. Paine also uses the identical formulation later in the same chapter of the *Rights of Man* (ibid., 305).

17. Paine, *Writings*, 2: 5–6.

18. Ibid., 237–238.

19. Ibid., 265.

20. Ibid., 4.

21. Paine, *Writings*, 4: 193–194.

22. Paine, *Writings*, 2: 79.

23. Ibid., 20–21.

24. Burke, *Writings*, 8: 213. Similarly, Burke writes in a 1790 letter to Thomas Mercer that over the course of centuries, "that which might be wrong in the beginning is consecrated by time and becomes lawful" (Burke, *Correspondence*, 6: 95).

25. Burke, *Writings*, 6: 316–317.

26. There are, of course, other exceptions to this rule, including most notably Machiavelli on numerous occasions in his descriptions of Rome in the *Discourses on Livy*.

27. Burke, *Writings*, 8: 331.

28. Paine, *Writings*, 4: 150.

29. Burke, *Writings*, 8: 112.

30. Ibid.

31. Burke, *Correspondence*, 6: 48.

32. Burke, *Appeal*, 168–169.

33. Bromwich, "Burke and the Argument from Human Nature," in Crowe, ed., *An Imaginative Whig*, 48.

34. Burke, *Appeal*, 179. Emphasis in original.

35. Ibid., 163–164.

36. Burke, *Writings*, 8: 206.

37. Ibid., 111.

38. Ibid., 112.

39. Ibid., 189.

40. Ibid., 115.

41. Burke, *Writings*, 1: 198.

42. Burke, *Writings*, 2: 196.

43. See especially Burke's adamant rejection of Rousseau's sentimentalism in his 1791 "Letter to a Member of the National Assembly" (Burke, *Writings*, 8: 312–317).

44. Burke, *Writings and Speeches*, 11: 237.

45. Burke, *Writings*, 8: 128.

46. Burke, *Writings*, 2: 252.

47. "Character of Mr. Burke," in Hazlitt, *The Collected Works of William Hazlitt*, 7: 306.

48. Burke, *Writings*, 8: 101, and 3: 396.

49. Burke, *Writings*, 8: 131 (emphasis in original).

50. Ibid., 133.

51. Ibid., 137.

52. This case is nicely outlined in Fennessy, *Burke, Paine, and the Rights of Man*, 121–123.

53. Burke, *Writings*, 8: 128.

54. Ibid.

55. Ibid., 126–127.

56. Burke, *Correspondence*, 6: 86–87.

57. Paine, *Writings*, 4: 24.

58. Burke, *Writings*, 8: 128.

59. Ibid., 84.

60. Burke, *Writings*, 9: 188.

61. Ibid.

62. Burke, *Appeal*, 87–88.

63. Burke, *Writings*, 9: 634.

Chapter 3: Justice and Order

1. Paine, *Writings*, 4: 26.

2. Burke makes this clearest in a letter to his friend Phillip Francis in 1791 (Burke, *Correspondence*, 6: 90–91).

3. Burke, *Appeal*, 89.

4. Paine, *Writings*, 4: 40.

5. The term "procedural conservative" is used especially in Hampsher-Monk, *The Political Philosophy of Edmund Burke*.

6. Charles Vaughn, one of the great twentieth-century readers of Burke, argued that Burke "stood side by side with Hume and Bentham in their assault upon abstract ideas of right, in their constant reference of everything to expediency" (Vaughan, *Studies in the History of Political Philosophy Before*

and After Rousseau, 2: 19). John Morley, perhaps Burke's best nineteenth-century biographer, called himself "a Burkean and a Benthamite," on similar grounds (Morley, *Recollections*, 1: 232–233). The majority of Burke's twentieth-century interpreters took him at least to be dramatically deemphasizing the significance of a moral standard in politics. Burkeanism, in this sense, is considered a *disposition*, not a theory, of politics, and mostly a disposition about change, which, as Hampsher-Monk, *The Political Philosophy of Edmund Burke*, 28, has put it recently, "claims to identify no ideal."

7. Mansfield, *Statesmanship and Party Government*, 245.

8. Burke, *Writings*, 9: 455.

9. Burke, *Appeal*, 176–177.

10. Burke, *Writings*, 9: 456.

11. This school of Burke scholars was exemplified by Peter Stanlis and his important 1958 book *Edmund Burke and the Natural Law*.

12. Ibid., 84.

13. "If I were to call for a reward," Burke wrote when reflecting on his career in his final year of life, "it would be for the services in which for fourteen years, without intermission, I showed the most industry and had the least success. I mean the affairs of India; they are those on which I value myself the most; most for the importance; most for the labor; most for the judgment; most for constancy and perseverance in the pursuit" (Burke, *Writings*, 9: 159).

14. Burke, *Writings*, 6: 459.

15. Burke, *Writings*, 9: 572.

16. Burke, *Correspondence*, 4: 416.

17. Burke, *Writings*, 9: 463.

18. Burke, *Writings*, 8: 145.

19. Ibid.

20. Ibid., 142–143.

21. Ibid., 146.

22. Ibid., 290.

23. Ibid., 148.

24. Ibid., 142. At several periods in his career, and especially in the early 1770s and again in the wake of the French Revolution, Burke was exceptionally hostile to all forms of atheism, employing a tone and vehemence rarely found in even in his most passionate writings on other subjects. "The most horrid and cruel blow that can be offered to civil society is through atheism," he argues in his Speech on the Relief of Protestant Dissenters in 1773.

"These are the people against whom you ought to aim the shaft of law; these are the men to whom, arrayed in all the terrors of government, I would say 'you shall not degrade us into brutes' . . . the infidels are outlaws of the constitution not of this country but of the human race. They are never, never, never to be supported, never to be tolerated. Under the systematic attacks of these people, I see some of the props of good government already begin to fail; I see propagated principles which will not leave to religion even a toleration. I see myself sinking every day under the attacks of these wretched people" (Burke, *Writings*, 2: 88).

25. "The institutions savour of superstition in their very principle; and they nourish it by a permanent and standing influence," Burke writes of French Catholic priests. "This I do not mean to dispute; but this ought not to hinder you from deriving from superstition itself any resources which may thence be furnished for the public advantage" (Burke, *Writings*, 8: 207–208).

26. Ibid., 151.

27. Burke, *Appeal*, 199.

28. Burke, *Writings*, 6: 350.

29. Burke, *Writings*, 8: 213.

30. "We cannot change the nature of things, and of men, but must act upon them the best we can," Burke writes (Burke, *Correspondence*, 6: 392).

31. Burke, *Correspondence*, 2: 281–282. He makes a nearly identical point in Burke, *Writings*, 9: 269.

32. Burke, *Writings*, 2: 282.

33. Burke, *Writings*, 3: 120.

34. Burke, *Writings*, 2: 196.

35. Burke, *Writings*, 8: 220.

36. Burke, *Correspondence*, 6: 48.

37. Burke, *Writings*, 8: 205.

38. Burke, *Writings*, 5: 382.

39. Burke, *Correspondence*, 3: 403.

40. Burke, *Writings*, 8: 100.

41. Ibid.

42. Ibid., 88.

43. Ibid., 101.

44. Ibid., 103. Or as he puts it earlier in the *Reflections*, "I do not hesitate to say that the road to eminence and power from obscure condition ought not to be made too easy, nor a thing too much of course. If rare merit be the rarest of all rare things, it ought to pass through some sort of probation. The temple of honor ought to be seated on an eminence. If it be opened

through virtue, let it be remembered, too, that virtue is never tried but by some difficulty and some struggle. . . . Everything ought to be open—but not indifferently to every man" (Ibid. 101).

45. Ibid., 95.

46. Burke, *Appeal*, 198.

47. Stanlis, *Edmund Burke and the Natural Law*, 186.

48. Burke, *Appeal*, 168.

49. "Men qualified in the manner I have just described, form in nature, as she operates in the common modification of society, the leading, guiding, and governing part. It is the soul to the body, without which the man does not exist. To give therefore no more importance, in the social order, to such descriptions of men, than that of so many units, is an horrible usurpation" (Burke, *Appeal*, 168–169).

50. Burke, *Writings*, 8: 100–101.

51. Ibid., 233.

52. Ibid., 97.

53. Ibid., 174.

54. Ibid., 259.

55. Ibid., 128.

56. David Bromwich, in Crowe, ed., *An Imaginative Whig*, 46, notes Burke's several allusions to "the natural equality of all mankind" and suggests that "Burke must have meant, above all, equality before the law." But in the context in which these references appear, especially the context of Hastings's actions in India, this explanation seems implausible. Burke appears, rather, to refer to a general equality of material nature, which he does not, however, take simply to imply a political or social equality.

57. Burke, *Correspondence*, 3: 403.

58. Burke, *Writings*, 8: 110.

59. Ibid., 127.

60. Ibid., 87.

61. Paine, *Writings*, 2: 50.

62. Ibid., 19.

63. Ibid., 12.

64. Ibid., 195.

65. Paine, *Writings*, 9: 243.

66. Paine, *Writings*, 4: 234.

67. Ibid., 297–298.

68. Ibid., 247.

69. "That property will ever be unequal is certain," Paine writes in his

Dissertations on First Principles of Government in 1795. "Industry, superiority of talents, dexterity of management, extreme frugality, fortunate opportunities, or the opposite, or the means of those things, will ever produce that effect, without having recourse to the harsh, ill-sounding names of avarice and oppression" (Paine, *Writings*, 9: 262).

CHAPTER 4: CHOICE AND OBLIGATION

1. Paine, *The Complete Writings of Thomas Paine*, 2: 1,298–1,299.
2. Paine, *Writings*, 4: 59.
3. Ibid., 59–60.
4. Ibid., 62.
5. Ibid.
6. Ibid., 12.
7. Paine, *Writings*, 9: 260.
8. Ibid., 161.
9. Burke, *Writings*, 8: 66.
10. Ibid.
11. Ibid., 73.
12. Burke, *Writings and Speeches*, 7: 93.
13. Burke, *Writings*, 8: 81 (emphasis in original).
14. Burke, *Writings*, 3: 315.
15. Burke, *Writings*, 8: 174.
16. Ibid. Burke is describing the case made by Aristotle in *The Politics*, 1.319a–1.320a.
17. Burke, *Writings*, 8: 174.
18. Burke, *Appeal*, 157.
19. Ibid., 157–158.
20. Ibid., 162.
21. Ibid., 160.
22. Ibid., 161.
23. Burke, *Writings*, 8: 316.
24. Burke, *Writings and Speeches*, 7: 95.
25. Morley, *Burke*, 239.
26. Burke, *Writings*, 8: 244.
27. Paine, *Writings*, 4: 56.
28. Burke, *Appeal*, 159–160.
29. Burke, *Writings*, 8: 229.
30. Ibid., 8: 147.
31. Burke, *Appeal*, 114.

32. Ibid., 163.

33. Paine, *Writings*, 4: 52.

34. Burke, *Writings*, 8: 109.

35. Ibid., 109–110.

36. Ibid., 110–111.

37. Ibid., 110.

38. Burke, *Writings*, 3: 69.

39. Paine, *Writings*, 4: 148–149.

40. Burke, *Writings*, 8: 290–291.

41. Burke, *Correspondence*, 6: 42.

42. Burke, *Writings*, 3: 59.

43. Burke, *Writings*, 8: 332.

44. Ibid., 291.

45. Burke, *Writings*, 3: 318.

46. Ibid., 59.

47. Fennessy, *Burke, Paine and the Rights of Man*, 38.

48. Paine, *Writings*, 5: 32–33. Nearly identical sentiments are expressed in Paine, *Writings*, 8: 269, and 3: 191.

49. Paine, *Writings*, 4: 239.

50. Burke, *Writings*, 8: 97.

51. Ibid., 129.

52. Burke, *Appeal*, 161.

53. Paine, *Writings*, 5: 6.

54. Paine, *Writings*, 8: 240.

55. Burke, *Writings*, 9: 137.

56. Burke, *Writings*, 9: 180.

57. Burke, *Writings*, 8: 209.

58. Burke, *Writings*, 9: 145.

59. West, *Adam Smith*, 201.

60. Paine, *Writings*, 4: 71.

61. Ibid., 227–228.

62. Paine, *Writings*, 9: 84.

63. Paine, *Writings*, 5: 15.

64. Ibid., 57–58.

65. Ibid., 58.

66. Paine, *Writings*, 10: 11–12.

67. Ibid., 16–17.

68. Ibid., 25–26.

69. Ibid., 28.

CHAPTER 5: REASON AND PRESCRIPTION

1. Burke, *Appeal*, 147–148.
2. Burke, *Writings*, 2: 196.
3. Burke, *Writings and Speeches*, 7: 97.
4. Ibid., 41.
5. Burke, *Writings*, 3: 317.
6. Ibid., 157.
7. Burke, *Writings*, 2: 282.
8. Burke, *Correspondence*, 2: 372–373.
9. Burke, *Writings*, 1: 228.
10. Burke, *Writings and Speeches*, 7: 41.
11. Burke, *Writings*, 8: 58.
12. Burke, *Writings*, 3: 313.
13. Burke, *Writings*, 8: 326. Note, however, that in his writings about America, India, and France, Burke always worked from his desk and never traveled to the scene of the action. Paine, meanwhile, although he surely valued abstract principles of justice more highly, wrote of America from Philadelphia and of the French Revolution from the heart of the action in Paris. Almost without exception, he wrote of events in which he was a participant.
14. Ibid., 231–232.
15. Ibid., 232.
16. Ibid., 193.
17. Burke, *Correspondence*, 6: 46.
18. Burke, *Writings*, 8: 165.
19. Burke, *Writings*, 2: 188.
20. Burke, *Writings*, 1: 207.
21. Burke, *Writings*, 3: 589.
22. Burke, *A Note-Book of Edmund Burke*, 68.
23. Burke, *Writings*, 8: 138.
24. Burke, *Appeal*, 199.
25. Burke, *Writings*, 8: 138.
26. Burke, *Appeal*, 192–193.
27. Burke, *Writings*, 8: 217.
28. Burke, *Writings*, 3: 69.
29. Burke, *Writings*, 8: 217.
30. Paine, *Writings*, 3: 10.
31. Burke, *Writings*, 3: 163.
32. Burke, *Writings*, 2: 317.

33. Ibid., 318.

34. Ibid., 315.

35. Ibid., 320; and Burke, *Correspondence*, 4: 79.

36. Burke, *Appeal*, 197.

37. Ibid., 196.

38. Burke, *Writings*, 3: 139.

39. Burke, *Writings and Speeches*, 7: 104.

40. Burke, *Writings*, 8: 86.

41. Burke, *Writings and Speeches*, 7: 104.

42. Burke, *Writings*, 8: 137.

43. Ibid., 83.

44. Burke, *Correspondence*, 6: 158.

45. Burke, *Writings*, 2: 456.

46. Burke, *Writings*, 8: 138.

47. Burke, *Correspondence*, 4: 295.

48. Burke, *Writings*, 8: 150.

49. Burke, *Writings*, 3: 492.

50. Burke, *Writings*, 8: 72.

51. Toward the end of his life, Burke indeed describes that preservation as his very chief concern. In his final year in Parliament, at a time when he was persuaded that the radicals would overwhelm the English constitution, he wrote to Lord Loughborough, "I am heartily sick of politics, and would give any thing for the means of burying myself in a quiet obscurity, until the Jacobins shall pull me, with others much my betters, out of it. However, my views are very single; my principles are very much fixed; my time of political service and natural existence are very short. With those things strong before my eyes I have but one idea, in which I wish to be serviceable as long as I live and can serve, which is to preserve the order of things into which I was born" (Burke, *Correspondence*, 7: 518–519).

52. Burke, *Writings*, 8: 83–84.

53. Ibid., 82.

54. Burke, *Writings*, 2: 194.

55. Burke, *Correspondence*, 7: 521–522.

56. Burke, *Appeal*, 91.

57. Burke, *Writings*, 2: 175.

58. Burke, *Appeal*, 163.

59. Burke, *Writings and Speeches*, 7: 14.

60. Of course, Burke himself argues a great deal for and about prescrip-

tion—a paradox of which he sometimes seems aware but which he could not avoid or resolve.

61. Burke, *Writings*, 3: 319.

62. Burke, *Writings*, 8: 142.

63. Burke, *Appeal*, 190–191.

64. Burke, *Writings*, 8: 214.

65. Burke, *Correspondence*, 3: 355.

66. Paine, *Writings*, 4: 306.

67. Paine, *Writings*, 5: 45.

68. Ibid., 1.

69. Paine, *The Complete Writings of Thomas Paine*, 2: 1,480.

70. Paine, *Writings*, 4: 199–200.

71. Ibid., 263.

72. Ibid., 188.

73. Ibid., 263.

74. Ibid., 234.

75. Ibid., 156.

76. Ibid., 21–22. Paine here uncharacteristically (and therefore quite possibly intentionally) distorts the quotation he offers. In the relevant passage from the *Reflections on the Revolution in France*, Burke is making a case against judging governments in the abstract: "Abstractly speaking, government as well as liberty, is good; yet could I, in common sense, ten years ago have felicitated France on her enjoyment of a government (for she then had a government) without inquiry what the nature of that government was, or how it was administered? Can I now congratulate the same nation upon its freedom? Is it because liberty in the abstract may be classed amongst the blessings of mankind that I am seriously to felicitate a madman who has escaped from the protecting restraint and wholesome darkness of his cell, on his restoration to the enjoyment of light and liberty?" (Burke, *Writings*, 8: 58). In other words, Burke asks a rhetorical question to which he clearly intends a negative answer, but Paine presents the remark (having altered the grammar and removed the question mark) as though it were a positive assertion. It is an extraordinary fact of the literature regarding Paine's *Rights of Man* and the Burke-Paine debate that this distortion is very rarely noticed.

77. Paine, *Writings*, 4: 17.

78. Paine, *Writings*, 5: 211–112.

79. Paine, *Writings*, 9: 248.

80. Paine, *Writings*, 4: 291.

81. Paine, *Writings*, 2: 235. Though he does largely avoid quotations, Paine does at various places in his writings quote and refer approvingly to Locke, Montesquieu, Rousseau, Grotius, Adam Smith, and others.

82. Paine, *Writings*, 6: 267.

83. Ibid., 268.

84. Ibid, 2.

85. Ibid., 10.

86. Ibid., 265.

87. Ibid., 273 and 277.

88. Ibid., 47.

89. Ibid., 3.

90. Paine, *Writings*, 4: 189–190.

91. Burke, *Writings*, 8: 110.

92. Paine, *Writings*, 4: 147.

93. Paine, *Writings*, 5: 103n.

94. Paine, *Writings*, 4: 244–245.

95. Ibid., 276.

96. Ibid., 215–216.

97. Paine, *Writings*, 5: 107.

98. Paine, *Writings*, 8: 240.

99. Paine, *Writings*, 4: 286.

100. Ibid., 286–287.

101. Paine, *Writings*, 10: 275–276.

102. Paine, *Writings*, 8: 371.

103. Paine, *Writings*, 4: 164.

104. Ibid., 164–165.

105. Ibid., 234.

106. Ibid., 103.

107. Ibid., 150–151.

108. Ibid., 63–64.

109. Paine, *Writings*, 2: 5–6.

110. Burke, *Writings*, 8: 112.

111. Paine, *Writings*, 4: 244.

112. Burke, *Writings and Speeches*, 7: 133.

113. Burke, *Writings*, 8: 293.

114. Paine, *Writings*, 4: 258.

115. Paine, *Writings*, 9: 273.

116. Paine, *Writings*, 2: 52.

117. Paine, *Writings*, 4: 293.

118. Ibid., 80–81.
119. Ibid., 260.
120. Ibid., 245.
121. Ibid., 83.
122. Ibid., 214.
123. Paine, *Writings*, 5: 2–3.
124. Ibid., 97–98.
125. Paine, *Writings*, 9: 270–271.
126. Ibid., 272.
127. Paine, *Writings*, 4: 306.
128. Ibid.
129. Paine, *Writings*, 5: 92–93.
130. Paine, *Writings*, 4: 220.
131. Paine, *Writings*, 2: xx.
132. Paine, *Writings*, 8: 195.
133. Ibid., 269.
134. Paine, *Writings*, 5: 232–233.
135. Ibid., 233.
136. Ibid., 234.
137. Burke, *Writings*, 3: 126–127.
138. Burke, *Writings*, 2: 428.
139. Burke, *Writings*, 3: 135.
140. Burke, *Writings*, 2: 194.
141. Ibid., 428.
142. Ibid., 428 and 461.
143. Ibid., 111.
144. Burke, *Appeal*, 106–108.

CHAPTER 6: REVOLUTION AND REFORM

1. Cited in Foner, *Tom Paine and Revolutionary America*, 270.
2. Ibid., 236–237.
3. Ibid., 19–20.
4. Ibid., 46.
5. Paine, *Writings*, 4: 212.
6. Paine, *Writings*, 9: 276.
7. Paine, *Writings*, 4: 66.
8. Ibid., 232.
9. Ibid., 241.
10. Ibid., 200.

11. Paine, *The Complete Writings of Thomas Paine*, 2: 281.

12. Paine, *Writings*, 3: 146.

13. Paine, *Writings*, 5: 100–101.

14. Paine, *Writings*, 4: 249.

15. Paine, *Writings*, 5: 46.

16. Paine, *Writings*, 2: 90.

17. Ibid., 224.

18. Paine, *Writings*, 9: 271–272.

19. Paine, *Writings*, 10: 173–174.

20. Burke, *Correspondence*, 6: 70.

21. Paine, *Writings*, 4: 3.

22. Burke, *Writings*, 9: 277.

23. Ibid., 174.

24. Ibid., 253.

25. Ibid., 264.

26. Ibid., 267.

27. Burke, *Writings*, 8: 136.

28. Most notoriously in the *Reflections*; see especially ibid., 89.

29. Ibid., 175–176.

30. Ibid., 292.

31. Burke, *Appeal*, 89.

32. Burke, *Writings*, 8: 173.

33. Ibid., 114.

34. Ibid., 218.

35. Ibid., 81.

36. Ibid., 245.

37. Burke, *Appeal*, 195–196.

38. Ibid., 83.

39. Burke, *Writings*, 8: 230.

40. Burke, *Correspondence*, 7: 388.

41. At one point in the *Letters on a Regicide Peace*, Burke actually defines Jacobinism (a term he uses often in his French writings) by pointing to this practice: "Jacobinism is the revolt of the enterprising talents of a country against its property" (Burke, *Writings*, 9: 241).

42. Ibid., 291.

43. Burke, *Writings*, 8: 115.

44. Burke, *Appeal*, 89.

45. Burke, *Writings*, 8: 129.

46. Ibid., 266.

47. Burke, *Writings*, 9: 288.

48. Burke, *Writings*, 8: 190.

49. Burke, *Appeal*, 196.

50. Burke, *Writings*, 8: 188.

51. Burke, *Writings*, 9: 173–174.

52. Ibid., 386. This passage has been the subject of a great deal of scholarly controversy. Some readers (following especially Matthew Arnold) see it as self-criticism on Burke's part, arguing that he is essentially championing a cause he knows is lost. Others see it as a clarion call for early resistance to the revolution, lest it establish itself too firmly in European politics, and a warning to those inclined to think that if the revolution fails, its evident faults will necessarily persuade people of the essential error of its ways, and so no great effort is required to combat it. I am mostly of the latter view, as the context of the essay strongly suggests that Burke is arguing that the struggle against the revolution must be won at the level of ideas, because once the ideas have sunk in, no amount of practical failure will persuade its adherents of its falsehood. But Burke's remark certainly contains something of a melancholy reflection on the difficulty of his own cause. (See also Leo Strauss, *Natural Right and History*, 318.)

53. Burke, *Writings*, 8: 180 (emphasis in original).

54. Ibid., 72.

55. Ibid., 216.

56. Ibid., 206.

57. Ibid., 72.

58. Burke, *Writings*, 9: 287.

59. Burke, *Writings*, 3: 492.

60. Burke, *Writings*, 9: 154–155.

61. Ibid., 545.

62. Ibid., 483.

63. Burke, *Writings*, 8: 290.

64. Ibid., 72.

65. Ibid., 77.

66. Burke, *Appeal*, 136n.

67. Burke, *Writings*, 9: 326–327.

68. Paine, *Writings*, 4: 101.

69. Ibid.

70. Paine, *Writings*, 5: 43n.

71. Ibid., 245.

72. Paine, *Writings*, 4: 77.

73. Ibid., 17.

74. Paine, *Writings*, 5: 103.

75. Ibid., 15.

76. Paine, *Writings*, 4: 201.

77. Paine, *Writings*, 5: 99.

78. Ibid., 92.

79. Burke, *Writings*, 8: 105.

Chapter 7: Generations and the Living

1. Paine, *Writings*, 4: 54.

2. Ibid., 7.

3. Ibid., 55.

4. Paine, *Writings*, 9: 248.

5. Paine, *Writings*, 4: 8.

6. Paine, *Writings*, 9: 251.

7. In fact, Burke appears to be arguing only that the Parliament of 1688 did not do the opposite, that is, Parliament did not decree that the people owed *no* allegiance to the royal family and have a permanent right to elect their own monarch (Burke, *Writings*, 8: 70).

8. Paine, *Writings*, 4: 6.

9. Ibid., 7–8.

10. Ibid.

11. Paine, *Writings*, 9: 255.

12. Ibid., 13.

13. Paine, *Writings*, 2: 74.

14. Paine, *Writings*, 5: 212.

15. Paine, *Writings*, 4: 306.

16. Ibid., 248.

17. Ibid., 259.

18. Ibid., 257–258.

19. Ibid., 12.

20. Ibid.

21. Paine, *Writings*, 10: 17–18.

22. Paine, *Writings*, 4: 9.

23. Paine, *Writings*, 8: 342.

24. Ibid., 342–343. Three years after Paine's proposal quoted here, Thomas Jefferson made a similar suggestion on similar grounds in a letter to James Madison, on September 6, 1789. His letter came complete with actuarial calculations that placed the length of one generation at nineteen years

and thus made for somewhat shorter-lived laws than Paine had envisioned. "The earth belongs always to the living generation," Jefferson wrote, and "one generation is to another as one independent nation to another" (Jefferson, *Writings*, 959).

25. Paine, *Writings*, 8: 343.

26. Ibid., 345.

27. Burke, *Writings*, 3: 147.

28. Burke, *Writings*, 7: 692.

29. Burke, *Writings*, 8: 146.

30. Ibid., 83.

31. Ibid., 145.

32. Burke, *Correspondence*, 2: 377.

33. Burke, *Writings*, 8: 138–139.

34. Burke, *Writings*, 9: 183.

35. Burke, *Appeal*, 133–134.

36. Burke, *Writings*, 8: 84.

37. Ibid., 145.

38. Ibid., 217–218.

39. Burke, *Appeal*, 90–91.

40. Ibid., 197.

41. Burke, *Correspondence*, 6: 109.

CONCLUSION

1. Lambert, *Edmund Burke of Beaconsfield*, 168–169, offers a concise summary of the facts surrounding this request (which was recorded in writing by several of those involved).

2. Paine, *Writings*, 10: 369.

3. Obama's self-description is reported by *New York Times* columnist David Brooks in Gabriel Sherman, "The Courtship," *The New Republic*, August 31, 2009.

4. Burke, *Writings*, 2: 194.

BIBLIOGRAPHY

Aldridge, Alfred. *Man of Reason: The Life of Thomas Paine*. London: Cresset Press, 1960.

———. *Thomas Paine's American Ideology*. Wilmington: University of Delaware Press, 1984.

Ayer, A. J. *Thomas Paine*. New York: Atheneum, 1988.

Ayling, Stanley. *Edmund Burke: His Life and Opinions*. New York: St. Martin's Press, 1988.

Baumann, Arthur. *Burke: The Founder of Conservatism*. London: Eyre and Spottiswoode, 1929.

Berthold, S. M. *Thomas Paine: America's First Liberal*. Boston: Meador Publishing Company, 1938.

Best, Mary. *Thomas Paine: Prophet and Martyr of Democracy*. New York: Harcourt, Brace and Co., 1927.

Bisset, Robert. *Life of Edmund Burke*. 2 vols. London: G. Cawthorn, 1800.

Blakemore, Steven. *Intertextual War: Edmund Burke and the French Revolution in the Writings of Mary Wollstonecraft, Thomas Paine, and James Mackintosh*. Madison, NJ: Fairleigh Dickinson University Press, 1997.

Bogus, Carl. "Rescuing Burke." *Missouri Law Review* 72, no. 2 (spring 2007): 387–476.

Bolingbroke, Viscount Henry. *The Philosophical Writings of the Late Henry St. John, Viscount of Bolingbroke*. London: David Mallet, 1754.

Boswell, James. *The Hypochondriak*. Edited by Margery Bailey. Palo Alto, CA: Stanford University Press, 1928.

Brooke, John. *The Chatham Administration*. London: MacMillan & Co., 1956.

Browne, Ray. *The Burke-Paine Controversy: Texts and Criticism*. New York: Harcourt, Brace and Co., 1963.

Browne, Stephen. *Edmund Burke and the Discourse of Virtue*. Tuscaloosa: University of Alabama Press, 1993.

Burke, Edmund. *The Correspondence of Edmund Burke*. 10 vols. Edited by Thomas Copeland. Chicago: University of Chicago Press, 1958–1978.

———. *Further Reflections on the Revolution in France*. Edited by Daniel Ritchie. Indianapolis: Liberty Fund, 1992.

———. *A Note-Book of Edmund Burke*. Edited by H. V. F. Somerset. Cambridge: Cambridge University Press, 1957.

———. *On Empire, Liberty, and Reform: Speeches and Letters of Edmund Burke*. Edited by David Bromwich. New Haven, CT: Yale University Press, 2000.

———. *Reflections on the Revolution in France*. Edited by Frank M. Turner. New Haven, CT: Yale University Press, 2004.

———. *Selected Letters of Edmund Burke*. Edited by Harvey Mansfield. Chicago: University of Chicago Press, 1984.

———. *A Vindication of Natural Society*. Edited by Frank Pagano. Indianapolis: Liberty Fund, 1982.

———. *The Writings and Speeches of Edmund Burke*. 12 vols. Boston: Little, Brown, & Co., 1901.

———. *The Writings and Speeches of Edmund Burke*. Edited by Paul Langford. 9 vols. Oxford: Oxford University Press, 1991–.

Bury, J. B. *The Idea of Progress*. New York: Kessinger, 2004.

Butler, Marilyn, ed. *Burke, Paine, Godwin and the Revolution Controversy*. Cambridge: Cambridge University Press, 1984.

Butterfield, Herbert. *George III and the Historians*. London: Collins, 1957.

Cameron, David. *The Social Thought of Rousseau and Burke: A Comparative Study*. London: Weidenfeld and Nicolson, 1973.

Canavan, Francis. *Edmund Burke: Prescription and Providence*. Durham, NC: Carolina Academic Press, 1987.

———. *The Political Economy of Edmund Burke*. New York: Fordham University Press, 1995.

———. *The Political Reason of Edmund Burke*. Durham, NC: Duke University Press, 1960.

———. "The Relevance of the Burke-Paine Controversy to American Political Thought." *Review of Politics* 49, no. 2 (spring 1987): 163–176.

Carnes, Mark. *Rousseau, Burke, and the Revolution in France.* New York: Pearson Longman, 2005.

Chalmers, George. *The life of Thomas Pain, the Author of Rights of Man: With a Defense of his Writings.* London: John Stockdale, 1791 (in the collections of the Library of Congress, Washington DC).

Chapman, Gerald. *Edmund Burke: The Practical Imagination.* Cambridge, MA: Harvard University Press, 1967.

Churchill, Winston. *Thoughts and Adventures.* London: Butterworth, 1932.

Claeys, Gregory. *The French Revolution Debate in Britain.* London: Palgrave Macmillan, 2007.

———. *Thomas Paine: Social and Political Thought.* Boston: Unwin Hyman, 1989.

Cobban, Alfred. *Edmund Burke and the Revolt Against the Eighteenth Century: A Study of the Political and Social Thinking of Burke, Wordsworth, Coleridge, and Southey.* New York: Barnes & Noble, 1960.

Cone, Carl. *Burke and the Nature of Politics.* 2 vols. Lexington: University of Kentucky Press, 1954.

———. *The English Jacobins.* New York: Scribner, 1968.

Conniff, James. *The Useful Cobbler: Edmund Burke and the Politics of Progress.* Albany: SUNY Press, 1994.

Conway, Moncure. *The Life of Thomas Paine.* New York: B. Blom, 1970.

Copeland, Thomas. *Our Eminent Friend Edmund Burke: Six Essays.* New Haven, CT: Yale University Press, 1949.

———. "The Reputation of Edmund Burke." *Journal of British Studies* 1, no. 2 (1962): 78–90.

Courtney, Ceceil. *Montesquieu and Burke.* Oxford: Blackwell, 1963.

Creel, George. *Tom Paine: Liberty Bell.* New York: Sears Publishing Company, 1932.

Crowe, Ian, ed. *Edmund Burke: His Life and Legacy.* Dublin: Four Courts Press, 1997.

———. *An Imaginative Whig: Reassessing the Life and Thought of Edmund Burke.* Columbia: University of Missouri Press, 2005.

Del Vecchio, Thomas. *Tom Paine: American.* New York: Whittier Books, 1956.

Descartes, Rene. *Discourse on Method.* Translated by Richard Kennington. Newburyport, MA: Focus Publishing, 2007.

Dishman, Robert, ed. *Burke and Paine on Revolution and the Rights of Man*. New York: Charles Scribner's Sons, 1971.

Dreyer, Frederick. *Burke's Politics: A Study in Whig Orthodoxy*. Waterloo: Wilfrid Laurier University Press, 1979.

Dyck, Ian, ed. *Citizen of the World: Essays on Thomas Paine*. New York: St. Martin's Press, 1988.

Edwards, Samuel. *Rebel! A Biography of Tom Paine*. New York: Praeger, 1974.

Elder, Dominic. *The Common Man Philosophy of Thomas Paine*. Notre Dame, IN: Notre Dame Press, 1951.

Evans, Christopher. *Debating the Revolution: Britain in the 1790s*. London: I.B. Tauris & Co., 2006.

Fasel, George. *Edmund Burke*. Boston: Twayne Publishers, 1983.

Fennessy, R. R. *Burke, Paine, and the Rights of Man: A Difference of Political Opinion*. The Hague: M. Nijhoff, 1963.

Fidler, David, and Jennifer Welsh, eds. *Empire and Community: Edmund Burke's Writings and Speeches on International Relations*. Boulder, CO: Westview Press, 2001.

Foner, Eric. *Tom Paine and Revolutionary America*. New York: Oxford University Press, 2005.

Ford, Karen, ed. *Property, Welfare, and Freedom in the Thought of Thomas Paine*. Lewiston, NY: Edwin Mellen Press, 2001.

Ford, Karen. "Can a Democracy Bind Itself in Perpetuity: Paine, the Bank Crisis and the Concept of Economic Freedom." *Proceedings of the American Philosophical Society* 142, no. 4 (1998): 557–577.

Franklin, Benjamin. *The Works of Benjamin Franklin*. Edited by John Bigelow. New York: Putnam's Sons, 1904.

Freeman, Michael. *Edmund Burke and the Critique of Political Radicalism*. Chicago: University of Chicago Press, 1980.

Frohnen, Bruce. *Virtue and the Promise of Conservatism: The Legacy of Burke and Tocqueville*. Lawrence: University of Kansas Press, 1993.

Fruchtman, Jack. *Thomas Paine and the Religion of Nature*. Baltimore: Johns Hopkins University Press, 1993.

Godwin, William. *Memoirs of Mary Wollstonecraft*. New York: Haskel House, 1927.

Halevy, Elie. *The Growth of Philosophic Radicalism*. New York: Beacon Press, 1966.

Hampsher-Monk, Iain. *The Political Philosophy of Edmund Burke*. New York: Longman, 1987.

Hawke, David. *Paine*. New York: Harper and Rowe, 1974.

Hazlitt, William. *The Collected Works of William Hazlitt*. Edited by A. R. Waller and Arnold Glover. London: J.M. Dent, 1902.

Herzog, Don. "Puzzling Through Burke." *Political Theory* 19, no. 3 (August 1991): 336–363.

Hitchens, Christopher. *Thomas Paine's Rights of Man: A Biography*. Boston: Atlantic Monthly Press, 2007.

Hobbes, Thomas. *Leviathan*. Edited by Michael Oakshott. New York: Simon & Schuster, 1997.

Hoffman, Steven, and Paul Levack, eds. *Burke's Politics*. New York: Knopf, 1949.

Insole, Christopher. "Two Conceptions of Liberalism: Theology, Creation, and Politics in the Thought of Immanuel Kant and Edmund Burke." *Journal of Religious Ethics* 36, no. 3 (2008): 447–489.

Jefferson, Thomas. *The Papers of Thomas Jefferson*. 10 vols. Edited by Julian Boyd. Princeton, NJ: Princeton University Press, 1950.

———. *The Political Writings of Thomas Jefferson*. Chapel Hill: University of North Carolina Press, 1993.

———. *Writings*. New York: Library of America, 1984.

Kant, Immanuel. *First Introduction to the Critique of Judgment*. New York: Bobbs-Merril, 1965.

Kaye, Harvey. *Thomas Paine: Firebrand of the Revolution*. Oxford: Oxford University Press, 2000.

Keane, John. *Tom Paine: A Political Life*. New York: Grove Press, 2003.

Kirk, Russell. *The Conservative Mind*. Chicago: Regnery, 1953.

———. *Edmund Burke: A Genius Reconsidered*. New Rochelle, NY: Arlington House, 1967.

Kramnick, Isaac. *Edmund Burke*. Englewood Cliffs, NJ: Prentice-Hall, 1974.

———. *The Rage of Edmund Burke: Portrait of an Ambivalent Conservative*. New York: Basic Books, 1977.

Lambert, Elizabeth. *Edmund Burke of Beaconsfield*. Newark: University of Delaware Press, 2003.

Leffmann, Henry. *The Real Thomas Paine: A Philosopher Misunderstood*. Philadelphia: University of Pennsylvania, 1922.

Lock, F. P. *Edmund Burke*. 2 vols. Oxford: Oxford University Press, 1998 and 2006.

Locke, John. *Second Treatise of Government*. Edited by C. B. Macpherson. New York: Hackett, 1980.

MacCoby, Simon, ed. *The English Radical Tradition*. New York: Kessinger, 2006.

MacCunn, John. *The Political Philosophy of Burke*. New York: Russell & Russell, 1965.

Macpherson, C. B. *Burke*. Oxford: Oxford University Press, 1980.

Mansfield, Harvey. "Burke and Machiavelli on Principles in Politics." Chap. 3 in *Machiavelli's Virtue*. Chicago: University of Chicago Press, 1996.

———. *Statesmanship and Party Government: A Study of Burke and Bolingbroke*. Chicago: University of Chicago Press: 1965.

McCue, Jim. *Edmund Burke and Our Present Discontents*. London: Claridge Press, 1997.

Meng, John. "The Constitutional Theories of Thomas Paine." *Review of Politics* 8, no. 3 (July 1946): 283–306.

Morley, John. *Burke*. New York: Harper and Brothers, 1887.

———. *Recollections*. 10 vols. New York: Macmillan, 1917.

Murphey, Dwight. *Burkean Conservatism and Classical Liberalism*. Wichita, KS: New Liberal Library, 1979.

Namier, Lewis. *The Structure and Politics of the Accession of George III*. London: MacMillan & Co., 1929.

Nelson, Craig. *Thomas Paine: Enlightenment, Revolution, and the Birth of Modern Nations*. New York: Viking, 2006.

Newman, Bertram. *Edmund Burke*. London: G. Bell & Sons, 1927.

O'Brien, Conor C. *The Great Melody*. London: Minerva, 1993.

O'Gorman, Frank. *Edmund Burke*. Bloomington: Indiana University Press, 1973.

Osborn, Annie. *Rousseau and Burke: A Study of the Idea of Liberty in Eighteenth-Century Political Thought*. New York: Russell & Russell, 1964.

Paine, Thomas. *The Complete Writings of Thomas Paine*. 2 vols. Edited by Philip Foner. New York: Citadel Press, 1945.

———. *Essential Writings of Thomas Paine*. New York: Signet Classics, 2003.

———. *Life and Writings of Thomas Paine*. 10 vols. Edited by Daniel Wheeler. New York: Vincent Parke and Co., 1915.

———. *Paine: Political Writings*. Edited by Bruce Kuklick. Cambridge: Cambridge University Press, 2000.

Pappin, Joseph. *The Metaphysics of Edmund Burke*. New York: Fordham University Press, 1993.

Parkin, Charles. *The Moral Basis of Burke's Political Thought*. Cambridge: Cambridge University Press, 1956.

Philip, Mark. *Thomas Paine*. Oxford: Oxford University Press, 2007.

Price, Richard. *The Correspondence of Richard Price*. Edited by Bernard Peach. Durham, NC: Duke University Press, 1991.

Purdy, Strother. "A Note on the Burke-Paine Controversy." *American Literature* 39, no. 3 (November 1967): 373–375.

Ritchie, Daniel, ed. *Edmund Burke: Appraisals and Applications*. New Brunswick, NJ: Transaction Publishers, 1990.

Robbins, Caroline. "The Lifelong Education of Thomas Paine: Some Reflections upon His Acquaintance Among Books." *Proceedings of the American Philosophical Society* 127, no. 3 (1983): 135–142.

Rogers, Samuel. *Recollections of the Table Talk of Samuel Rogers*. London: Edward Moxon, 1856.

Rothbard, Murray. "A Note on Burke's *A Vindication of Natural Society*." *Journal of the History of Ideas* 19 (June 1958): 114–118.

Sloan, Herbert. *Principle and Interest: Thomas Jefferson and the Problem of Debt*. Charlottesville: University of Virginia Press, 2001.

Stanlis, Peter. *Edmund Burke and the Natural Law*. Ann Arbor: University of Michigan Press, 1958.

———. *The Relevance of Edmund Burke*. New York: P.J. Kennedy, 1964.

———, ed. *Edmund Burke, the Enlightenment, and the Modern World*. Detroit: University of Detroit Press, 1967.

Strauss, Leo. *Natural Right and History*. Chicago: University of Chicago Press, 1953.

Strauss, Leo, and Joseph Cropsey, eds. *History of Political Philosophy*. 3rd ed. Chicago: University of Chicago Press, 1987.

Taylor-Wilkins, Burleigh. *The Problem of Burke's Political Philosophy*. Oxford: Clarendon Press, 1967.

Todd, W. B. "The Bibliographical History of Burke's *Reflections on the Revolution in France*." *Library* 6 (1951): 100–108.

Turner, John. "Burke, Paine, and the Nature of Language." *Yearbook of English Studies* 19 (1989): 36–53.

Vaughan, Charles. *Studies in the History of Political Philosophy Before and After Rousseau*. 2 vols. New York: Russell & Russell, 1925.

Vickers, Vikki. *Thomas Paine and the American Revolution*. New York: Routledge, 2006.

Walpole, Horace. *Horace Walpole's Correspondence*. 48 vols. Edited by W. S. Lewis. New Haven, CT: Yale University Press, 1937.

Washington, George. *The Writings of George Washington*. Edited by Jared Sparks. Boston: Little, Brown & Co., 1855.

Welsh, Cheryl. *Edmund Burke and International Relations*. New York: St. Martin's Press, 1995.

Wecter, Dixon. "Burke's Birthday." *Notes and Queries* 172 (1937): 441.

West, E. G. *Adam Smith*. New York: Arlington House, 1969.

Williams, Gwyn. *Artisans and Sans-Culottes: Popular Movements in France and Britain During the French Revolution.* New York: Norton, 1969.

Williamson, Audrey. *Thomas Paine: His Life, Work, and Times.* London: Allen and Unwin, 1973.

Woll, Walter. *Thomas Paine: Motives for Rebellion.* New York: P. Lang, 1992.

INDEX